WORLD PEACE

VOLUME SIX

FOOD SECURITY AND PEACE

Suresh Chandra Mallick
Pritam Mallick

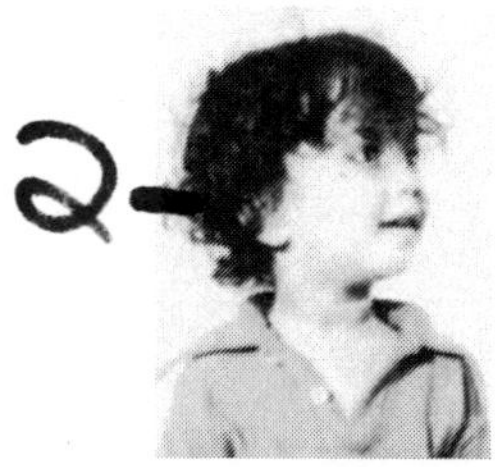

FOOD SECURITY AND PEACE

Institute of Development Studies and Policy research, Pritam Bhawan, 93 Dharma Vihar, P.O. Khandagiri, Bhubaneswar 751030 (Orissa), INDIA

© ISBN: 978-81-924851-5-7 -6

First Edition
2017

International Publisher and Distributor

Price: US $

Dedicated to

H. E. Lionel Zinsou
The Prime Minister of Norway

PROLOGUE

A hungry world is an unstable world; a cursed world and a fragmented world but it can be made a 'world of peace', if all countries emphasize on democracy, food security, good governance and a policy to safeguard the poorest among the poor and hungry people. The world possesses abundant natural resources - fertile soil, vast water resources, unlimited human resources, bright sunlight and fresh air. The intelligent people identified useful plants, birds, and animals for our foodstuffs. Our philosophers, scientists, writers and thinkers made further progress in all branches of knowledge for enjoyment and progress. The twentieth century witnessed two fierce fighting World Wars and the twenty-first century faces over-exploitation of natural resources, severity of pollution and climate change. Even today, more than one billion people are hungry. So food security for all people has posed serious problems in all developing countries and it would aggravate further because of poverty, unemployment, urbanization, population explosion, industrialization, and reduction of agricultural land.

History repeats itself. Like yester years the rich, powerful and intelligent people desire to control the whole world and shed crocodile tears for the poor, hungry and innocent people. The World Trade Center, the World Bank and the FAO have not yet been successful in decreasing the number of hungry people although their statements are palatable to all. The recent slogan is a food plan for '9 billion people' in 2050. These organizations predict problems and try to solve them by creating further problems.

In this manuscript, we have suggested the ways by which 'food security' could be possible in all countries. It is a fact that countries plagued with food imports are not only importing food to feed their people, but also importing unemployment and socio-economic fallout. These countries add frustration among youths and multiply further poverty and hunger. These developing countries are wedded to massive corruption, no-work culture, gossiping, false propaganda, lawlessness, black money and administrative failures. These countries suffer from growth of muscle power in political parties and imposition of martial laws.

Chapter-I incorporates the necessity of food security in all the countries. If any country is incapable of producing the required quantities of cereals permanently, the surplus countries should extend helping hands to mitigate the sufferings their brethren from hunger. The food-insecure countries must produce required food materials such as cereals, milk, meat, fruits or eggs in the country. Poverty is a product of bad governance; hence the government must be accountable for this. Chapter II incorporates food security measures of the developed countries such as USA, UK, Australia and Canada and their role in assisting the food-insecure countries. Chapter-III highlights food-insecurity in Pakistan, Brazil, Ethiopia, Bangladesh and Malawi. It seems they cannot move without foreign assistance because the governments are more worried to rule the country rather than creating their own abilities to be self-sufficient in food grains.

The chapter-IV includes 'Food Security in India'. India claims to be an advanced and the greatest democratic country in the world. But there are 430 million of poor people, which are food insecure. So food insecurity in India is also the highest in the world.

Chapter-V has highlights committee reports and declarations on Food Security. Chapter-VI analyses the contributions of world organizations, international organizations and countries for global food security. These institutions contribute funds for strengthening food security and offer advices to the poor countries. The developed countries have emphasized on the dangers of food-insecurity. Chapter VII suggests that food security must be the prime duty of each state. So the Low-income countries should implement pro-poor, pro-rural and pro-agricultural policies to award food security and peace to all people in the world.

We acknowledge the contribution of authors, who have written articles, research papers, reports, resolutions, and books for food security. We are indebted to authors and organizations for incorporating their suggestions such as the UN, countries, and research institutions, Researchers, Newspapers, Commissions and international Summits with deep gratitude.

We are grateful to Wikipedia, Google in search, and a number of Newspapers for collection of facts and figures on food security. We have referred books journals and Go ogle search for enriching this manuscript. The authors are grateful to Dr. Bikram Mallick, Sarat C Mallick, Bina Mallick, Priyam Mallick and Priyambada Mallick for their cooperation during preparation of the manuscript. We will appreciate for constructive criticism aiming at improvement of the subsequent editions of the book. We would be happy, if a small step towards world peace is contemplated through this endeavour.

Suresh Chandra Mallick
Pritam Mallick

ACRONYMS

A C I A. R:	Australian Centre for International Agricultural Research
A G R A	Alliance for a Green Revolution in Africa
A S A R E CA	Association for Strengthening Agricultural Research in Eastern and Central Africa
A D L I:	Agriculture Development Led Industrialization
A D M A R C:	Agricultural Development and Marketing Corporation
B P L:	Below Poverty Line
C A P:	Common Agricultural Policy
C A A D P:	Comprehensive Africa Agriculture Development Program
C H M S:	Canadian Health Measures Survey
C F S:	Committee on Food Security / Committee on World Food Security
C S I S:	Center for Strategic and International Studies
C G I A R:	Consultative Group on International Agricultural research
C I M M Y T:	International Center for Maize and Wheat Research (Improvement Center)
C S I S	Center for Strategic and International Studies
D C I:	Development Cooperation Instrument
D D G	Dried Distillers' Grains

D E F R A:	Department of Environment, Food and Rural affairs (of the U K Government)
D P P C:	Disaster Preparedness and Prevention Commission
D R R:	Disaster Risk Reduction
E I	Employment Insurance
E D F	European Development Fund
E E Z	Exclusive Economic Zone
E N P I	European Neighborhood and Partnership Instrument
F A O	Food and Agriculture Organization
F F W	Food for Work
F I V I M S	Food Insecurity and Vulnerability Information and Mapping Systems
F S C O	Food Security Coordination Office
F S A	Food Security Analysis
G A T T	General Agreement on Tariff and Trade
G I S	Geographical Information System
G M	Genetically Modified
G M O	Genetically Modified Organism
G A F S P	Global Agriculture and Food Security Program
G P S	Global Positioning System
G N P	Gross National Product
H F A	Hyogo Framework for Action
H I P C	Heavily Indebted Poor Countries
H L T F	U N System - High Level Task Force
I A A S T D	International Assessment of Agricultural knowledge, Science and Technology for Development
I C A R R D	International Conference on Agrarian Reform and Rural Development
I C D S	Integrated Child development Scheme
I C R I S A T	International Center for Research in the Semi-Arid Tropics
I D P s	Internally Displaced Persons
I D D	Iodine Deficiency Disorder
I G D	Initiative for Global Development
I P C	Committee for Food Security
I P P C	International Plant Protection Convention

I F A D	International Fund for Agricultural Development
I F P R I	International Food Policy Research Institute
I S A AA	International services for the Acquisition of Agri-biotech Application
I C E S C R	International Covenant on Economic, Social and Cultural Rights
I M F	International Monetary Fund
J C G	Joint Consultative Group
L D C	Least Developed Countries
L I F D C	Low Income Food Deficit Countries
M D G	Millennium Development Goals
M I S	Managed Investment scheme
M V A C	Malawi Vulnerability Assessment Committee
N A C	National Advisory Committee
N A F T A	North American Free Trade Alliance
NA WA P P A	North American Water and Power Alliance
N N F B	National Nutrition Food Basket
N E P A D	New Partnership in Africa's Development
N R E G A	National Rural Employment Guarantee Scheme
O D A	Official Development Assistance
O E C D	Organization for Economic Cooperation and Development
O I E	Office International des Epizooties
P A D E T ES	Participatory Demonstration and Training Extension System
P C P A	Plant Variety Protection Act
P H L I N O	Hydraulic Project for the Northwest of Mexico
P P A	Plant Patent Law
P D S	Public Distribution System
S A F A N S	South Asia Food and Nutrition Security (Initiative)
S G R	Strategic Grain Reserve
S A E R P	Sustainable Agriculture and Environmental Rehabilitation Program

R R C	Relief and Rehabilitation Commission
T R I P S	Trade Related Intellectual Property Rights
U N E P	United Nations Environment Programme
U N I C E F	United Nations' Children's emergency Fund
U P O V	Union for the Protection of New Varieties of Crops
U S D A	United States Department of Agriculture
U D H R	Universal Declaration of Human Rights
W C A R R D	World Conference on Agrarian Reform and Rural Development
W D M	World Development Movement
W F S	World Food Summit
W I P O	World Intellectual Property Rights Organization
W F P	World Food Program
W H O	World Health Organization
W T O	World Trade Organization
Y B F	Young and Beginning Farmers

+++++

CONTENTS

INTRODUCTION

Food Security has emerged as the greatest challenge to the world organizations, governments, economists, and political leaders in the twenty-first century. Food security is a human right; but more than one billion people are yet to avail proper diet. Food security is not a utopian thought; it is a necessity. We have land, human resources, capital, expertise, and willpower to produce more quantities of agricultural produce to feed all; but we have failed in achieving the target. When one billion people suffer from obesity, one billion people are facing chronic hunger. The Millennium Development Goals include reduction of hunger, but the world statistics explain that the number of food-insecure people is increasing each year.

It is because the governments are fighting against the effects of hunger rather than the causes of hunger.

The UN, the US or the UK and all governments are more worried to maximize agricultural production through investments in research, use of bio-technique, infrastructure development, irrigation, warehouses and cold storages. The governments employ more technical staffs to undertake extensive extension programs to disseminate scientific knowledge to the farmers. The hike of pay of government employees and Members of Parliament in India has increased inflation rather than agricultural production. The government sells subsidized rice and wheat to solve hunger of 430 million of poor people. But this has resulted in low agricultural production. Agricultural labourers are not interested to work in agricultural fields. The farmers are not interested to invest in agriculture, as it is a loss bearing profession. Increase of salary of government officials, investment in infrastructure, agricultural exhibitions or knowledge sharing with farmers makes advertisements of the government but the result is abysmal.

The farmers can maximize agricultural production provided they are offered higher prices for wheat and rice. In India, the procurement price for paddy (rice with husk) or wheat is fixed US$ 25 per quintal (or Indian Rupees 1250 per quintal), but it should be US$ 75 /quintal (or 3750 INR per quintal). Unless agriculture is a profitable enterprise, agricultural production cannot be increased. People need employment and agriculture can accommodate more workers as against service sector or industrial sector per millions of dollars invested.

In all low-income countries, farm labourers are moving to towns and cities. It would result in more than 50 percent of people in towns within a short period all over the world. This is not a favourable step for the world as a whole. Why all countries would be industrialized? Who would control pollution? Which country would supply foods to other countries during national calamity? There could be better equations if farm price is increased. Subsidy in agriculture in both industrialized countries and low-income countries must be withdrawn completely to achieve food security. This could be possible through an international law.

This is not a good step for the world as a whole. Why the governments in low-income countries invite the industrialists to start mega industries? Why the governments snatch away agricultural lands from the peasants forcefully with police forces at higher costs? Why forestlands are converted into industrial areas? What is the fate of peasants and agricultural labourers? **There could be better equations if farm price of cereals is increased**. **Subsidy in agriculture must be withdrawn completely to achieve peace and arrest corruption in the countries.** The government must make agriculture a profitable business. The Government must take steps for creating employment opportunities of rural youths in agriculture and agricultural trade.

Similarly, each country should give importance to meet its own demand of food grains. No country should be permitted to undertake international trade in food grains (rice and wheat). All other agricultural commodities could be traded internationally for earning foreign exchange. In case of natural calamities such as flood, cyclone, earthquakes of other disasters, food grains could be donated to the victim countries without the cost of the grains. Each country must try to increase agricultural output for its food security. Hence, all the low-income countries should adopt pro-poor, pro-rural and pro-agricultural policies for food security. Subsidy, bad governance and wrong policies of the government increase corruption, inefficiency, foreign funding, interest payments, press capturing, farmers' suicides and terrorism. The world now faces challenges of disparity, poverty, hunger, unemployment, and war. The world needs to solve the problems of billions of people, which are underfed, under-nourished and uncared for. Food insecurity and crime go hand in hand in most of the developing countries.

Let the developing countries utilize their own resources and expertise to achieve food security for their people. Food security can ensure peace and independence of the country. Food security to all would pave the way for WORLD PEACE.

World Hunger: Facts and statistics

World hunger is the greatest cataclysm and misfortune to achieve world peace. Unless all governments and world organizations realize the harmful effects of hunger, we possibly cannot achieve a conflict free world order. Some of the facts are as follows:

Every year 15 million children die of hunger.

In the Asian, African and Latin American countries, well over 500 million people are living in what the World Bank has called "absolute poverty".

For the price of one missile, a school full of hungry children could eat lunch every day for 5 years.

Throughout the 1990's more than 100 million children died from illness and starvation. Those 100 million deaths could be prevented for the price of ten Stealth bombers, or what the world spends on its military in two days!

The World Health Organization estimates that one-third of the world is well fed, one-third is under-fed one-third is starving- since you've entered this site at least 200 people have died of starvation. Over 4 million will die this year.

One in twelve people worldwide are malnourished, including 160 million children under the age of 5.
- - United Nations Food and Agriculture

The Indian subcontinent has nearly half the world's hungry people. Africa and the rest of Asia together have approximately 40 percent, and the remaining hungry people are found in Latin America and other parts of the world. - - Hunger in Global Economy

Nearly 1.3 billion people live on less than $1 per day, while the world's 358 billionaires have assets exceeding the combined annual incomes of countries with 45 percent of the world's people. - UNICEF

3 billion people in the world today struggle to survive on US $2 /day.

In 1994 the Urban Institute in Washington DC estimated that one out of 6 elderly people in the U.S. have an inadequate diet.

In the U.S. hunger and race are related. In 1991, 46 percent of African-American children were chronically hungry, and 40 percent of Latino children were chronically hungry compared to 16 percent of white children.

The infant mortality rate is closely linked to inadequate nutrition among pregnant women. The US ranks 23rd position among industrial nations in infant mortality. African-American infants die at nearly twice the rate of white infants.

One out of every eight children under the age of twelve in the U.S. goes to bed hungry every night.

Half of all children under five years of age in South Asia and one third of those in sub-Saharan Africa are malnourished.

In 1997 alone, vitamin A supplementation programs in developing countries saved the lives of at least 300,000 young children.

Malnutrition is implicated in more than half of all child deaths worldwide – a proportion unmatched by any infectious disease since the Black Death.

About 183 million children weigh less than what they should weigh for their age.

To satisfy the world's sanitation and food requirements would cost only US $13 billion - what the people of the United States and the European Union spend on perfume each year.

The assets of the world's three richest men are more than the combined GNP of all the least developed countries on the planet.

Hunger kills a man every 3.6 seconds.

Food aid is the best form of gift.

A hungry man could commit any sin.

+++++

Chapter I

FOOD SECURITY: A BASIC RIGHT

Food security exists when all people at all times have physical, social and economic access to sufficient, safe and nutritious food to meet their dietary needs and food preferences for an active and healthy life. The four pillars of food security are availability, access, utilization and stability.

– Committee for Food Security

Food security refers to the availability of food and one's access to it. A household is considered food secure when its members do not live in hunger or fear of starvation. According to the World Resources Institute, global per capita food production has been increasing substantially for the past several decades. In 2006, it is reported that globally, the number of people who are overweight has almost equaled with the numbers of undernourished people – the world has one billion people who are overweight, and another one billion people who are undernourished. China, the world's most populous country, is suffering from an obesity epidemic. The target set at the 1996 World Food Summit was to halve the number of undernourished people by 2015 from their number in 1990-92. The (estimated) number of undernourished people in developing countries was 824 million in 1990-92. In 2009, the number had climbed to 1.02 billion people. The World Food Security goal is not yet achieved.

In developing countries, often 70 percent or more of the population lives in rural areas. In that context, agricultural development among smallholder farmers and landless people provides a livelihood for people allowing them the opportunity to stay in their communities. In many areas of the world, land ownership is not available, thus, people who want or need to farm to make a living have little incentive to improve the land.

In the US, there are approximately 2,000,000 farmers, which is less than 1 percent of the population. A direct relationship exists between food consumption levels and poverty. Families with the financial resources to escape extreme poverty rarely suffer from chronic hunger; while most of the poor families not only suffer from chronic hunger, but also they are at risk during food shortage and famines.

In this chapter the importance of food security has been highlighted for effective policy framework by all developing countries. Moreover, the causes of food insecurity, hunger and malnutrition, and effects of natural calamities are incorporated.

Food insecurity:

Embedded In Inequalities, Greed and Ecological Ruin

IT is a stark irony of our times that despite the most amazing advances in science and technology, the world is becoming increasingly vulnerable in terms of meeting its most essential need ~ food. The number of chronically hungry people now exceeds one billion. Despite the bulging surpluses of not only grain but also milk, sugar and wine in some countries, large-scale hunger still continues to plague the world.

The recent wave of price increases in staple food items has spread discontent in many countries. The food price index of the United Nations Food and Agriculture Organization (FAO) in December 2010 surpassed its previous peak of June 2008. Wheat prices doubled in the second half of 2010.

Despite the deepening food crisis that has affected the world's poor, it is strange that the richest countries are busy converting more and more food into fuel. According to the report, 'Meals per gallon', released by the UK charity Action Aid, bio-fuels are conservatively estimated to have been responsible for at least 30 per cent of the global food price spike in 2008. This pushed 100 million people into poverty and drove some 30 million more into hunger.

Speculative tendencies have also played an important role in the worldwide rise in food prices. As economist Jayati Ghosh says, "It is likely that a combination of panic buying and speculative financial activity is playing a role in driving world food prices up well beyond anything that is warranted by real quantity movements.... We now have direct recent experience of how financial speculation in commodity markets cannot only create unprecedented volatility, but also affect prices in developing countries, with extreme effects on hunger and nutrition for at least half of humanity."

At a time of near famine conditions in several countries of Africa, many agri-business companies have moved in to seize millions of acres of land which directly and indirectly have been the source of food and subsistence for millions of people in the Dark Continent. Far from being contained, inequalities in the access to farmland have been accentuated. Farmers in remote rural areas are feeling the adverse impact of increasingly unfair trade practices under the WTO regime and the various free trade agreements.

Perhaps the most widely prevalent threat to the food and agricultural system exists in the form of massive loss of fertile farmland to non-agricultural uses as well as large-scale degradation of land. A world-level assessment of human-induced soil degradation, which was prepared by the International Soil Reference and Information Centre in the Netherlands, concluded that 1.96 billion hectares of soil were degraded to some degree and out of this 300 million hectares have suffered strong to extreme degradation. "It seems incredible that something as basic as the very soil on which we stand should be disappearing at such a rate", warned an editorial in the prestigious journal, New Scientist.

The Green Revolution generally involved the spread of intensive monocultures, but this is harmful for the long-term fertility of land.

The World Resources Report (WRR) explains:

Soil under intensive monoculture tends to lose organic matter and their ability to retain moisture thus becoming more susceptible to erosion and ultimately losing their fertility and productivity. Spread of intensive monoculture generally involves a higher reliance on chemical pesticides.

A very small part of the pesticide applied on a field - less than 0.1 per cent in many insecticides - actually reaches its target organism. The rest plays the role of polluting the land and water, poisoning birds and other forms of life.

As WRR says, "Wholesale elimination of helpful soil dwelling insects and microorganisms that build soil and plant nutrition sometimes occurs, essentially sterilizing the soil."

Excessive use of chemical fertilizers and relative neglect of organic manure also leads to loss of fertility of land. The problems get worse when an unbalanced mix of fertilizers results in nutrient deficiencies in the soil, particularly the deficiency of micro-nutrients.

In several countries excessive application of fertilizers, particularly nitrogen has become a serious problem and the pollution of water sources by nitrates is posing a serious threat.

Particularly linked to the degradation of land is a steady decline in the quality of food. The London Food Commission concluded that at least 92 pesticides, cleared for use in Britain, have been linked to cancer, birth defects or genetic mutation in animal studies. A report of the National Academy of Sciences, USA, said that pesticides in food might cause more than one million additional cases of cancer. This problem is likely to be exacerbated in poorer countries because several of the more hazardous and persistent pesticides banned in rich countries are exported ~ or rather dumped on ~ to the poor nations.

Excessive use of chemical fertilizers can also result in a loss of nutritive value and create some serious health problems. According to the distinguished nutrition expert, C. Gopalan, "the use of high doses of chemical fertilizers, which is part of the modern intensive agricultural technology, had not always gone hand-in-hand with appropriate measures for soil testing and soil replenishment, with the result that, as shown by the studies of FAO, there are disturbing evidences of micro-nutrient depletion of soils in some areas; these are likely to be eventually reflected in impaired nutritive value of food grains grown in such soils."

There has been a substantial increase in recent years in the number and quantity of additives used by the food processing industry, including flavours, colours, emulsifiers, preservatives and an amazing range of other additives. The London Food Commission noted that about 3,800 additives were being used to perform about a hundred functions. Only about a tenth of the additives are subject to government control. The commission wrote: "A single meal may contain a cocktail of 12 to 16 additives. The combinations of additives may react with each other and with foods to produce new chemical substances." A wide range of health hazards has been reported for an equally wide variety of food additives.

Ninety per cent of the world's most important food crops are threatened by loss of bees, birds, bats, and other pollinators, according to two US scientists who conducted a campaign to protect pollinators. "It is clearly a concern on the global level", says Stephen Buchmann, a world-renowned entomologist who launched the forgotten pollinator campaign with Gary Nabhan.

Thus the food situation in the short-term as well as in the long term is endangered by a host of factors related to inequalities, greed and ecological ruin. Unfortunately some of the solutions that are being offered such as genetically modified crops will only worsen the health hazards as well as the stability of food production.

What will actually help to increase food security is an approach based on strengthening the base of small farmers, including the landless farm workers who should be provided some land. These farmers are capable of following the agro-ecology approach to increase food production. Olivier De Schutter, UN Special Rapporteur on the right to food, has presented his annual report to the UN Human Rights Council, focusing on agro-ecology and the right to food. He writes: "Agro-ecology mimics' nature, not industrial processes".

It replaces the external inputs like fertiliser with knowledge of how a combination of plants, trees and animals can enhance productivity of the land. Yields went up 214 per cent in 44 projects in 20 countries in sub-Saharan Africa using agro-ecological farming techniques over a period of three to 10 years....Today's scientific evidence demonstrates that agro-ecological methods outperform the use of chemical fertilizers in boosting food production in regions where the hungry live."

A good food and agricultural system is one which makes available satisfactory livelihood to members of the farming community and wholesome, nutritious food to all people in a sustainable way. It must ensure the welfare of farm animals; protect the soil and its fertility for future generations. It is in this broad perspective that the solutions to the food crisis should be explored.[1]

Food Security

Food security is possible if three minimum conditions are fulfilled. These are:

(a) **Food is available:** The amount and quality of food available globally, nationally and locally can be affected temporarily or for long periods by many factors including climate, disasters, war, civil unrest, population size and growth, agricultural practices, environment, social status and trade.

---

[1] Bharat Dogra (2011), "Food Insecurity - Embedded In Inequalities, Greed And Ecological Ruin", The Statesman, December 8, 2011

(b) **Food is affordable**: When there is a shortage of food prices increase and while richer people will likely still be able to feed themselves, poorer people may have difficulty obtaining sufficient safe and nutritious food without assistance.

(c) **Food is utilized**: At the household level, sufficient and varied food needs to be prepared safely so that people can grow and develop normally, meet their energy needs and avoid disease.

Food security includes the ready availability of nutritionally adequate and safe foods, and an assured ability to acquire acceptable foods in socially acceptable ways (without emergency food supplies, scavenging, stealing, or other coping strategies).

- - (USDA)

Commonly, the concept of food security is defined as including both physical and economic access to food that meets people's dietary needs as well as their food preferences. In many countries, health problems related to dietary excess are an ever increasing threat, In fact, mal-nutrition and food borne diarrhea are become double burden.[2]

Food security is a complex sustainable development issue, linked to health through malnutrition, but also to sustainable economic development, environment, and trade. There is a great deal of debate around food security with some arguing that:

(a) There is enough food in the world to feed everyone adequately; the problem is distribution.

(b) Future food needs can – or cannot – be met by current levels of production.

(c) National food security is paramount – or no longer necessary because of global trade.

---

[2]World Health Organization

(d) Globalization may – or may not – lead to the persistence of food insecurity and poverty in rural communities.

Food security is clearly linked to health: such as enough food, equal distribution and nutrition needs of all members of the household. Agriculture remains the largest employment sector in most developing countries and international agriculture agreements are crucial to a country's food security. Some critics argue that trade liberalization may reduce a country's food security by reducing agricultural employment levels. Concern about this has led a group of World Trade Organization (WTO) member states to recommend that current negotiations on agricultural agreements allow developing countries to re-evaluate and raise tariffs on key products to protect national food security and employment. They argue that WTO agreements, by pushing for the liberalization of crucial markets, are threatening the food security of whole communities.

In 1996, more than 854 million people did not get enough regular healthy food; had ill health and experienced a shorter life expectancy. By 2011, about 1.02 billion of people do not possess the ability to have sufficient food. Children, and especially very young children, who suffer from food insecurity, would be less developed than children of the same age who have sufficient food. They would most likely be shorter and weigh less, and be less able physically and intellectually, because of poor nutrition.

Food security can be improved

(1)**Improving food production:** Increasing the amount of food available is necessary to feed the growing population. The Green Revolution of the 1970s and 1980s led to huge increases in output, largely due to the cultivation of high-yielding varieties of rice and wheat, the expansion of land under production and irrigation, greater use of fertilizers and pesticides and greater availability of credit. In many countries these gains have reached their limit, and social and environmental issues must now be addressed. Further increases in food production depend on better integration of traditional knowledge with research; improving farming practices through training and the use of technology to increase outputs from current land without further loss of productive land; land reform to provide secure access to land for more people; and the provision of low-cost finance to help farmers invest in higher quality seeds and fertilizers and small irrigation pumps.

While genetically modified seeds are being hailed as a means of improving crop outputs, there are also concerns about the ownership of seeds, adequate compensation for traditional knowledge and possible side effects.

(2) **Economic growth and trade liberalization:** Increasing food production leads to greater availability of food and economic growth in the domestic and/or overseas markets. Generating income can provide access to more and varied foods and provide cash for use in other areas of the economy, such as small enterprise and manufacturing, which in turn helps reduce poverty. Trade liberalization is opening up markets slowly, but there are costly barriers to overcome. Work is underway through the Doha Round of multilateral trading negotiations in the World Trade Organization to make trade rules fair, encourage trade liberalization and assist developing countries to participate in the global trade environment.

(3)**Distribution:** While there are sufficient resources in the world to provide food security for all, policy and behavioral changes are necessary to guarantee a fair share for all people, especially the poor. Building on a series of global conferences, in particular the 1992 International Conference on Nutrition and the 1996 and 2002 World Food Summits, countries have developed national nutrition plans and policies in nine major strategic action areas that:

(a) Include mainstream nutrition goals in development policies and programs;
(b) Improve household food and nutrition security;
(c) Protect consumers through improved food quality and safety;
(d) Prevent and manage infectious diseases;
(e) Promote breastfeeding;
(f) Care for the socio-economically deprived and nutritionally vulnerable;
(g) Prevent and control specific micronutrient deficiencies;
(h) Promote appropriate diets and healthy lifestyles; and
(i) Access, analyze and monitor nutrition situations.

The progress towards achieving these goals, however, has been much slower than intended.

(4) **Food aid:** The need for food during emergencies such as drought, disaster, population displacement and conflict is addressed by the distribution of basic food supplies and fuel. Early warning systems can predict problem areas, allowing action to be taken to keep people in their homes and help them back to food self-sufficiency as quickly as possible. Food sourced locally rather than internationally minimizes the costs and disruption to local markets. In severe situations feeding may be necessary but often food aid is linked with work, health or education to avoid dependency and address the long-term causes of food insecurity.[3]

---

[3]Global agenda

Hunger and Malnutrition: Hunger denotes want or scarcity of food. If someone cannot supply food to his family members, the family is in hunger. Similarly if a state cannot supply food to the inhabitants, the state faces hunger.

Hunger[4] creates starvation of people, loss of health, diseased and even deaths. Malnutrition is a general term that indicates a lack of some or all-nutritional elements necessary for human health.

There are two basic types of malnutrition.[5]

(a) The first and most important is protein-energy malnutrition–the lack of enough protein (from meat and other sources) and food that provides energy (measured in calories) which all of the basic food groups provide. This is the type of malnutrition that is referred to when world hunger is discussed.

(b) The second type of malnutrition, also very important, is micronutrient (vitamin and mineral) deficiency. This is not the type of malnutrition that is referred to when world hunger is discussed, though it is certainly very important.

Recently there has also been a move to include obesity as a third form of malnutrition. Considering obesity as malnutrition expands the previous usual meaning of the term, which referred to poor nutrition due to lack of food inputs. It is poor nutrition, but it is certainly not typically due to a lack of calories, but rather too many although poor food choices, often due to poverty, are part of the problem. Obesity will not be considered here, although obesity is certainly a health problem and is increasingly considered as a type of malnutrition.

---

[4] World Hunger Facts 2009

[5] Wikipedia, the free encyclopedia

Protein-energy malnutrition: It is the most lethal form of malnutrition/hunger. It is basically a lack of calories and protein. Food is converted into energy and the energy contained in food is measured by calories. Protein is necessary for key body functions including provision of essential amino acids and development and maintenance of muscles.

The FAO has estimated that more than 1.02 billion Hungry People are living in our planet.

(a) Developed Countries 15 million
(b) North East and North Africa – 42 million
(c) Latin America and the Caribbean 53 million
(d) Sub –Saharan Africa – 265 Million
(e) Asia and the Pacific – 642

No one really knows how many people are malnourished. The statistic most frequently cited is that of the United Nations Food and Agriculture Organization, which measures 'under nutrition'. The most recent estimate, released on October 14, 2009 by FAO, says that 1.02 billion people are undernourished, a sizable increase from its 2006 estimate of 854 million people. The increase has been due to three factors:

(a) Neglect of agriculture relevant to very poor people by governments and international agencies;
(b) The current worldwide economic crisis, and
(c) The significant increase of food prices in the last several years, which has been devastating to those with only a few dollars a day to spend.

1.02 billion People constitute 15 percent of the estimated world population of 6.8 billion. Most of the undernourished people reside in developing countries. The FAO estimate is based on statistical aggregates. It looks at a country's income level and income distribution and uses this information to estimate how many people receive such a low level of income that they are malnourished. Under nutrition is a relatively new concept, but is increasingly used. It should be taken as basically equivalent to malnutrition. **Children are the most visible victims of under nutrition.**

Children who are poorly nourished suffer up to 160 days of illness each year. Poor nutrition plays a role in at least half of the 10.9 million child deaths each year – five million deaths. Under nutrition magnifies the effect of every disease, including measles and malaria. The estimated proportions of deaths in which under nutrition is an underlying cause are roughly similar for diarrhea (61 percent), malaria (57 percent), pneumonia (52 percent), and measles (45 percent). Malnutrition can also be caused by diseases, such as the diseases that cause diarrhea, by reducing the body's ability to convert food into usable nutrients.

According to the most recent estimate that Hunger Notes could find, malnutrition, as measured by stunting, affects 32.5 percent of children in developing countries – one of three (de Onis 2000). Geographically, more than 70 percent of malnourished children live in Asia, 26 percent in Africa and 4 percent in Latin America and the Caribbean. In many cases, their plight began even before birth with a malnourished mother. Un-nutrition among pregnant women in developing countries leads to 1 out of 6 infants born with low birth weight. This is a risk factor for neonatal deaths, but also causes learning disabilities, mental, retardation, poor health, blindness and premature death.

True individual freedom cannot exist without economic security and independence. People who are hungry and out of a job are the stuff of which dictatorships are made.

Franklin D. Roosevelt

The world produces enough food to feed everyone. World agriculture produces 17 percent more calories per person today than it did 30 years ago, despite a 70 percent population increase. This is enough to provide everyone in the world with at least 2,720 kilocalories (kcal) per person per day (FAO 2002, p.9). The principal problem is that many people in the world do not have sufficient land to grow, or income to purchase enough food.

Causes of hunger: The world organizations and all governments must fight against hunger, as it is the root cause of all ills, all conflicts and all evils. The causes are:

(a)**Poverty:** The causes of poverty include poor people's lack of resources, an extremely unequal income distribution in the world and within specific countries burdened with conflict, and hunger. As of 2008 (2004 statistics), the World Bank has estimated that there were an estimated 982 million poor people in developing countries, but in 2009, the FAO estimates of 1.02 billion undernourished people. Progress in poverty reduction has been concentrated in Asia, and especially, East Asia, with the major improvement occurring in China. In Sub-Saharan Africa, the number of people in extreme poverty has increased.

(b) **Harmful economic systems:** The principal underlying cause of poverty and hunger is the ordinary operation of the economic and political systems in the world. Essentially control over resources and income is based on military, political and economic power that typically ends up in the hands of a minority, who live well, while those at the bottom barely survive, if they do.

(c)**Conflict:** At the end of 2005, the global number of refugees was at its lowest level in almost a quarter of a century. Despite some large-scale repatriation movements, the last three years have witnessed a significant increase in refugee numbers, due primarily to the violence-taking place in Iraq and Somalia. By the end of 2008, the total number of refugees under UNHCR's mandate exceeded 10 million. The number of conflict-induced internally displaced persons (IDPs) reached some 26 million worldwide at the end of the year. Conflict causes displacement, poverty and hunger and it losses peace.

(d) **Hunger is also a cause of hunger**: By causing poor health, low levels of energy, and even mental impairment, hunger can lead to even greater poverty by reducing people's ability to work and learn.

(e) **Climate change**: Climate change is increasingly viewed as a current and future cause of hunger and poverty. Increasing drought, flooding, and changing climatic patterns requiring a shift in crops and farming practices that may not be easily accomplished are three key issues

(f) **Micronutrients:** Quite a few trace elements or micronutrients–vitamins and minerals–are important for health. 1 out of 3 people in developing countries are affected by vitamin and mineral deficiencies, according to the World Health Organization. Three, perhaps the most important in terms of health consequences for poor people in developing countries, are:

Vitamin: Vitamin A deficiency can cause night blindness and reduces the body's resistance to disease. In children Vitamin A deficiency can also cause growth retardation. Between 100 and 140 million children are vitamins A deficient. It is estimated that an estimated 250,000 to 500 000 vitamin A-deficient children become blind every year, and half of them die within 12 months of losing their sight.

Iron: Iron deficiency is a principal cause of anemia. Two billion people—over 30 percent of the world's population—are anemic, mainly due to iron deficiency, and, in developing countries, frequently exacerbated by malaria and worm infections. For children, health consequences include premature birth, low birth weight, infections, and elevated risk of death. Later, physical and cognitive developments are impaired, resulting in lowered school performance. For pregnant women, anemia contributes to 20 percent of all maternal deaths.

Iodine: Iodine deficiency disorders (IDD) jeopardize children's mental health– often their very lives. Serious iodine deficiency during pregnancy may result in stillbirths, abortions and congenital abnormalities such as cretinism, a grave, irreversible form of mental retardation that affects people living in iodine-deficient areas of Africa and Asia. IDD also causes mental impairment that lowers intellectual prowess at home, at school, and at work. IDD affects over 740 million people, 13 percent of the world's population. Fifty million people have some degree of mental impairment caused by IDD.

The State of Food Insecurity in the World

World hunger is increasing: The World Food Summit (WFS) goal of halving the number of undernourished people in the world by 2015 is becoming more difficult to reach for many countries. FAO's most recent estimates put the number of hungry people at 923 million in 2007, an increase of more than 80 million since the 1990–92 base period. Long-term estimates (available up to 2003–05) show that some countries were well on track towards reaching the WFS and Millennium Development Goal (MDG) targets before the period of high food prices; however, even these countries may have suffered setbacks.

High food prices share much of the blame: The most rapid increase in chronic hunger experienced in recent years occurred between 2003–05 and 2007. FAO's provisional estimates show that, in 2007, 75 million more people were added to the total number of undernourished relative to 2003–05. While several factors are responsible, high food prices are driving millions of people into food insecurity, worsening conditions for many who were already food-insecure, and threatening long-term global food security.

The poorest, landless and female-headed households are the hardest hit: The vast majority of urban and rural households in the developing world relies on food purchases for most of their food and stands to lose from high food prices. High food prices reduce real income and worsen the prevalence of food insecurity and malnutrition among the poor by reducing the quantity and quality of food consumed.

Initial governmental policy responses have had limited effect: To contain the negative effects of high food prices, governments have introduced various measures, such as price controls and export restrictions. While understandable from an immediate social welfare perspective, many of these actions have been ad hoc and are likely to be ineffective and unsustainable. Some have had damaging effects on world price levels and stability.

High food prices are also an opportunity: In the long run, high food prices represent an opportunity for agriculture (including smallholder farmers) throughout the developing world, but they will have to be accompanied by the provision of essential public goods. Smallholder gains could fuel broader economic and rural development. Farming households can see immediate gains; other rural households may benefit in the longer run if higher prices turn into opportunities for increasing output and creating employment.

A comprehensive twin-track approach is required: Governments, donors, the United Nations, non- governmental organizations, civil society and the private sector must immediately combine their efforts in a strategic, twin-track approach to address the impact of high food prices on hunger. This should include:

(a)Measures to enable the agriculture sector, especially smallholders in developing countries, to respond to the high prices; and

(b)Carefully targeted safety nets and social protection programs is a must for the most food-insecure and vulnerable. This is a global challenge requiring a global response.[6]

World Population Reaches Seven Billion:
predictions of doom are nothing new

Thomas Malthus predicted that the Earth would be unable to support the growing population. On Monday, November7, 2011, the world's population crossed a new milestone.

In 1798, an English clergyman, the Rev Thomas Malthus, predicted that one day the population of the world would outstrip the globe's ability to feed it. He based this on a simple and, on the face of it, unarguable premise:

Population grows exponentially – increasing by a set percentage per year – while food production grows arithmetically, by a set quantity per year.

Even the smallest exponential progression will, given enough time, outstrip any arithmetical one. Eventually, by the relentless laws of mathematics and

[6]The State of Food Security in the World 2008, FAO, Rome

demography, humanity would overreach itself and face mass starvation.

His warnings were echoed nearly two centuries later, by an American academic, Paul Ehrlich. His 1968 book, **The Population Bomb**, warned that by the end of the 20th century, humanity would face a population explosion followed by a sudden, devastating collapse. The book opened with the words: "The battle to feed all of humanity is over. In the 1970s hundreds of millions of people will starve to death in spite of any crash programs embarked upon now. At this late date nothing can prevent a substantial increase in the world death rate." He predicted four billion deaths, including those of 65 million Americans. The book was a huge success, making Prof Ehrlich a global celebrity. He wasn't alone in his predictions: the year before, two American brothers, William and Paul Paddock, had written another smash hit, Famine – 1975! Malthusian collapse was big box office.

According to the United Nations Population Fund, on Monday, October 31, global population will reach seven billion. That's more than double what it was when 'The Population Bomb' was published. The world is growing by 80 million people per year – more than two every second. Clearly, the dire predictions of Malthus and Ehrlich have not come to pass: England and America are not starving, and there has been no great population collapse. So what has happened?

In short; **Malthus** was wrong not because of his mathematics, but because of his inability to see into the future. His belief that humanity's ability to feed itself would grow only arithmetically did not take into account – how could it? – The rise of agricultural efficiency, of industrial farming, of fertilizers and chemicals. At the time he wrote, 20,000 square meters of agricultural land were required to feed one person. That figure was only 2,000 square meters in 2002

By the time Ehrlich wrote in 1968, industrial farming was widespread: still, he predicted a nightmare far more imminent and inevitable than any of Malthus's claims. But Ehrlich was even more dramatically wrong. In the 43 years since he set down his terrifying vision, population has doubled: but not only has the world not starved, the amount of food available per head has increased by more than a quarter. According to the UN, the percentage of the population which is "undernourished" has fallen from 33 per cent to 16 since 1968. Global food production has easily kept pace with population: again, thanks to advances in agricultural technology, specifically those which drove the so-called Green Revolution. Through aggressive use of selective breeding and agricultural chemicals, and the development of new breeds of wheat and rice, what seemed to be looming disaster was averted. Rice yields per hectare in Asia tripled, and food costs plummeted. The "father of the Green Revolution", an American agronomist and plant geneticist called **Norman Borlaug,** won the Nobel Peace Prize. He was described as the "Forgotten benefactor of mankind" by Atlantic Monthly, and credited having prevented a billion deaths.

That Malthus and Ehrlich were both so wrong is a tribute to human ingenuity. It's also a warning to those who try to forecast the future. Neither of them predicted the revolutions in food production. Neither did they foresee another, even simpler, change in human behaviour: a global drop in fertility. The average woman now has just 2.52 children – down from 4.85 when Ehrlich was writing. In Europe and the United States, that has dropped to 1.53 and 2.07 respectively. This is thanks to contraception, to greater urbanization and economic development, and to the education of women.

However, the fact that previous soothsayers have been wrong does not mean that the future is necessarily secure. It means that humanity is overconfident in its ability to predict it. Dan Gardner, the author of Future Babble, a book about the unreliability of such predictions, points out that it's not new: "If you look at the history of demographic predictions, they are not only often wrong, they are routinely wrong. And we swing from one to the other: we swing from fear of overpopulation to under-population and back again. If you go back to the 1930s, you'll find many smart people – George Orwell among them – saying that it's terrifying that Britain will be completely depopulated by the 1980s."

It wasn't just the doomsayers in the 1970s that were making bad guesses. "As well as the Malthusians like Ehrlich, there was another group, the Cornucopian's, who claimed 'Ehrlich and the rest are wrong: don't worry, everything's going to be great,' " says Gardner. "Now, things turned out OK, but for completely different reasons from the ones the Cornucopian's suggested." Among their more "goofy" theories was a suggestion that undersea kelp farms would solve the food crisis.

"If people had said 'human ingenuity is a magnificent thing, and in the face of necessity who knows what we'll come up with', that would have been exactly right," says Gardner. "Unfortunately, that's not what the Cornucopian's said. What they said was 'here is how we are going to fix it', and they were wrong. It's the mirror image mistake of Ehrlich and the Malthusians: complete overconfidence in their ability to predict future events." They just didn't make as much of a splash. "If you want to sell books, donot be an optimist," Gardner points out.

As we reach the seven billion mark, both camps are still in action, predicting either doom or plenty. Matt Ridley, the author of The Rational Optimist, is probably the most well-known of the modern Cornucopian's: Paul Ehrlich, meanwhile, still flies the flag for the Malthusians, saying as recently as 2009 that The Population Bomb was "too optimistic" about the future, and that since it was published there have been "famines, essentially continuously in parts of Africa".

While his prediction of billions of deaths has not come to pass, 300 million people have died of hunger and hunger-related diseases since 1968. He added that "the world now may be on the brink of another major rise" in the death rate from starvation.

So what does this tell us about the world that lays ahead for baby number 7,000,000,000? Mainly those humans will continue to make bad predictions. The UN projects population reaching a peak of 9.22 billion in 2075, but as Gardner says:

Demography is a wonderful field that provides a lot of insights, but it is not a crystal ball: any sort of projection that goes out to, say, 100 years is essentially a guess.

Making predictions, though, is not without consequence. "If you want Ehrlich's worst prediction," says Gardner, "I can summarize it in one word: India." In 1974, Ehrlich, and the Paddocks, thought that India was doomed, and soon. But they didn't think that the world should work to save it: they suggested a system of "triage", in which rich countries should stop sending money to the terminal cases and try to save the others. Luckily, they were not listened to: the scientist who introduced Borlaug's Green Revolution to India, Prof Monkombu Swaminathan, says that if they had been, tens of millions might have starved. Instead, India is one of the few countries whose economies are booming: it is now a major donor, rather than recipient, of food aid.

"These overconfident predictions could have destroyed India," says Gardner. "This is not an academic issue, or a ha-ha-you-lost, we-won thing, this is serious stuff."

We must not be complacent: more than a billion people worldwide are starving or undernourished, and the world's population is growing by more than 200,000 people a day. Human ingenuity is needed now as much as ever. But the seven billionths human is not necessarily a harbinger of disaster: and anyone who confidently says otherwise doesn't know what they're talking about.[7]

Peace March for Food Security

Sharma[8] opines that unless the problem of 'food insecurity' is solved, people would perish without food. With an estimated 24,000 people succumbing globally to hunger every day, more than 120 million people could perish by the year 2015 from this shameful scourge. In Gleneagles, however, the leaders of the world's richest economies did not even provide lip service to the hungry and malnourished.

Like thousands of British who had assembled at the meadows in Edinburgh two days before the G-8 Summit officially began at the Gleneagles resort in Scotland, this writer was amazed at the perseverance, determination and patience of the people who had lined up for a peaceful march snaking its way through the city. Carrying placards, banners and wearing mostly white, they waited for the police to give the thumbs up signal to move. Such was the enthusiasm to make their voices heard that they

---

[7] Tom Chivers, (2011), " The World's population id 7 Billions", The Sunday Pioneer, Agenda, November 6, 2011 / The Telegraph

[8]Devendra Sharma, GATT to WTO and In the Famine Trap, August 6, 2005, India Together

braved the slow movement of the march. It took us nearly three and a half hours to traverse not more than 100 meters and yet people were clam and cheerful.

An estimated 250,000 people took part in the peaceful march.

For those who assembled in Edinburgh, the peaceful march was the only democratic way to express their anguish at the faulty global policies exacerbating hunger and poverty. Unfortunately, the world leaders who swear in the name of democracy are the first ones to turn a blind eye to the traditions of democracy once they are in power. This is exactly what happened at Gleneagles. Democracy no longer means hearing and protecting the voice of the masses. As the G-8 clearly demonstrates, democracy is all about protecting and strengthening the stock markets.

A last minute gesture by Japan provided the G-8 countries some saving grace. Japan agreed to fill the gap to raise the aid packet to Africa to US $50 billion by the year 2010. Like all other policy decisions that emanate from the rich economies this too came with strings attached. **"Private enterprise is the prime engine of growth and development,"** the communiqué issued at the end of the Summit said. In other words, the G-8 leaders allowed the private sector to join the World Bank/IMF to continue the plunder of Africa. As Peter Hard staff from the World Development Movement (WDM) summed it up:

Ask not what we can do for the poor, but what the poor can do for us.

Time and again, the emphasis shifted to global trade and investment. More than writing off the outstanding debt (surpassing some US $295 billion for Africa) and providing aid, trade was projected as the right approach to growth. With no commitment to do away with the huge agricultural subsidies being provided by the OECD countries, equal to US $321 billion a year, the development paradigm being suggested for some of the world's poorest countries will only multiply poverty and hunger. Farm subsidies for the wealthy in their own countries are almost six times what have been promised as aid for Africa.

Agricultural subsidies depress global prices and enable the food companies to dump highly subsidized farm products in developing countries. For the countries deluged with food imports, importing food is like importing unemployment. The socio-economic fallout adds to poverty and hunger.

After all, what is the justification for Europe to produce 200 per cent surplus milk for the next ten years? With countries like India already surplus in milk, and with China not requiring milk for human consumption, the entire surplus is meant for the African countries. The G-8 leaders therefore need to cap agricultural production in their own countries.

Numerous studies have shown how agriculture subsidies are being used to destroy farm livelihoods in the developing countries, thus posing a serious threat to food sovereignty. Except for lip service to do away with export subsidies, nothing tangible and date-bound is being spelled out. At the same time the thrust on private investment is meant to push the genetically modified food industry into Africa. With Europe refusing to accept GM foods on conditions of human and environment safety, the G-8 leadership is finding ways and means to find a market for the unwanted genetically manipulated food. Africa therefore is the perfect food dump. Such an approach runs counter to achieving food self-sufficiency.

What the G-8 leadership refuses to accept is that the only way out of darkness for Africa is to strengthen its agriculture so as to emerge food-secure. Africa will have to follow the same approach that the two most populated countries – India and China – followed in the early 1970s. Both the countries closed the national borders and provided the right kind of policy mix that enabled farmers to produce more. The rest is history.

If a third of the planet's population could emerge out of starvation and hunger by restructuring domestic policies that ensured food self-sufficiency, Africa too will have to follow the same approach. Never before has such a huge mass of people been lifted out of poverty and hunger without ensuring food self-sufficiency, and never in future the same Herculean task can be accomplished by privatization and agribusiness. Coupled with the right kind of domestic policies, food self-reliance is the only way to Make Hunger History, the title of a lively event in Edinburgh. Once hunger is abolished, poverty too will become history; this was the powerful message at Gleneagles.

But the leaders might as well have been playing on the links. Riding on the swelling public opinion in support of the Make Poverty History campaign, G-8 leaders arrived at the Gleneagles resort with a simple task: sow the seeds of hope for the billions living in abject poverty and destitution. Instead, they opted to uphold the commercial interests of big businesses and transnational corporations. Except for making empty statements about the shameful scourge of poverty and the need to bring ailing Africa back into the fold of economic development, the international community failed to take any significant step. The message of the G-8 Summit is very clear:

Africa will have to live on hope. Unfortunately, the world leaders who swear in the name of God to promote democracy are the persons, who forget their promises once they are in power.

Natural Calamities

There is a growing trend towards greater and more catastrophic natural disasters. Of the ten disasters with the highest death tolls since 1975, half have occurred in the five-year period between 2003 and 2008, with the developing world witnessing nine of the ten worst. A range of factors such as climate change and the decline of ecosystems; increasing urbanization and poor urban governance; and low incomes and fragile rural livelihoods compound such terrible natural events.

This first edition of the biennial Global Assessment Report on Disaster Risk Reduction (DRR) aims to review and analyze the natural hazards threatening humanity and seeks to provide new evidence on how, where and why disaster risk is increasing globally. The report focuses on:

(a) Global disaster risk: patterns, trends and drivers
(b) Deconstructing disaster: risk patterns and poverty trends at the local level
(c) Progress in the implementation of the Hyogo Framework for Action (HFA): a ten-year framework adopted by 168 countries in order to mitigate the effect of natural disasters.

Addressing the underlying risk factors- Economic development increases a country's exposure at the same time as it decreases its vulnerability. However, in low- and middle-income countries with rapidly growing economies, exposure increases at a far faster rate than vulnerability decreases, leading to increased risk overall.

Risk drivers: economic and social development plays a crucial role. These include income and economic strength; and governance factors such as the quality of institutions, openness and government accountability.

Climate change: more than two thirds of the mortality and economic losses from internationally reported disasters is associated with meteorological, climatologically and hydrological hazard.

Poverty and poor governance: the translation of poverty into risk is conditioned by the capacity of urban and local governments to plan and regulate urban development, enable access to safe land and provide hazard mitigating infrastructure and protection for poor households.

Areas of HFA progress reported: progress has been made in strengthening capacities, institutional systems and legislation to address deficiencies in disaster preparedness and response. However, little progress is being made in the mainstreaming of DRR into economic, social, urban, rural, and environmental and infrastructure planning.[9]

Community- and local-level approaches, particularly when supported by effective decentralization processes and government-civil society partnerships, can increase the relevance; effectiveness and sustainability of DRR across all practice areas, reduce costs and build social capital.

Food for Peace

In 1954, President Dwight D. Eisenhower signed what was then known as the Agricultural Trade Development and Assistance Act, or Public Law 480.

In 1961, the law got another name when President Kennedy expanded the program and renamed it **"Food for Peace."**

---

[9] Global assessment report on disaster risk reduction: risk and poverty in a changing climate, Prevention Web (2009), Eldis Poverty reporter June 11, 2009

John Fitzgerald Kennedy set out the logic for the program saying, "Food is strength, and food is peace, and food is freedom, and food is a helping to people around the world whose goodwill and friendship we want."

Yet the program has always had a purpose beyond the humanitarian one. As Eisenhower said, the legislation will "lay the basis for a permanent expansion of our exports of agricultural products with lasting benefits to us and people of other lands." In other words, let's help our farmers at the same time as we help hungry people in places that might breed war and terrorism without our help.

Food for Peace was actually an outgrowth of the Marshall Plan to help rebuild war torn countries after World War II. So, in the early years, most of the food aid went to Italy, Japan, Germany, Austria, England and Finland.

Then, as those countries rebuilt and droughts, local wars and other emergencies developed in other places, the list of recipient countries changed and expanded. Recipient countries have included most of Europe, all of Africa, the Mid East, Asia, South and Central America, Mongolia and even Russia. Since 1954, 135 countries have received food through the program. We had grain on the ground we didn't know what to do with. And there was a growing awareness of hungry people around the world. I mean the first impulse is to get those things together, pronto!

Throughout the 60s, 70s and 80s, India was the largest recipient of American food aid. The level of aid was highest in the 60s when over $1.5 billion in aid helped stave off starvation in the subcontinent. In addition to providing direct aid, the Food for Peace program worked closely with Green Revolution programs that introduced new varieties of wheat and rice to the country. Today, India is close to graduating from foreign food aid altogether.

In Ethiopia, cycles of drought and famine have repeated over the last 30 years. Each time, Food for Peace stepped in to alleviate the worst conditions, and recently scientists have learned how to predict the conditions that lead to famine. In 2003, Food for Peace actually began shipping commodities into the country before the crisis peaked and saved thousands of lives.

The largest part of the program is administered by USAID, the U.S. Agency for International Development, which was also set up by President Kennedy. Over the years, the bulk of the money appropriated has gone to buy farm products from almost every one of the 50 U.S. states, shipping the commodities to the countries that need aid, and contracting with NGOs (non-governmental organizations) to actually distribute the food to needy people.

The program claims that 99 percent of the food aid arrives at its destination and is eaten by the people it was intended for. In recent years, the program has emphasized longer-term development projects that build the agricultural ability of the recipient countries. In a sense, this is an extension of the Green Revolution approach to help countries become self-sufficient for their own food. In the past 50 years, Food for Peace has sent 106 million metric tons overseas feeding billions of hungry people.

That's an average of a little over 2 million metric tons a year. That may sound like a small amount, given the current world population of over 6.7 billion people. But, those 2 million metric tons of food actually fill the equivalent of 80,000 trucks each carrying five hundred 110-pound bags. Over 50 years, that's enough trucks to stretch around the equator.[10]

Food Security up to 2050

The UK prepares to produce more food, more sustainably for the coming years. The UK has a moral obligation to contribute to the global challenge of securing future food supplies.

The Select Committee Chairman the Rt Hon Michael Jack MP opined that if people go hungry then political stability goes out of the window. This is a key lesson that DEFRA must learn from last year's food price hike when some countries ran short of food. What happened showed just how fine the line is between full supermarket shelves and empty stomachs. [11]

The Committee wants the UK to make the most of its temperate climate and the natural advantages this gives it for producing food. In contrast, it does not favour targets for food production and recognizes that DEFRA cannot command farmers to increase output of specific commodities. MPs urge DEFRA to provide clear leadership, and guidance on the nature and size of the challenge. The report says that the Department must concentrate on building capacity in the food and farming industries so that they can respond to market signals in ways that will reduce the risk of food shortages.

The UK can play a leading role both in Europe and globally in making sure that our farmers and food industry can contribute effectively towards meeting the challenge of a world that will need to double its food output by 2050 whilst coping with the pressures

---

[10]Farming in the 1950s and 1960s, Weasels; Living History Farm, Nebraska

[11]Defra Committee, Session 2008-09, July 21, 2009

Note: Defra refers to Department of Environment, Food and Rural affairs of the U.K. Government

of climate change as well as global plant and animal diseases. Every region of the UK has a contribution to make.

The report emphasizes that producing sufficient food is only part of the challenge. How food is produced is equally important. The Committee notes that increases in production will have to take place in the context of reducing greenhouse gas emissions from the food system, reducing reliance on fossil fuel-derived inputs, and conserving soil and water. Consumers are increasingly interested in how their food is produced. The report says that consumer engagement will be vital if DEFRA is to achieve its vision for the UK food system.

The report does not advocate food self-sufficiency for the UK and emphasizes the importance of strong trading relationships with a variety of countries. It notes that DEFRA's response to the challenge of securing food supplies must take place in a European and global context. It calls for the focus of the reformed Common Agricultural Policy to be on sustainable food production, whilst encouraging European farmers to make their contribution to meeting the world's future food demands.

The Committee also highlights the development of "food colonialism" or "land grabbing" – a phenomenon that involves the large-scale acquisition of land overseas by wealthy investors in order to grow food for people in the investor country. The Committee is concerned about the pressure this could place on the global food system over time and believes that DEFRA must take the implications of this phenomenon seriously.

The report provides long-term leadership and advises that DEFRA must tackle existing weaknesses in the UK food system. In particular, it calls for an urgent increase in spending on public-sector food and farming research.

The long-term securing of the UK's food supplies is a fundamental responsibility of Government. In addressing these challenges DEFRA must ensure that the nation's farmers have the support and resources they need to secure long-term sustainable increases in agricultural production. This challenge will not be met unless DEFRA properly safeguards our world-class agricultural science base. It must heed the words of Professor Kell, the Chief Executive of the Biotechnology and Biological Sciences Research Council, and put in an extra £100 million.

A clear plan of action is needed now, not the formation of ever more Government-run committees. DEFRA must show real leadership in ensuring that all parts of Government play their role in meeting this challenge. It will take national, European and global co-operation-not confrontation-if the world is to feed itself sustainably in the future.

Food security – A major concern

Dr. Manmohan Singh, Prime Minister of India has opined that the sense of comfort over India's food security is somewhat misplaced and both the availability of produce and controlling prices remain challenges needing focused attention on farm productivity. Our experience in the past two years has brought to the fore the importance of food security and the need for containing prices. For some time past, there was a false sense of security that availability of food has ceased to be a concern. Similarly, many felt that we have been able to control prices.

The state governments, too, to focus their energies on farm productivity and there is great scope for improving the yields of major crops through greater efforts in achieving this. Our agricultural productivity still ranks far below the best in the world. India handled the challenges posed by the global slowdown in a much better fashion than many other economies, through inclusive growth.

Fast economic growth has little meaning if it does not lead to the well-being of the poor and the disadvantaged of farmers, workers, children, students and women. The benefits of the development process have to percolate to every part of our country. The bureaucracy should ensure that the numerous welfare programs of the federal and state governments are implemented in the spirit in which they have been conceived without roadblocks and leakages through decentralized governance. All this constitutes a huge task that requires dedication, commitment and persistence. The central government does recognize that there is always room for improvement in these schemes and programs.

The prime minister also expressed concern over poor infrastructure in the country and said states that have lagged behind must go that extra mile to remove all the bottlenecks. Shortages of electricity, poor roads, over-crowded ports, delayed flights, all retard our economic efficiency and damage our international image. States that have relatively better infrastructure attract investment while the others lag behind. This is a lesson, which all States have to imbibe.[12]

Strengthening Cooperation for Global Food Security

Hui Liangyu says emphatically that food is essential to the survival of people and grain is the principal food. Freedom from hunger is the most fundamental human right. Food security is the basis for economic

---

[12]First Annual Conference of Chief Secretaries, New Delhi, Times of India February 1, 2010

development and social stability. It is also an important prerequisite for national independence and world peace. At present, the international community is under the dual pressure of an international financial crisis and a global food crisis. Some developing countries have seen their development process severely hindered and social stability threatened. The international community should view and address food security as a matter vital to human survival and development, and safeguard food security in the world through strengthened cooperation. To this end, we wish to put forward the following suggestions.

First, increase input raises food production. The developing ones should be in ways suited to their national circumstances, invest more in agriculture, break the technical bottlenecks inhibiting output growth, build up the capability to resist natural disasters, plant diseases and insect pests and strive for higher yield and greater self-sufficiency. Developed countries and international organizations should provide developing countries with financial, technological, market and capacity-building assistance with due respect for the sovereignty of the recipient countries and more emphasis on building their own "blood-generating" capacity.

Second, create a sound market environment for mutual benefit and win-win progress. The causes of a food crisis are complicated, including unbalanced supply and demand, as well as distorted international agricultural market and financial speculation. All countries should jointly oppose trade protectionism in all forms and manifestations and push for a positive outcome of the Doha Round negotiations. Developed countries should demonstrate greater sincerity in the negotiations, slash agricultural subsidies, remove trade barriers and give greater market access to developing members so that a fair, reasonable, sustainable and stable international agricultural trading order can take shape. It is imperative to enhance financial regulation over agricultural markets and effectively curb speculative activities. This should become one of the priorities in reforming the international financial regulatory system.

Third, press ahead with reform and improve the global governance mechanism. China supports the strengthening of the global governance mechanism for food security and the early establishments of a food security safeguard system encompassing early warning, emergency relief and macro-control and regulation functions. China favors the adoption of a comprehensive, coordinated and sustainable strategy for global food security that ensures efficiency and equal participation of all parties. China supports the strengthening of the UN food and agriculture agencies through reform and endorses a bigger role of the Committee on World Food Security and the Task Force on the World Food Security Crisis of the United Nations.

Fourth, adopt a holistic approach for comprehensive and balanced growth. In the final analysis, the food issue is a development issue. Food security is closely related to economic growth, social progress, and climate change and energy security. All countries should pay great attention to the impact of climate change on agriculture and other sectors, intensify global cooperation on climate change under the principle of "common but differentiated responsibilities", and strive for a positive outcome of the up-coming Copenhagen Conference. The international community should take seriously the long-term implications of the development of the bio-fuel sector and guide it toward sustainability based on the principle of "not competing for food with humans and not competing for land with food". Energy security should by no means come at the cost of food security.

This year marks the 60th anniversary of the founding of the People's Republic of China. Over the past 60 years, we have placed great importance on agriculture and food. Providing sufficient food for over 1 billion people has been on top of our agenda. Our policy is to realize basic food self-sufficiency, strengthen the fundamental role of agriculture and pursue agricultural modernization with Chinese features. We have enhanced water conservancy for rural farmlands, accelerated the advance of agro-science and technology, and motivated farmers to produce more. As a result, we have made notable achievements in agriculture and rural development. China feeds about 20 percent of the world's population with about 9 percent of the world's arable lands and about 6.5 percent of the world's fresh water. The Chinese people, who once lived in hunger, now enjoy moderate prosperity. We have met ahead of schedule the targets for eradicating extreme poverty and hunger under MDGs. It is a historic transformation. It is a miracle. It is the Chinese people's great contribution to global food security, world peace and development.

China now has a favorable food security situation. The comprehensive grain production capacity is on a steady rise. Grain reserves are abundant. Staple agricultural produce is in sufficient supply. Food prices are basically stable. Grain output has been increasing for five years in a row since 2004, reaching a record high of over 500 million tons in 2008. We expect another bumper harvest this year. For many years, China has been able to meet its own food demand on its own. Every year we export an average of 8 million tons of staple grains such as wheat, rice and corn. Our agricultural markets are fairly open with the average tariff level only one fourth of the world's average. We have every reason to be confident that we can ensure food security by mainly relying on domestic production.

However, we are keenly aware that China has a large population, agricultural infrastructure is weak, economic and social development in rural areas has fallen behind and there is a growing income gap between urban and rural areas. The international financial crisis has brought us new pressures and challenges. Therefore, we have made it clear in our response to the international financial crisis that in boosting domestic demand, rural areas have the greatest potential; for steady and relatively fast economic growth, agriculture is the foundation; and in improving people's well-being, farmers are the top priority. We have increased input, enhanced agricultural infrastructure and projects designed to improve rural residents' livelihood, and maintained good momentum of steady and relatively fast development of agriculture and rural areas. These have been a strong support for the stabilization and improvement of China's economy. We are confident that the goal of 8 percent GDP growth for this year can be met.

As a developing country, China has done its best to provide help to other developing countries and contribute to world food and agriculture development. Over the years, we have made contributions to international institutions for food and agriculture and provided emergency humanitarian food assistance to some countries in need. Meanwhile, we have been committed to helping other developing countries improve their capacity of food production with our advantage in agro-technologies. In nearly 100 countries in Asia, Africa, Latin America, the Pacific and other regions, we have set up agricultural technology demonstration centers, experiment stations and dissemination stations, sent over 30,000 agricultural experts and technical personnel, and helped train a great number of local agricultural technical personnel.

China will continue to enhance exchanges and cooperation with other countries in food and agricultural development. We are ready to continue to provide agricultural assistance to other developing countries to the best of our ability within the framework of South-South cooperation, including expanding agricultural technology demonstration centers, sending more agricultural experts, offering more agricultural training programs, and providing emergency humanitarian assistance in food. Last year, we decided to double the number of agricultural experts and technical personnel sent abroad and provide agricultural training programs in China for 3,000 people from other developing countries. China has signed the agreement and started to contribute $30 million to the Food and Agriculture Organization of the United Nations to establish a trust fund for projects and activities to help developing countries improve their capacity of agricultural production. We will as always increase our support on a continued basis for international institutions for food and agriculture. China is ready to work with the international community to safeguard world food security and build a harmonious world of enduring peace and common prosperity.[13]

Food safety before food security

It was in April-May 1968, that the country witnessed the wonderful spectacle of large arrivals of wheat grain in the mandis of Punjab like Moga and Khanna. Wheat production in the country rose to nearly 17 million tonnes that year, from the previous best harvest of 12 million tonnes. Indira Gandhi released a special stamp titled "Wheat Revolution" in July 1968, to mark this new phase in our agricultural evolution. The nation rejoiced at our coming out of a "ship to

---

[13]Address at the World Food Summit by Hui Liangyu, Vice Premier of the State Council of the People's Republic of China, November 16, 2009

mouth" existence. Later in 1968, Dr. William Gaud of the US referred to the quantum jumps in production brought about by semi-dwarf varieties of wheat and rice as a "green revolution." This term has since come to symbolise a steep rise in productivity and, thereby, of production of major crops.

Wheat production this year may reach a level of 85 million tonnes, in contrast to the seven million tonnes our farmers harvested at the time of independence in 1947. I visited several grain mandis in Moga, Khanna, Khananon and other places in the Punjab during April 23-27, 2011 and experienced, concurrently, a feeling of ecstasy and agony. It was heart-warming to see the great work done by our farm men and women under difficult circumstances when, often, they had to irrigate the fields at night due to a lack of availability of power during the day.

The cause of agony was the way the grains produced by farmers with loving care were being handled. The various State marketing agencies and the Food Corporation of India (FCI) are trying their best to procure and store the mountains of grains arriving every day. The gunny bags containing the wheat procured during April-May 2010, are still occupying a considerable part of the storage space available at several mandis. The condition of the grains of earlier years presents a sad sight. The impact of moisture on the quality of paddy is even worse.

Malathion sprays and fumigation with Aluminium Sulphide tablets are used to prevent grain spoilage. Safe storage involves attention to both quantity and quality. Grain safety is as important as grain saving. Due to rain and relatively milder temperature, grain arrivals were initially slow, but have now picked up. For all concerned with the procurement, dispatch and storage of wheat grains in the Punjab-Haryana-Western U.P. region, which is the heartland of the green revolution, the task on hand is stupendous.

Farmers in Punjab contribute nearly 40 percent of the wheat and 26 percent of the rice needed to sustain the public distribution system. The legal entitlement to food envisaged under the proposed National Food Security Act cannot be implemented without the help of the farm families of Punjab, Haryana and other grain surplus areas.

Farmers are currently facing serious problems during production and post-harvest phases of farming due to inadequate investment in farm machinery and storage infrastructure. The investment made and steps taken to ensure environmentally sustainable production and safe storage and efficient distribution of grains will determine the future of both agriculture in Punjab and national food security.

On the production side, the ecological foundations essential for sustainable food production are in distress. There is an over-exploitation of the aquifer and nearly 70 percent of irrigated area shows a negative water balance. The quality of the water is also deteriorating due to the indiscriminate use of pesticides and mineral fertilizer.

Over 50,000 ha of crop land in the south-west region of Punjab are affected by water logging and salinisation. Deficiencies of Nitrogen, Phosphorous and Zinc are affecting 66, 48 and 22 percent of soils in Punjab respectively. No wonder factor productivity, i.e., return from a unit of input, is going down. Unless urgent steps are taken to convert the green revolution into an ever-green revolution leading to the enhancement of productivity in perpetuity without associated ecological harm, both agriculture in Punjab and our public distribution system will be in danger.

The investment made and steps taken to ensure environmentally sustainable production and safe storage and efficient distribution of grains will determine the future of both agriculture in Punjab and national food security.

Worried about the future fate of farming as a profession, the younger generation is unwilling to follow in the footsteps of their parents and remain on the farm. This is the greatest worry. If steps are not taken to attract and retain youth in farming, the older generation will have no option but to sell land to real estate agents, who are all the time tempting them with attractive offers. Global prices of wheat, rice and maize are almost 50 percent higher than the minimum support price paid to our farmers. Our population is now over 1.2 billion and we can implement a sustainable and affordable food security system only with home-grown food.

A disturbing finding of Census-2011 is the deteriorating sex ratio in the Punjab-Haryana region. The female-male ratio among children has come to its lowest point since independence. Already, women are shouldering a significant portion of farm work. If the current trends of youth migrating from villages coupled with a drop in the sex ratio continue, agricultural progress will be further endangered.

The prevailing preference for a male child is in part due to the fear of farm land going out of a family's control, when the girl child gets married. I hope the loss of interest in taking to farming as a profession among male youth will remove the bias in favour of male children. I foresee an increasing feminisation of agriculture in the green revolution areas. While the drop in the sex ratio should be halted, steps are also needed to intensify the design, manufacture and distribution of women friendly farm machinery.

Tasks ahead

The first task is to defend the gains already made in improving the productivity and production of wheat, rice, maize and other crops. For the purpose of providing the needed technologies, it will be advisable to set up soon a Multi-disciplinary Research and Training Centre for Sustainable Agriculture at the Punjab Agricultural University, Ludhiana.

This centre can be organised under the National Action Plan for the Management of Climate Change developed under the Chairmanship of the Prime Minister, which includes a Mission for Sustainable Agriculture. Such a centre should initiate a Land and Water Care Movement in the Punjab in association with the farming community. The other urgent task is the promotion of appropriate changes in land use. Over 2.7 million ha are now under rice leading to the unsustainable exploitation of the ground water. Our immediate aim should be to find alternative land use for about a million ha under rice.

It is time that we organise a National grid of grain storages, starting with storage at the farm level in well designed bins and extending to rural godowns and regional ultra-modern silos.

This will be possible only if farmers can get income similar to that they are now earning from rice. Possible alternative crops will be maize and arhar (Pigeon pea). Quality Protein Maize will fetch a premium price from the poultry industry which is fast growing in the Punjab. Arhar being a legume will also enrich soil fertility as well as soil physical properties. Other high value but low water requiring crops like pulses and oilseeds can also be promoted.

At the same time, there could be diversified basmati rice production in over a million ha. In addition to Pusa Basmati 1121 which occupies the largest area now, Pusa Basmati-I (1460) and Pusa Basmati 6 (1401) can be promoted. These have resistance to bacterial leaf blight. Varietal diversity will reduce genetic vulnerability to pests and diseases.

For handling the over 26 million tonnes of wheat which will be purchased during this season, a four-pronged strategy may be useful.

First, distribution through railway wagons could be expanded and expedited. One wagon can handle 2,500 tonnes. Currently 30,000 to 40,000 tonnes of wheat are being dispatched each day through wagons. With advanced planning, this quantity can be raised to over 1 lakh tonnes per day.They can be dispatched to different States for meeting the needs of PDS, Integrated Child Development Services (ICDS), School Noon Meal Programme, Annapoorna, etc.

Second, the present Common Agricultural Policy (CAP) and godown storage systems can be improved with a little more investment and planning. In Punjab there are 146 mandis and 1,746 Purchase Points. They could be grouped and their infrastructure improved.

Third, storage in modern silos, like the one put up at Moga by Adani Agri-logistics, and another one coming up in Amritsar, should be promoted. This will help to adopt an end- to-end system from the point of view of procurement, cleaning, quality assurance, safe storage and distribution. The cost of building silos to store a million tonnes of food grains may be about Rs.600 crore, if the required land is made available by state governments. An investment of about Rs.10,000 crore would help to establish a grid of modern grain storages with a capacity for storing, in good condition, over 15 million tonnes in the Punjab-Haryana-Western U.P. region.

Lastly, export options can be explored after taking steps to make food available to the hungry, as suggested by the Supreme Court. Also, we should ensure that adequate food grains will be available for implementing the proposed Food Security Act. Export should be done only if the global food prices are attractive and if the profit made is distributed as bonus to our farmers, as suggested by the National Commission on Farmers.[14]

It is time that we organise a National grid of grain storages, starting with storage at the farm level in well designed bins and extending to rural godowns and regional ultra-modern silos. Post harvest losses can then be minimised or even eliminated and food safety ensured. Unless the prevailing mismatch between production and post-harvest technologies is ended, neither the producer nor the consumer will derive full benefit from bumper harvests.

In short, mounts of food grains rotting in poorly managed godowns of Punjab tell the sad story of paucity amidst plenty. Hence, an organised foodgrain storage and distribution system would be key to food security.

Global Food Security for Tomorrow

M S Swaminathan has discussed on Global Food Security for tomorrow. He has expressed that the concept of Food Security has evolved during the last 3 decades to includc not only food availability, but also economic access to food and the biological absorption of food in the body. Adequate per capita availability of food is a function of the balance between food production on the one hand, and growth in population and purchasing power, on the other.

Urbanization enhances the consumption of animal products and thereby increases the demand for feed grains and fodder. The "green revolution" of the sixties and seventies helped developing countries to

[14]M.S. Swaminathan (2011), "Food safety before food security", the Hindu, May 11, 2011

gain a breathing spell during which they could attempt to achieve a balance between population growth and the population supporting capacity of the ecosystems. In spite of the success of the population stabilizing efforts in many developing countries, the UN projections indicate that the global population may range from 8 to 10 billion by 2050. I would like to discuss in this paper the challenge of achieving sustainable advances in farm productivity, leading to an "ever-green revolution" in the fields of farm families with smallholdings.

The Challenge of Sustainable Agriculture

On the eve of the UN Conference on Environment and Development held at Rio de Janeiro in June 1992, the Union of Concerned Scientists published an open letter titled, World Scientists' **Warning to Humanity**, which stated: "Human beings and the natural world are on a collision course. If not checked, many of our current practices put at serious risk for human society and the plant and animal kingdoms, may so alter the living world that it will be unable to sustain life in the manner that we know."

Over 1600 scientists from leading scientific academies of 70 countries signed this warning. The list included 104 Nobel Laureates. Colborn, Dumanaski and Myers (1996)[15] in their book "Our Stolen Future" and James Morgan (1999)[16] in his book "The Last Generation" also provide a picture of the grim future that waits the generations yet to be born, if we lose further time in restoring harmony between humankind and nature. It is now widely realized that the genes, species,

---

[15]Colborn Theo, Dumanoski Dianne and John Peterson Myers, 1996, "Our Stolen Future: Are we threatening our Fertility, Intelligence and Survival?" A Scientific Detective Story, Penguin Books, New York 316 pp

[16]Morgan James, 1999. The Last Generation; Krieger Publishing Company, Florida 246 pp. 10

ecosystems and traditional knowledge and wisdom that are being lost at an increasingly accelerated pace limit our options for adapting to local and global change, including potential changes in climate and sea level. The Hadley Centre of the UK Meteorological office has recently predicted that even if Governments cut green house gas emissions, sea levels may rise by at least 2 meters over, the next few hundred years.[17]

If the global community can limit emissions up to 550 ppm, which is twice the pre-industrial levels and 50 percent above today's, about 2 billion persons can be saved from water shortages, low crop yields and increased coastal flooding, especially in India and Africa.

The Global Biodiversity Assessment published in 1995 by the United Nations Environment Programme (Cambridge University Press) estimates that about 13 to 14 million species might exist on our planet. Of this, less than 2 million species have so far been scientifically described. Invertebrates and microorganisms are yet to be studied in detail. In particular, our knowledge of soil microorganisms is still poor. Also, biosystematics as a scientific discipline is tending to attract very few scholars among the younger generation.

Another important paradigm shift witnessed in recent decades in the area of management of natural resources is a change in the concept of "common heritage". In the past, the atmosphere, oceans and biodiversity used to be referred to as the common heritage of humankind. However, recent global conventions have led to an alteration in this concept in legal terms. Biodiversity is now the sovereign property of the nation in whose political frontiers it occurs. Further, the Trade Related Intellectual

---

[17]New Scientist (30 October 1999, No 2210) Going Under: We can save the Amazon, but not the South Pacific, pp. 5

Property Rights (TRIPS) provisions of the World Trade Agreement have made it mandatory to cover products of genetic improvement with either patents and *sui generis* methods of intellectual property rights protection. Under the UN Convention on the Law of the Sea, nations with coastal areas have access to a 200 mile Exclusive Economic Zone (EEZ).

The Climate Convention and the Kyoto protocol provide for both common and differentiated responsibilities to countries. Thus, the global commons can be managed in a sustainable and equitable manner only through committed individual and collective action among nations. In the Asia-Pacific Region, Australia can play a catalytic role in fostering cooperation in both avoiding and mitigating the adverse impact of climate change.

A Chinese proverb warns, **"If you do not change direction, you will end up where you are headed".** Since we do not want to reach where we are presently headed, what change of course should we bring about in the field of agriculture?[18]

Emerging Scientific Revolutions

Fortunately, as we approach the new century we are experiencing three major revolutions in science and technology, which will influence agriculture and industry in a fundamental manner. It will therefore be appropriate to make a brief reference to them.[19]

---

[18]UNESCO Chair in Eco-technology, M S Swaminathan Research Foundation, Chennai, India

[19]Agarwal, Anil and Sunita Narain (1997) Dying Wisdom: Rise, fall and potential of India's traditional water harvesting systems, Thomson Press (India) Ltd, Faridabad. 404 pp

(1)The gene revolution:

This provides a molecular understanding of the genetic basis of living organisms, as well as the ability to use this understanding to develop new processes and products for agriculture, industry, the environment, and for human and animal health.

The past ten years have seen dramatic advances in our understanding of how biological organisms function at the molecular level, as well as in our ability to analyze, understand, and manipulate DNA molecules, the biological material from which the genes in all organisms are made. The entire process has been accelerated by the Human Genome Project, which has poured substantial resources into the development of new technologies for working with human genes. The same technologies are directly applicable to all other organisms, including plants. Thus, a new scientific discipline of genomics has arisen.

This discipline has contributed to powerful new approaches in agriculture and medicine and has helped to promote the biotechnology industry. Several large corporations in Europe and the United States have made major investments in adapting these technologies to produce new plant varieties of agricultural importance for large-scale commercial agriculture. The same technologies have equally important potential applications for addressing food security in the developing world.

The key technological developments in this area are:

(a) Genomics: the molecular characterization of species.

(b) Bio-informatics: data banks and data processing for genomic analysis

(c) Transformation: introduction of individual genes conferring potentially useful traits into plants, trees, livestock and fish species.

(d) Molecular breeding: identification and evaluation of useful traits by use of marker assisted selection, which greatly speeds up traditional breeding processes.
(e) Diagnostics: identification of pathogens by molecular characterization
(f) Vaccine technology: use of modern immunology to develop recombinant DNA vaccines for improved control against lethal diseases of animals and fish.

Let me cite one example from the work of MSSRF scientists to illustrate the value of the new tools. As a part of the anticipatory research program to meet the consequences of sea level rise arising from global climate change, genes responsible for conferring the ability to withstand seawater intrusion were identified in a few mangrove species through molecular mapping. They have been transferred to annual economic plants through recombinant DNA technology.

The sequencing of the genome of rice (*Oryza sativa* L.cv. Nipponbare) by an international consortium supported by the Rockefeller Foundation and the International Rice Research Institute will permit allele mining for all genes of rice and possibly for other cereals. Thus, altogether unforeseen opportunities for creating novel genetic combinations have been opened up.

As mentioned earlier, there are widespread public concerns about the potential adverse impact of genetically modified organisms (GMOs) on human health, biodiversity and the environment. Several of these concerns are genuine. In order to take advantage of recombinant DNA technologies without associated harm to human or ecological health, it is important that every country has in place suitable institutional structures and regulations for bio-safety, bioethics and bio-surveillance. At the same time, there is need for greater investment of public funds for public good research, the results of which can reach the un-reached. For example, in food and agriculture, there is need to strengthen both National Agricultural Research Systems and the International Agricultural Research Centers supported by the CGIAR.

(2) The Eco-technology revolution:

It promotes the blending of the best in traditional knowledge and technology. Moreover biotechnology, space and information technologies, renewable energy and new materials have contributed tremendously. Knowledge is a continuum. There is much to learn from the past in terms of the ecological and social sustainability of technologies. At the same time, new developments have opened up new opportunities for developing technologies, which can lead to higher productivity without adverse impact on the natural resources base. Blending traditional and frontier technologies leads to the birth of eco-technologies with combined strengths in economics, ecology, social and gender equity, employment generation and energy conservation.

For example, in the area of water harvesting and sustainable use, there are many lessons to be learnt from the Australian experience. There is need to conserve traditional wisdom and practices, which are often tending to become extinct.

The decision of the World Intellectual Property Rights Organization (WIPO) to explore the intellectual property needs, rights and expectations of holders of traditional knowledge, innovations, and culture is hence an important step in widening the concept of intellectual property. FAO has been a pioneer in the recognition of the contributions of farm families in genetic resources conservation and enhancement by promoting the concept of "Farmers Rights". Like

WIPO, UPOV (Union for the Protection of New Varieties of Crops) should also undertake the task of preparing an integrated concept of breeders' and farmers' rights. UPOV itself should be restructured to become a Union for the Protection of Farmers' and Breeders' Rights.

(3)The information technology revolution:

It allows a very rapid growth in the systematic assimilation and dissemination of relevant and timely information, as well as a dramatically improved ability to access the universe of knowledge and communicate through low cost electronic networks. New communication and computing technologies are already influencing life on our planet in a profound manner.

(a)Access to the Internet will soon be universal, and it can provide unrestricted low-cost access to information, as well as highly interactive distance learning. The Internet will not only facilitate interactions among researchers, but also greatly improve their ability to communicate effectively with the potential users of their research knowledge.

(b)Computing makes it possible to process large capacity databases (libraries, remote sensing and GIS data, gene banks) and to construct simulation models with possible applications in ecosystem modeling, preparation of contingency plans to suit different weather probabilities and market variables.
(c)The software industry is continuously providing new tools that increase research productivity and create new opportunities for understanding complex agro-eco systems.

Remote sensing and other space satellite outputs are providing detailed geographic information useful for land and natural resources management. The promotion of eco-technology development and dissemination, the effective adoption of integrated systems of gene and natural resources management and the effective harnessing of information technologies should become essential elements of the "science and technology for basic human needs" movement.

In principle, these three types of advances – when coupled with improvements in the management and governance - greatly increase the power of a scientific approach to genetic improvement, the integrated management of natural resources and ecosystems, and the management of local and regional development strategies. Eco-technologies enable the adoption of ISO 9000 and ISO 14000 standards of environmental management. These scientific revolutions seem to be proceeding at an ever-increasing pace, with most of the action occurring in industrialized nations. Also, new discoveries of great relevance to sustainable food and health security are coming under the purview of proprietary science, since they are covered by Intellectual Property Rights. It is the duty of organizations devoted to public good to mobilize recent advances in science and technology for meeting the basic needs of the economically and socially underprivileged sections of the human family.

To sum up, there is no time to relax on the food production front. It is obvious that we have to produce more, but produce it in a manner that there is no adverse environmental or social impact. Water is likely to be a serious constraint in many countries. Hence, priority should be given to developing and spreading efficient water management techniques, including aquifer management, waste water recycling and conjunctive use of surface and rainwater. Future agricultural production technologies should be based on the foundation of integrated natural resources management.

The world can produce enough food for a population of 10 billion by harnessing the untapped yield reservoir existing even with currently available technologies, if greater attention is given to soil health care and water management. We must defend the productivity gains so far made, extend the gains to semi-arid and marginal environments, and work for new gains using blends of frontier technologies and traditional ecological prudence. The problem of generating adequate purchasing power to enable families living in poverty to have economic access to food will still confront us. This is where a job-led economic growth strategy based on micro-level planning, micro-enterprises and micro credit will be of great help. Integrated production and post-harvest technologies and on farm and off-farm employment strategies will be needed to provide livelihoods for all in rural areas.

With increasing globalization of economies, it will be necessary to agree at the international level that safeguarding and strengthening the livelihood security of the poor should be a major goal of liberalized trade. The current trend of increasing rich-poor divide will have to be stopped, if social conflicts are not to increase. Thus, we are really walking a tightrope in terms of achieving sustainable solutions to the problems of population, poverty and environmental degradation. The various international conferences held during this decade starting with the Children's' Summit held in New York in 1990 and ending with the World Conference on Science held at Budapest in 1999, have indicated possible solutions to these problems. It is now for nations to act individually and collectively so that the uncommon opportunities opened up by science and technology and democratic systems of governance for creating a food secure world are not missed.

The United Nations University which has so far provided innovative leadership in developing institutional structures and pedagogic approaches designed to reach the un-reached should not only continue its philosophy of working for a better common present and future for humankind, but should intensify its efforts to foster relevant partnerships and networks for launching and sustaining an ever-green revolution on the farms.

According to the Asian Development Bank, over 900 million out of the 1.3 billion persons currently living on a per capita daily income of less than US $1 are in Asia. One in three Asians is poor. Poverty is the main cause of food insecurity at the level of individuals today.

Most of the new jobs or livelihood opportunities in Asia will have to come from the on-farm and rural non-farm sectors. Macro-economic policies at the national and global levels should ensure that they help to strengthen micro-enterprises supported by micro credit. Technology and trade should become allies in the movement for a more equitable world.

It would be useful if UNU could organize a Virtual College together with WTO on the theme "**Trade as an instrument for poverty eradication**". This will help to strengthen the livelihood security of the poor, so very essential for food security. Through appreciate blends of technologies and public policies we now have uncommon opportunities for achieving the human quest for a hunger-free world by the year 2020.

Building livelihoods

Emergency[20] relief can only fulfill a limited role. For those that are forced to rely on humanitarian assistance for long period's aid must be provided for

---

[20]Austin J.R and T Morris (2009), "Building Livelihoods", Women's Commission for Refugee Women and Children, Conflicts and Disasters, document 43614, Eldis com

displaced persons to garner skills, training and economic opportunities in order to establish sustainable livelihoods. As a person uprooted by conflict will remain displaced for an average of 17 years, so new generations will need access to viable processes to become self-reliant and build lives. Such a focus is paramount if families and communities are going to be able to survive – and quite possibly thrive – in the camp environment.

This field manual has been developed in an attempt to provide practitioners with usable information and tools so that they can design and implement effective livelihood programs. The programs must:

(a) Be based on market demand and contextually appropriate
(b) Build on the existing skills and experience within the target population
(c) Enhance the dignity and options for the displaced.[21]

INDIA: **Food security is a basic right**

A national campaign throughout the month of July on issues related to food security and against rising prices will culminate in a five-day sit-in protest in Delhi beginning today. These are issues fundamental to the well-being of the majority of our people and therefore deserve national support.

With the specter of drought haunting the countryside, speculators, hoarders and black-marketers are back in business. Prices of essential commodities like pulses, edible oil, sugar and salt are going through the roof. Vegetables are out of reach of the average family with the price of a kilo of potatoes increasing

---

[21]Young, H, K. Jacobsen and A Osman (2009), "Livelihoods, Migration and Conflicts", Feinstein International Center, USA, Conflict and Disasters, eldis.com

by over 100% in the last month. The majority of Indians earn their living in the unorganized sector marked by low and fluctuating incomes with no dearness allowance. Any rise in prices causes havoc in the lives of millions of families.

According to earlier data, an Indian, on average, spent as much as 53 percent of total expenditure on food requirements. With relentless food inflation this percentage would be far higher now. In comparison, Americans, on average, spend 9.3 percent of their income on food; in Italy a family on average spends 25.7 percent, in Japan 19.1percent, in France 16.3percent, in the United Kingdom 11.5percent. While there is a difference in the method of calculation between India and the others, it does emphasize the Indian reality of higher food prices and lower levels of disposable income than other countries.

But the UPA government, preoccupied with its internal squabbles, cares little for the insecurity rising prices and consequent food deprivation causes Indian families. For the government this is collateral damage in its mission to implement pro-corporate reform (PCR) and cut food subsidy. This started in the initial period of PCR in the 1990s by the Introduction of the targeted system through the categorization of people as poor and non-poor, with only the former being eligible for subsidized grain. This is the bizarre logic of targeting. The sham estimates of poverty by the Planning Commission became the basis on which to exclude people. In spite of national outrage against the present poverty line figures of Rs 26 a day for an adult in rural India and Rs 32 for an adult in urban India (at 2010-11 prices) these still continue as the basis for access to the public distribution system.

The critical issue here is to reverse targeting and ensure a universal public distribution system. This is estimated to cost the exchequer an additional 250 billion INR to 300 billion INR (1 billion = 1000 million), a small price to pay for a country, which has the largest malnourished population in the world. But this is too much for the UPA government, which prefers to give tax concessions worth 5 trillion INR (1 trillion = 1000 billion) in a single year to the rich.

This approach is now reflected in its policy regarding the surplus food grain stocks it holds. The buffer stock in the month of July, according to the quarterly buffer stock norms India has, should be 33 million tonnes. Current stocks are as high as 82 million tonnes. Instead of distributing these surplus stocks to the millions of families wrongly defined as non-poor, the government has chosen to permit exports "to liquidate the stocks". Most of the exported food grain will be ultimately used as feed for livestock converted to animal products in developed countries.

The government sees nothing unethical about subsidizing grains for foreign cattle but not for its own people. The decision to export is influenced by agribusiness lobbies, which want to take advantage of rising wheat prices in the international market driven upwards by reported crop damage in major wheat growing areas across the globe. This is very similar to what happened during the NDA regime. At that time the food stocks were around sixty million tonnes and the government sold them off to foreign traders at BPL prices. It had also made open market sales to grain traders at subsidized prices giving them a subsidy of between 70 billion and 80 billion INR. At that time the Congress in opposition had protested. Today, the BJP in opposition is also protesting. But as the facts show, the policies regarding food are no different between the Congress and the BJP.

The right to food must be recognized as a basic right of people and must be backed by legislation. However, the Food Security Bill presently before the parliamentary standing committee makes a mockery of food security by legalizing the present injustices of the targeted system. The Left parties have opposed the Bill in its present form. Not only does the Bill retain the APL and BPL categories, it centralizes all powers in the hands of the central government and thus undermines any positive measures for food security taken by some of the state governments.

There are utter absurdities in definitions in the Bill. For example, in the section on special groups, a differentiation is made between those in starvation and those in destitution with the former being eligible to two free meals while the latter can get only one. Can any sane person find any difference between a person in starvation defined as "prolonged deprivation of food threatening survival", and destitution defined as those who "have no support for food and nutrition enabling their survival?"

But World Bank indoctrinated economists can find the subtle difference between equally hungry people to decide who will get two free meals and who only one. The present food Bill legalizes the injustices of a targeted distribution system.[22]

Conclusion

Food insecurity occurs because of change in climate, crop failure, poor governance, unsustainable agriculture, high disparity in income among the citizens, entry of FDI in agricultural marketing, unemployment among farm youths, inefficient management of market yards and low support prices of agricultural commodities, corruption in administration, free food, high subsidy to industrialists for agricultural inputs such as chemical fertilizers, pesticides, dependence on hybrid seeds on

---

[22]Brinda Karat (2012), "Food security is a basic right", Times of India, July 30, 2012; Note: 1 Trillion = 1000 billion;1 billion = 1000 million; INR= Indian rupees

government, lack of political interest in agriculture, conversion of agricultural land to non-agriculture for real estate business and industry.

Food insecurity is caused as farmers know that agriculture is a loss– bearing profession.

But it is possible to award food security to all people in each country. Food security is possible by empowering farmers, higher agricultural production, engagement of rural youths in agriculture, global cooperation for food security, food aid, birth control, increasing support prices for rice and wheat.

Peaceful marches are necessary to attract the attention of the government to demand justice for the rural people. In short, peaceful environment for farmers and farming is necessary for food security.

+++++

Chapter II

FOOD SECURITY IN DEVELOPED COUNTRIES

Food is strength, food is peace, food is freedom, and food is a helping hand to people around the world; we want their good will and friendship.

John Fitzgerald Kennedy

In a speech in South Dakota, 1960

A developed country is food secured; but all families are not food secured in a developed country. Rich people can meet their dietary needs but the poor people would face food shortage. There are approximately 2,000,000 farmers in the US, which constitutes less than 1 percent of the population. But they supply all food needs of the country and the U.S. donates food stuffs to other countries regularly. A country can be food secured if it is thinly populated, agricultural productivity is higher, and per capita income is higher and there exists a free market. The twenty-first century is facing the challenge of 'food security' because all the countries prefer industrial progress, military power and consumerism for economic development, but they neglect food production, allow subsidy in agriculture, control grain prices and face climatic hazards.

In this chapter, Food Security in the USA, Food insecurity, Community food safety, Food production in UK, What is food security, USAID, Food Security in Australia, Food Security in France, Approaches to address food security issues, Reactive control system, How to inform and educate consumers have been analyzed. This has been described in order to make a comparison against the food-insecure countries.

The United States of America

Population – 313,085,000 (2011) UN Report

The USA is self-sufficient in food production. It can feed its population for another century without any difficulty.

The country produces maize, indigenous cattle meat, cow milk, indigenous chicken meat, soybean, wheat, hen eggs, tomato, grape, potato, indigenous turkey meat, rice /paddy, lettuce, apples, sorghum, strawberries, and groundnuts. Only 1 percent of American people are engaged in agriculture and the country exports foodstuff to all countries during natural calamities. The USA is more worried to assist the deficit countries for attaining food security. The country accepts a major advisory role in food security for all food deficit countries.

Food insecurity

Food insecurity has been described as "a condition in which people lack basic food intake to provide them with the energy and nutrients for fully productive lives."

In 2005, 35.1 million Americans, which include 22.7 million adults and 12.4 million children, lived in households that were unable to afford the food they need for the year. Households that are more likely to experience food insecurity are female-headed with children, those with incomes below the poverty line, and those that reside either in principal cities or within rural areas. The top three states ranking in prevalence of food insecure households were New Mexico (16.8 percent), Mississippi (16.5 percent), and Texas (16.0 percent) during 2003-2005.

In 2011, nearly 46 million Americans, or 15 percent of the U S population, are now living on 'food stamps' doled by the government.

The number under Supplemental Nutrition Assistance Program (SNAP) has increased by 34 percent over two years. The American definition of low-income up to $1174 a month qualifies for food stamps. The average monthly food stamps benefit is put at $133.80 per person and $283.65 per household. The program costs the US exchequer $6 billion a month.

The USDA report cited below asks the question, "How often were people hungry in households that were food insecure with hunger?" Around 4 percent of people reported going hungry at least once a year, while on any given day the figure is estimated to be between 0.5 percent and 0.8 percent.

A March 1, 2009, Associated Press article cited many examples of hungry children in the United States. The article talked about all of the children's mothers, but did not mention any of their fathers. The article also said that some of the mothers were feeding their children junk food such as potato chips and hot dogs, instead of nutritious foods such as fruits, vegetables, and milk.

Many countries experience perpetual food shortages and distribution problems. These result in chronic and often widespread hunger amongst significant numbers of people. Human Populations respond to chronic hunger and malnutrition by decreasing body size, known in medical terms as stunting or stunted growth. This process starts *in utero* if the mother is malnourished and continues through approximately the third year of life. It leads to higher infant and child mortality, but at rates far lower than during famines. Once stunting has occurred, improved nutritional intake later in life cannot reverse the damage. Stunting itself is viewed as a coping mechanism, designed to bring body size into alignment with the calories available during adulthood in the location where the child is born. Limiting body size as a way of adapting to low levels of energy (calories) adversely affects health in three ways:

(a) Premature failure of vital organs occurs during adulthood. For example a 50 year old individual might die of heart failure because his/her heart suffered structural defects during early development.
(b) Stunted individuals suffer a far higher rate of disease and illness than those who have not undergone stunting.
(c) Severe malnutrition in early childhood often leads to defects in cognitive development.

How to make availability of adequate food stuffs to the Hungry people?

(a) The Governments of developing countries should accept pro-poor, pro-rural and pro-agricultural policies in planning and budget formulation
(b) The state can take up adequate steps to procure and distribute foodstuffs to all needy families.

(c) Hoarding of foodstuffs by few business houses must be avoided and the government must procure the cereals and distribute rice and wheat in public distribution system at fair prices.

(d) Irrigation facility, credit facility at lower interest rate, opening of regulated markets, adequate market intelligence, creation of employment opportunity and agricultural research must be strengthened to cater to the needs of all consumers.

Community Food Safety:

Community food security is a condition in which all community residents obtain a safe, culturally acceptable, nutritionally adequate diet through a sustainable food system that maximizes community self-reliance and social justice.

Following are six basic principles of community food security, as defined by the Community Food Security Coalition:

(a)**Low Income Food Needs:** Like the anti-hunger movement; CFS is focused on meeting the food needs of low income communities, reducing hunger and improving individual health.

(b) **Broad Goals:** CFS addresses a broad range of problems affecting the food system, community development, and the environment such as increasing poverty and hunger, disappearing farmland and family farms, inner city supermarket redlining, rural community disintegration, rampant suburban sprawl, and air and water pollution from unsustainable food production and distribution patterns.

(c) **Community focus:** A CFS approach seeks to build up a community's food resources to meet its own needs. These resources may include supermarkets, farmers' markets, gardens, transportation, community-based food processing ventures, and urban farms to name a few.

(d) **Self-reliance/empowerment**: Community food security projects emphasize the need to build individuals' abilities to provide for their food needs. Community food security seeks to build upon community and individual assets, rather than focus on their deficiencies. CFS projects seek to engage community residents in all phases of project planning, implementation, and evaluation.

(e) **Local agriculture** - A stable local agricultural base is the key to a community responsive food system. Farmers need increased access to markets that pay them a decent wage for their labor, and farmland needs planning protection from suburban development. By building stronger ties between farmers and consumers, consumers gain a greater knowledge and appreciation for their food source.

(f).**Systems-oriented CFS** projects typically are "inter-disciplinary, crossing many boundaries and incorporating collaborations with multiple agencies.

Economic approaches:

There are many economic approaches advocated to improve food security in developing countries. Three typical approaches are listed below.

(a)Westernized view: Conventional thinking in westernized countries is that maximizing the farmers profit is the surest way of maximizing agricultural production; the higher a farmer's profit, the greater the effort that will be forthcoming, and the greater the risk the farmer is willing to take.

This view holds that it is the government's job to place into the hands of farmers the largest number and highest quality tools possible such as improved production techniques, improved seeds, secure land tenure, accurate weather forecasts, etc. However, it is left to the individual farmer to pick and choose which tools to use, and how to use them, as farmers have intimate knowledge of their own land and local conditions.

As with other businesses, a percentage of the profits are normally reinvested into the business in the hopes of increasing production, and hence increase future profits. Normally higher profits translate into higher spending on technologies designed to boost production, such as drip irrigation system, agriculture education, and cold storages and warehouses. An increased profit also increases the farmer's incentive to engage in double cropping, soil improvement programs, and expanding usable area.

(b) Food justice: Fight Hunger is a United Nations World Food Program initiative.

An alternative view takes a collective approach to achieve food security. It notes that globally enough food is produced to feed the entire world population at a level adequate to ensure that everyone can be free of hunger and fear of starvation. That no one should live without enough food because of economic constraints or social inequalities is the basic goal.

This approach is often referred to as food justice and views food security as a basic human right. It advocates fairer distribution of food, particularly grain crops, as a means of ending chronic hunger and malnutrition. The core of the Food Justice movement is the belief that what is lacking is not food, but the political will to fairly distribute food regardless of the recipient's ability to pay.

(c) Food sovereignty: A third approach is known as food sovereignty; though it overlaps with food justice on several points, the two are not identical. It views the business practices of multinational corporations as a form of neocolonialism. It contends that multinational corporations have the financial resources available to buy up the agricultural resources of impoverished nations, particularly in the tropics. They also have the political clout to convert these resources to the exclusive production of cash crops for sale to industrialized nations outside of the tropics, and in the process to squeeze the poor off of the more productive lands. Under this view subsistence farmers are left to cultivate only lands that are so marginal in terms of productivity as to be of no interest to the multinational corporations.

It advocates banning the production of most cash crops in developing nations, thereby leaving the local farmers to concentrate on subsistence crops. In addition it opposes allowing low-cost subsidized food from industrialized nations into developing countries, what is referred to as "import dumping".

The agriculture-hunger-poverty nexus:

Eradicating hunger and poverty requires an understanding of the ways in which these two injustices interconnect. Hunger and malnourishment prevent poor people from escaping poverty because it diminishes their ability to learn, work, and care for themselves and their family members. Food insecurity exists when people are undernourished as a result of the physical unavailability of food, their lack of social or economic access to adequate food, and/or inadequate food utilization. Food-insecure people are those individuals whose food intake falls below their minimum calorie (energy) requirements, as well as those who exhibit physical symptoms caused by energy and nutrient deficiencies resulting from an inadequate or unbalanced diet or from the body's inability to use food effectively because of infection or disease.

An alternative view would define the concept of food insecurity as referring only to the consequence of inadequate consumption of nutritious food, considering the physiological utilization of food by the body as being within the domain of nutrition and health. Malnourishment also leads to poor health hence individuals fail to provide for their families. If left unaddressed, hunger sets in motion an array of outcomes that perpetuate malnutrition, reduce the ability of adults to work and to give birth to healthy children, and erode children's ability to learn and lead productive, healthy, and happy lives. This truncation of human development undermines a country's potential for economic development for generations to come.

There are strong, direct relationships between agricultural productivity, hunger, and poverty. Three-quarters of the world's poor live in rural areas and make their living from agriculture. Hunger and child malnutrition are greater in these areas than in urban areas. Moreover, the higher the proportion of the rural population that obtains its income solely from subsistence farming (without the benefit of pro-poor technologies and access to markets), the higher the incidence of malnutrition. Therefore, improvements in agricultural productivity aimed at small-scale farmers will benefit the rural poor first.

Increased agricultural productivity enables farmers to grow more food, which translates into better diets and, under market conditions that offer a level playing field, into higher farm incomes. With more money, farmers are more likely to diversify production and grow higher-value crops, benefiting not only themselves but the economy as a whole.

Prompted by rising food prices in 2008, riots and demonstrations erupted in over 40 countries around the world. Unable to afford adequate food, many of the poor in these countries and others are at higher risk for malnutrition, which can have devastating and long-lasting impacts on those suffering now and future generations. Food security is a foundation for building social and economic development. It means that all people in a society have access, at all times, to enough food for an active and healthy life. It depends on agriculture to provide sustenance, incomes and livelihoods for the world's rural poor - 2.1 billion living on less than $2 per day.

The food supply is increasingly global; recent high food prices hit American families too. Ensuring safe and affordable food at home and abroad requires addressing global agricultural challenges: declining growth in crop productivity while demand rises, emerging diseases and pests that threaten crop and livestock production, declining availability of water, and increasing climatic variability due to climate change.

USAID promotes food security by stimulating rural economies through broad-based agricultural growth, which increases incomes along with food production, reduces poverty, and brings down food prices in local markets for the urban poor.

USAID approach:

Improving food security is both a humanitarian and development priority. A successful attack on extreme poverty and chronic hunger requires assistance to increase availability, access to, and utilization of food. Economic growth through agriculture is a central and proven tool for many developing countries. To achieve global food security USAID works with developing countries, civil society, the private sector, and other development organizations to:

(a)Save lives and halt the slide into hunger and absolute poverty by providing emergency assistance, such as food aid, which protects limited resources of the poor from further erosion and provides a foundation for longer-term investments in agricultural productivity and social protection;

(b)Create dynamic rural economies by modernizing the agriculture of small-scale producers - throughout history, including in the U.S., agriculture has driven economic growth, increasing incomes of farm families, much of the poor in developing countries, and creating off-farm employment for the landless rural poor ;

(c)Support research and development of improved technologies and sustainable production practices, including biotechnology; expand access to quality seeds and fertilizers, agricultural services, and financing; strengthen farmer organizations and cooperatives as well as agribusiness and value chain development; link small producers to markets; and promote regional trade and market-based policies;

(d)Make rural growth work for the poorest - the extreme poor in rural areas are often landless or face other constraints that prevent them from being commercially viable agricultural producers. Enabling them to take advantage of economic opportunities requires targeted social and economic assistance — "productive safety nets" — ranging from vocational and skills training, to public works, to income generation and programs that provide temporary financial and food assistance;

(e)Improve nutrition security as integral to both humanitarian and agricultural development through approaches such as linking community-based agriculture, health and nutrition programs; diversifying food production with, for instance, home and school gardens; and breeding staple food crops for enhanced nutritional quality.

USAID response to the Food Crisis:

While food prices have declined from the crisis levels of early 2008, prices continue to be significantly higher in many developing countries. This food crisis and the growing implications of the financial crisis have added to the ranks of nearly a billion people living with chronic poverty and hunger. The U.S. continues to be the world's largest food aid donor providing, on average, over half of annual international food aid. In response to the food crisis, the U.S. Government committed over $5.5 billion for fiscal years 2008 and 2009 to fight world hunger. $4.75 billion of these funds were programmed by USAID, to:

Provide immediate and expanded humanitarian response:

In FY 2008, USAID provided $2.06 billion in emergency food assistance to 26 countries (Djibouti, Ethiopia, Kenya, Somalia, Sudan, Tanzania, Burundi, Central African Republic, D.R. Congo, Rwanda, Zimbabwe, Zambia, Uganda, Cameroon, Chad, Liberia, Afghanistan, Bangladesh, Burma, Nepal, Sri Lanka, Algeria, Syria, Yemen, Colombia, Ecuador), $129 million of which was designated for buying food locally in Somalia, Ethiopia, Nepal and Tajikistan, for emergency distribution, thus cutting shipping costs and stimulating local production.

Investing in staple food production for vulnerable states:

USAID is investing $130 million in FY 2009 for the production and trade of staple foods such as corn, wheat, cassava, sorghum and millet, initially focusing on five West African countries with the greatest need: Ghana, Liberia, Mali, Nigeria and Senegal.

Supporting trade liberalization to reduce price volatility:

USAID is working with host countries to reduce barriers to staple food trade and trade-distorting subsidies, help increase market access for agricultural products, and encourage open markets.

Increase availability and use of advanced agricultural technologies:

USAID provided $20 million in FY 2008 Famine Funds to the Consultative Group on International Agricultural Research (CGIAR) to disseminate "on the shelf" food staple technologies in sub-Saharan Africa and South Asia. The analysis ... points to the misleading nature of the concept of subsistence as Malthus originally used it and as it is still widely used today. Subsistence is not located at the edge of a nutritional cliff, beyond which lies demographic disaster. Rather than one level of subsistence, there are numerous levels at which a population and a food supply can be in equilibrium in the sense that they can be indefinitely sustained. However, some levels will have smaller people and higher normal mortality than others.

Biotechnology for smallholders in (sub) tropics:

The area sown to genetically engineered crops in developing countries is rapidly catching-up with the area sown in industrial nations. According to the International Service for the Acquisition of Agri-biotech Applications (ISAAA), genetically engineered (biotech, GM) crops were grown by approximately 8.5 million farmers in 21 countries in 2005, up from 8.25 million farmers in 17 countries in 2004. The largest increase in biotech crop area in any country in 2005 was in Brazil, provisionally estimated at 44,000 km^2 (94,000 km^2 in 2005 compared with 50,000 km^2 in 2004. India had by far the largest year-on-year proportional increase, with almost a threefold increase from 5,000 km² in 2004 to 13,000 km² in 2005.

Current high regulatory costs imposed on varieties created by the more modern methods are a significant hurdle for development of genetically engineered crops well suited to developing country farmers by modern genetic methods. Once a new variety is developed, however, seed provides a good vehicle for distribution of improvements in a package that is familiar to the farmer.

Currently there are some institutes and research groups that have projects in which biotechnology is shared with contact people in less-developed countries on a non-profit basis. These institutes make use of biotechnological methods that do not involve high research and registration costs, such as conservation and multiplication of legitimate concerns of the population and the germ plasm and phyto - sanitation.

The United Kingdom

Population – 62, 417,000 (2011) –UN Report

In 1996, the World Food Summit organized by FAO made the solemn commitment to halve the level of hunger and under nutrition in the world. For that purpose it adopted a program to achieve sustainable food security. That commitment was subsequently reaffirmed at the Millennium Summit in 2000, the World Food Summit: five years later in 2002 and the FAO High-Level Conference on World Food Security in June 2008. Unfortunately, FAO's most recent data on world hunger and malnutrition indicate a situation that is even more worrying than in 1996. In the last three years, food insecurity has risen throughout the world, mainly on account of the global crisis of 2007-2008, triggered by soaring food prices and exacerbated by the financial and economic crisis that has shaken the world for more than a year. Thus the number of people suffering from chronic hunger and poverty in 2009 has risen by 105 million since last year, bringing the total number of undernourished people to over one billion, in other words one out of every six inhabitants of the world. Virtually all of these people live in the developing countries: 642 million in Asia and the Pacific; 265 million in sub-Saharan Africa; 53 million in Latin America and the Caribbean; and 42 million in the Near East and North Africa.

In July, thirty countries were in a state of serious food crisis requiring emergency aid. They included twenty countries in Africa and ten in Asia and the Near East. The food insecurity crisis represents a grave threat to world peace and stability as we saw in 2007- 2008 with the food riots that broke out in 22 countries in all the regions of the world. We need to urgently secure broad international policy consensus to totally and rapidly eliminate hunger in the world and take all necessary measures to that end.

The challenge of eliminating hunger is not one of insufficient knowledge or resources available to the international community. The vision of a world free from hunger is feasible. Concrete changes in political strategy are indispensable to achieve that objective. The time has come to act responsibly and to address the many root causes of food insecurity by taking bold decisions and adopting lasting political, economic, financial and technical solutions.

The food crisis of 2007-2008 highlighted the inadequacy of current governance of world food security. Despite its many advantages, in particular, its intergovernmental nature as a forum of sovereign States, its universal composition and its neutrality, the CFS has been unable to fully accomplish its mission of monitoring food security. There are at least five reasons for this:

(a) It lacks a high-level international policy-making body in the sectors of international cooperation and of food and agriculture;
(b) It lacks an integrated framework for short-, medium-, and long-term sectoral scientific advice on hunger;
(c) It lacks authority to evaluate and coordinate policies affecting world food security, in particular as regards production, agro-industry, trade, social safety nets and financing;
(d) It lacks an effective mechanism to track food security decisions and actions at national and regional level; and
(e) It lacks the financial resources needed to carry out its mandate.

At the FAO High-Level Conference on World Food Security in June 2008, firm proposals were made to reinforce the governance of food security. One of these was to create a Global Network of High-Level Experts on Food and Agriculture and a Global Partnership to enhance consultation with all stakeholders and facilitate the coordination and implementation of actions on the ground.

These proposals were discussed at numerous intergovernmental meetings, including the G8 Summit in Hokkaido in July 2008, the Special Session of the FAO Conference in November 2008, at L'Aquila in July 2009, and last month at the G20 Summit in Pittsburgh. The proposals for CFS reform that are tabled today are the end product of an arduous task initiated and conducted by the member countries.

One aspect that clearly emerged from all the discussions was that we did not want to create new structures. Instead, we wanted to enhance, strengthen, coordinate, and in other words reform, what existed, so that our action could be more effective. At its Special Session in November 2008, the FAO Conference requested that the CFS - which is open to all Member Nations of FAO and all Member States of the United Nations as well as representatives of other international institutions, NGOs, the private sector and civil society, and which is tasked with monitoring the evolution of food security in the world – be able to fully play its role in the new system of world governance.

The new CFS should become a global forum for debate and convergence on the causes and consequences of food insecurity and the ways to address them. It should lay the principles for the formulation of appropriate policies and strategies and should have the means to monitor progress and to report on their implementation. The members of the CFS, under the leadership of its Bureau, agree over the need to engage in its profound renewal. They have initiated a process of reform based on three principles: first, to include all stakeholders in CFS discussions; second, to serve as a genuine global forum for Member States of the United Nations and Member Nations of FAO; and third, to adopt new processes of governance and decision-making. Thus, the Bureau has decided to create a Contact Group made up of representatives of Member States and Nations, international organizations and financial institutions, NGOs, civil society and the private sector.

A renewed and revitalized structure for the governance of food security should aim to:

(a) Keep agriculture and food security at the top of the international agenda for the eradication of hunger and malnutrition in the world;
(b) Fully understand the factors that affect world food security, the associated risks and remedial actions;
(c) Ensure close links between technical expertise and policy-making;

(d) See that the international community adopts a coherent and systematic approach to food security with the capacity:
(e) To respond rapidly to situations of food crisis and emergency in order to mitigate their negative effects;
(f) To stimulate investment in agriculture and rural development and mobilize the funding required to ensure the food security of local populations;
(g) To help bolster the governance of food security in a framework of coherence and synergy of policies, strategies and actions at all levels: national, regional and international.

If they are to be credible, CFS discussions and decisions must rest on solid scientific and technical evidence. Hence the importance of establishing a high-level network of experts is necessary. Its principal task will be to provide Member Nations, CFS organizations and other interested parties with information analyses and summaries that can help produce scientific advice on technical and economic matters. Such knowledge will shape policies, strategies and programs to enhance food security and nutrition at global, national and local level.

FAO has long worked with sector-specific expert bodies and groups, in a precise juridical framework and following detailed procedures. It has thus received advice on policy and guidelines in many fields, including food, agricultural crops, animal production, forestry, fisheries and aquaculture, but also the agricultural commodity trade. Many of these bodies and groups have functioned continuously for decades.[23]

---

[23]Committee on World food Security, Thirty-fifth Session, Rome, 14, 15 and 17 October 2009, Opening Statement by director General (Wednesday 14 October 2009)

This mechanism must be strengthened and its inherent expertise must be better integrated for the benefit of the Committee on Food security (CFS). The United Kingdom has prepared a comprehensive study on 'Securing Food supplies up to 2050: The Challenges Faced by the United Kingdom' for the year 2050 for its own food security and for other countries to meet the challenges of food scarcity in the world.[24]

The world faces what one of our witnesses described as "an unprecedented double challenge": it needs to produce more food, but in a way that does not degrade the natural resources on which agricultural depends, and which decreases the food chain's reliance on fossil fuels and reduces greenhouse gas emissions. Meeting this challenge will require a fundamental shift in thinking about food, on the part of Governments and consumers. Two projections voiced at the UN Food and Agriculture Organization's "World Food Security" conference in June 2008 attracted particular attention. The Secretary-General of the United Nations, Ban Ki-moon, announced that food production would need to increase by 50 percent by 2030 to meet rising demand and the Director-General of the Food and Agriculture Organization, Jacques Diouf, stated that food production would need to double by 2050 to feed a world population of 9 billion. It is important to bear in mind that these are projections rather than targets.

They are a useful way of focusing attention on food production. However, they should also be used to draw attention to population growth, diet and waste at all stages of the food chain, and the need for policy responses in these areas. More information is needed about future patterns of consumption: what will be required is not simply an increase in production

---

[24]Department for Environment, Food and Rural Affairs (Defra), Fourth Report of Session 2009-2009 (Volume I), July 13, 2009

across the world, but an increase in the production of particular commodities to meet demand in particular parts of the world.

The UK has a choice about how to respond, both to secure its own food supplies and to increase the security of global supplies. We have considered the options and believe that the UK has a moral duty to make the most of its position in the globe and its natural advantages for producing certain types of food. The UK should not attempt to be totally self-sufficient, but it should aim to increase its production of those fruit, vegetables and cereals that are suited to being grown here. It is essential that this increase in production be carried out sustainably.

The Department for Environment, Food and Rural Affairs (DEFRA) of UK has a responsibility to provide strong leadership on food policy to co-ordinate the response from other departments and to enable people to invest and plan. The UK has neglected food policy in the past. Following the loss of most of its climate change responsibilities to the Department for Energy and Climate Change, the UK has the chance to refocus its attention on food. The UK is taking increased interest, but there is a great deal still to do. The UK must produce a vision and strategy for food that provides a long-term framework for the UK food and farming sectors, stretching beyond the short-term nature of the political cycle. The strategy should pull together the work of the various Government groups that are currently involved in food policy. The strategy cannot be expected to supply all the answers, but it should provide clear direction and indicate what further work is needed and the deadlines for its completion.

The UK must also provide leadership in Europe, to shape emerging European Union policy on the security of food supplies. The reform of the Common Agricultural Policy is an opportunity to ensure that

European agriculture is in a position to produce as much food as it can, sustainably, and in response to market signals. The CAP should provide incentives and mechanisms to encourage farming that uses less water and fossil fuels, produces less greenhouse gas emissions and does not degrade soils. The UK must provide clear leadership; tackle the existing weaknesses in food system that will otherwise prevent it from achieving its long-term objective of securing food supplies. UK public-sector research into food and farming is still world-class in some respects. However, there is an urgent need to:

(a) Increase the budget for public-sector food and farming research;
(b) Ensure that research priorities reflect the importance of securing food supplies; and
(c) Increase transnational services and research so that research does not "sit on the shelf" once it has been completed.

The UK must also act to address the potential skills gap in farming and in applied research. The UK has a role to play in fostering long-term, stable relationships in the food supply chain. Consumers will play a vital part in enabling to achieve its vision for the UK food system. They will need to be encouraged to think more about the environmental consequences of where and how their food is produced, and to be provided with sufficient information to enable them to make responsible choices. Increasing interest in local and home production on the part of some consumers is particularly encouraging in this context, because it is a way of reconnecting people with the process of producing the food that they eat. The role of local and home production, and of educating children about food, should be included in vision and strategy for food.

Food Production in the U.K:

The UK is self-sufficient in food production. It can feed its population for another 50 years without any difficulty.

The country produces the following commodities. The commodities are: Cow Milk, Wheat, Indigenous Chicken Meat, Potato, Indigenous Pig Meat, Indigenous Sheep Meat, Rapeseed, Barley, Hen Eggs, Sugar Beets, Indigenous Turkey Meat, Pulses, Carrots, Mushrooms, Green Peas, Greasy Wool and Vegetable Fresh

Australia

Population: 22,606, 754 (2011) U N report

A new Senate inquiry is to examine how Australia can produce enough food for it and maintain its major export capacity in the face of global warming.

The inquiry will be chaired by Senator Bill Heffernan, Liberal Senator for NSW, and represents the first time that the Senate has examined the issue of food security in Australia. The inquiry will hopefully determine how to produce food that is affordable to consumers, viable for production by farmers and has a sustainable impact on the environment. Senator Heffernan suggests that the Senate will look into a number of areas in their endeavour to provide a bank of information for future policy decisions to be made.

The Committee will look at:

(a) The impact of climate change both globally and nationally,
(b) The effect of carbon trading,
(c) Market distortions by, and including, commodity traders and speculators, consolidated retailers, supply and demand,
(d) Global cartels and their impact on fuel, fertilizer and chemical prices and supply,
(e) Tax distortions and the impact of their incentives in the market, e.g. Managed Investment Schemes (MIS),

(f) Supply chain efficiencies and
(g) Availability of agricultural land and water and other related matters.

Shadow Minister for Environment, Heritage, the Arts and Indigenous Affairs, Dr Sharman Stone, believes:

(a) The inquiry is pivotal, as it should provide greater understanding of the future of food-related industries here in Australia.
(b) Australians have long taken for granted the diversity, quality and low prices of foods grown locally.
(c) Government policy, in particular in relation to research and development, climate change and emissions trading schemes as they relate to agriculture, will all play a significant part in the future capacity of Australia's farmers to feed us and to continue to export globally.

This inquiry comes at a critical time for Australia's farmers. The cost of farm inputs has risen alarmingly, (and) fuel, fertilizers, veterinary services and supplies are all thinning margins. Urban, mining and forestry encroachment is reducing the arable land supply and labour shortages and the age of those in farm and food production are all adding to the mix of a sector needing very special attention if it is to flourish into the future. I encourage all sectors of Australian food producers and those with a concern for our natural environment to make their submissions to the committee.

The inquiry comes at a time when food prices have been skyrocketing, COAG meets to discuss the future of the Murray-Darling basin, and drought continues to cause great hardship in many rural farming areas. Additionally, many countries have been restricting exports to ensure that food security in their country is not threatened. Such policy measures have, however, been met with concern as they threaten to undermine the benefits of globalization and lead to higher food prices.

The World Bank President, Robert Zoellick, indicated that 26 net food-exporting countries have maintained or introduced such measures and he is worried that they have only increased food costs. For globalization to work successfully and achieve its promise, it must be inclusive and sustainable.[25]

Australia's response

The Australian Government helps developing countries in its region to reduce poverty and address food security by promoting trade liberalization, peace and stability, good governance, security of land tenure, rural development and agricultural research. Australia also provides emergency food aid to developing countries in need. In May 2003, the Australian Government announced a A$1 billion food security pledge for the five years from 1 July 2003 to 30 June 2008 for programs and initiatives that enhance the food security of people in the developing world. Specific programs to improve food security for those in need include:

(a) Helping people improve their farms and productivity;
(b) Constructing food stores and improving roads so that food can be moved to where it is needed or where it can be sold;
(c) Promoting national and international trade to encourage economic growth and poverty reduction;
(d) Improving the status of women and girls so they have more control over the areas in which they have traditionally been involved and can access new areas;

---

[25] Daniel Palmer, "Senate enquiry into Australia's Food Security", AFN thought for Food, July 3, 2008

(e) Ensuring that people, and especially children, receive food in emergency situations;

(f) Promoting rural development, including sustainable agricultural, fishery and forestry production and management of natural resources;

(g) Preparing for disasters and emergencies to meet transitory and emergency food requirements in ways that encourage recovery and rehabilitation

Each year Australia contributes up to 150,000 tonnes of Australian produced wheat and rice to the World Food Programme. This operates like a 'food bank' that can be used during both humanitarian emergencies and development situations to help households shift towards more sustainable livelihoods.

World Food Day, 16 October, highlights the need to ensure that all people have physical and economic access at all times to enough nutritious, safe food to lead healthy and active lives.

(a) More than half the world's population lives in low-income, food-deficit countries that are unable to produce or import enough food to feed their people.

(b) More than one-third of all children are malnourished and 6 million children a year die of causes related to malnutrition.

(c) Most of the world's hungry people are found in the developing world, but 34 million live in the developed world.

(d) Soil degradation, chronic water shortages, inappropriate agricultural policies and population growth threaten food production in many countries.

(e) While growing export crops such as coffee, cocoa and sugar produces export income, it can lead to a decrease in basic food production, causing hardship for people who are poor.

(f) Between 1960 and 1990 world cereal production more than doubled, food production increased by one-third per head, daily intake of calories increased by one-third, and real food prices fell by almost half.

(g) There is enough food in the world for everyone to have enough to eat, but it is unevenly distributed.[26]

Food Production in Australia:

Australia is self-sufficient in food grains production. It can feed its people for another century without difficulty.

The Australians are food-secured. The country supplies food to other deficit countries under Australian Aid organization. The country produces the following commodities. The commodities are: Indigenous Cattle Meat, Wheat, Cow Milk, indigenous Sheep Meat, Indigenous Chicken Meat, Greasy Wool, Grapes, Sugar cane, Barley, Indigenous Pig Meat, rapeseed, Sorghum, Potato, Hen Eggs, Tomato, Lupins, Oats, Rice/ Paddy, Oranges, Apples.

Canada

Population34, 350, 000(2010) –U N report

Canada's Action Plan for Food Security is Canada's response to the World Food Summit (WFS) commitment made by the international community to reduce by half the number of undernourished people no later than the year 2015. It builds on a wide range of existing international commitments which affect food security, including agreements on international trade and environmental issues, conventions on

---

[26] Australian AID, Government of Australia, Publication Division

human rights (including women's and children's rights), social development, education, housing and urban development. In addition, it builds on commitments and actions that flow from current domestic programs such as Canada's own Nutrition for Health:

(a) An Agenda for Action;
(b) Gathering Strength: Canada's Aboriginal Action Plan; Revisions to legislation, including the Fisheries Act; and
(c) Canada's evolving economic, social and environmental programs and policies.

This Plan is the work of a Joint Consultative Group (JCG) composed of both government and civil society representatives. During the drafting discussions, it became apparent to the JCG that it was dealing with a wide range of issues, many of which are complex and interconnected. The structure of this document is based on the WFS Plan of Action endorsed by 187 countries at the World Food Summit in Rome in 1996. The WFS Plan of Action contains seven commitments, which also form the backbone of this document. It recognizes that food security implies access to adequate food and sufficient food supplies. Poverty reduction, social justice and sustainable food systems are essential conditions.

The Plan acknowledges the important role that civil society plays in contributing to food security and recognizes the achievements of the academic community and private sector in expanding production and improving access to food since the global effort to end hunger began in earnest some 50 years ago. Information sharing, partnerships and inter-sectoral cooperation play a key role in Canada's approach.

The Plan is a work in progress, which forms a basis for further discussions on the specifics of implementation, including timing, roles and responsibilities, coordination mechanisms and related actions. It is open-ended and flexible, adaptable to changing conditions and responsive to evolving needs. It is not an exhaustive inventory of existing programs or planned actions; rather, it is a blueprint that sets out the highest priorities as identified by members of the JCG. These priorities are outlined below.

Commitments

Priority 1: The right to food reiterates Canada's belief that this right is an important element in food security and underscores the need to better define the meaning of this right, and the actions required to implement it. Actions include civil society support to the International Code of Conduct on the Human Right to Adequate Food, and all sector participation in national and international efforts to clarify the meaning of the right to food towards its full and progressive realization.

Priority 2: The reduction of poverty is an important element in the strategy for addressing food insecurity in both domestic and international actions, based on the notion that a key condition for food security is access to sufficient resources to purchase or grow food. International actions are influenced by Canada's poverty reduction focus in its development assistance program; actions include maintaining or exceeding the 25 percent Official Development Assistance (ODA) target for investments in basic human needs such as food and nutrition, education and primary health care. The Plan also reaffirms Canada's commitment to engaging citizens in policymaking and program design in the area of poverty reduction.

Priority 3: Promotion of access to safe and nutritious food is seen as a critical component of food security. In developing countries, actions on micronutrient and vitamin supplementation of foods contribute to improved nutrition. Breastfeeding is also highlighted as critical to infant health and nutrition worldwide. In Canada, commitment to this is furthered through actions to support working mothers, hospital programs, mother and child health care and other initiatives in support of the International Code of Marketing of Breast-milk Substitutes. Beyond the promotion and protection of breastfeeding and other food security conditions, caring practices, and health and education measures are important for the nutrition security of mothers and children, particularly, but not only, in developing countries.

Priority 4: Food safety underlines the new threats to global food supply posed by the rapid increase and deep market penetration of new and exotic foods from a variety of trading partners, which may constitute a safety or disease hazard; by environmental contaminants, especially in traditional food sources in Canada's Far North, which are also a threat to safety; and emergencies or disasters, which can cause problems such as contamination from hazardous chemicals or disease-causing micro-organisms. In addition, lack of knowledge about preparation and storage of foods is identified as a threat, mainly at the household level. Actions to ensure safe supplies and safe handling include enhanced public education, better product labeling, enhanced biotechnology assessment, improved monitoring methods and stronger multi-sectoral partnerships.

Priority 5: Traditional food acquisition methods of Aboriginal and coastal communities acknowledge the important role that hunting, fishing, gathering, bartering and trading play in the food security of many communities in Canada and abroad. By sharing their awareness of traditional foods and their knowledge of sustainable natural resource practices, indigenous people have an important contribution to make in achieving the World Food Summit's goal. Actions related to the reduction of environmental contaminants, sustainable management of resources (including fisheries) and appropriate supplementation with high-quality commercial foods, strengthen access to food for these communities.

Priority 6: Food production emphasizes the critical role of research, rural development and investment in the productivity of the agriculture and agri-food sector. This priority makes a strong link between the sustainable management of productive resources and the production of sufficient quantities of safe and nutritious food for all. It demonstrates the need to support local production, particularly in developing countries, where agrarian reform, participation of affected communities (including women producers) and fulfillment of basic human needs are essential to successful rural development programs. In Canada, actions aimed at enhancing agricultural production include: supporting sustainable resource management, continuing to invest in and build research capacity and encouraging investment in rural areas.

Priority 7: Emphasis on environmentally sustainable practices explores some of the most pressing challenges to food production. Canada's actions in support of this priority are channeled through its support to a wide variety of commitments under current international agreements. Internationally, this covers specific challenges to developing countries in such areas as water resource management, community forestry, sustainable population growth and respect and preservation of indigenous knowledge. For Canada, additional actions complement these agreements to enhance stewardship of natural resources in the areas of northern contaminants, sustainable fisheries management, biotechnology, climate change and biodiversity.

Priority 8: Fair trade outlines the potential impact of liberalized trade regimes on incomes and overall welfare, and indicates the possibility that there may be adjustment costs in non-competitive sectors. Actions within this priority involve enhancing trade in the food and agri-food sectors, particularly for developing countries, while achieving a better understanding of the impacts of liberalized trade on people vulnerable to food insecurity.

Priority 9: Acknowledgement of peace as a precursor to food security underlines the need for safe and secure access to means of production, especially arable land and harvestable waters. Actions within this priority strengthen emergency measures, conflict prevention, peace building and disaster preparedness in Canada and abroad.

Priority 10: A monitoring system for food insecurity identifies the need for a comprehensive set of agreed-upon indicators to determine the nature, extent and evolution of food insecurity, both to develop appropriate responses and to monitor their effectiveness. This Plan provides for both government and civil society to work toward developing indicators for national and international systems and using them for monitoring purposes.[27]

II. Income Related Household food Security in Canada

---

[27]Agriculture and Agricultural Food, Canada: For the purpose of this document, "civil society" refers to organizations and associations of people, formed for social or political purposes, which are not created or mandated by governments. Included are non-governmental organizations, trade unions, cooperatives, churches, grass-roots organizations, academic institutions, and business associations.

The report provides national and provincial estimates of the income-related food security status of Canadian households, including among the adult and child members of those households. It contributes to a wider understanding of the prevalence of food insecurity in Canada by identifying population sub-groups in which food insecurity is more prevalent and by highlighting socio-demographic factors associated with food insecurity. It will serve as an important reference on household food security in Canada in 2004.[28]

Focus of the Report

It is recognized that "food security exists when all people, at all times, have physical and economic access to sufficient, safe and nutritious food to meet their dietary needs and food preferences for an active and healthy life" (Food and Agriculture Organization 1996). This report reflects the characteristics of food security specifically, the financial ability of households to access adequate food, which is strongly related to household income.

The report includes for the first time in Canada, national and provincial data from a standard multiple-indicator measure of household food security used internationally, particularly in the United States. The food security questionnaire included in the survey was adapted from the 18-item United States Food Security Survey Module. This report describes a new approach to interpreting the food security data, including the application of household survey weights. Until now, monitoring changes in income-related food insecurity in Canada has been a challenge due to differences in questions and/or methodology used in the various surveys. The food security module

---

[28]Canadian Community Health Survey, Cycle 2.2, Nutrition (2004)—Income-Related Household Food Security in Canada

included in the report will be repeated in subsequent cycles presenting opportunities to study the same dimensions of food security over time.

Descriptive analyses were undertaken to determine the prevalence of income-related food insecurity among households, adults and children in Canada. Additional analyses were undertaken by selected socio-demographic variables to identify sub-groups of the population in which household food insecurity is more prevalent.[29]

Key Findings

Key findings of these analyses include the following:

Although most Canadian households had consistent access to food in 2004, more than 1.1 million households (9.2 percent) were food insecure at some point in the previous year as a result of financial challenges they faced in accessing adequate food. In these households, at least one adult or child member experienced multiple conditions characteristic of food insecurity.

Overall, 2.7 million Canadians, or 8.8 percent of the population, lived in food insecure households in 2004.

Across the country, rates of household food insecurity ranged from 8.1 percent in Saskatchewan to 14.6 percent in Nova Scotia.

---

[29] Bickel G, Nord M, Price C et al. *Guide to Measuring Household Food Security, Revised 2000*. Alexandria, VA: Food and Nutrition Service, United States Department of Agriculture, 2000. Available at: www.fns.usda.gov/fsec/files/fsguide.pdf (accessed May 2, 2006).

Among households with children, 5.2 percent experienced food insecurity at the child level—that is, at least one child in each of these households experienced food insecurity in the previous year. More than 700,000 children lived in households in which either adults or children experienced food insecurity at some time in 2004, including 366,200 who lived in households in which one or more of the children were food insecure.

Food insecurity was generally more prevalent among adults (9.0 percent) than among children (5.2 percent) in the household—especially when the experience of food insecurity was severe (adults 2.9 percent, children 0.4 percent).

The prevalence of food insecurity was higher among households with certain characteristics, including:

(a)Those with incomes in the lowest (48.3 percent) and lower middle (29.1 percent) categories of household income adequacy, compared with those in the middle (13.6 percent), upper middle (5.2 percent) and highest (1.3 percent) categories of household income adequacy,

(b)Those relying on social assistance (59.7 percent) or worker's compensation/employment insurance (29.0 percent) as their main source of household income, compared with those with salary/wages (7.3 percent) and those with pensions/seniors' benefits (4.9 percent) as their main source of income, off-reserve aboriginal households (33.3 percent), compared with non-Aboriginal households (8.8 percent), those who do not own their dwelling (20.5 percent), compared with those who do own their dwelling (3.9 percent), and those with children (10.4 percent), compared with those without children (8.6 percent).

Among households with children, the prevalence of food insecurity was higher among:

(a) Those led by a lone parent (22.5 percent), especially a female lone parent (24.9 percent), compared with households led by a couple (7.6 percent),
(b) Those with three or more children (15.0 percent), compared with those with one or two children (9.6 percent), and
(c) Those with at least one child under the age of 6 years (13.0 percent), compared with those without a child less than 6 years of age (8.8 percent).
(d) Among households without children, the prevalence of food insecurity was higher among unattached individuals (13.7 percent), compared with couple households (3.5 percent).

Implications

For the first time in Canada, data are available from a sophisticated multiple-indicator survey tool that enables a more confident estimate of the prevalence of household food insecurity. Although most Canadian households had consistent access to food in 2004, the findings of this analysis confirm what other studies have reported—that food insecurity is a reality for many socio-economically vulnerable Canadian households.

The report provides a descriptive overview of income-related household food security in Canada, highlighting population sub-groups for whom food insecurity is more prevalent. Employing new methods for interpreting the food security data, it offers guidance to others who undertake their own research using these data for more in-depth analyses to better understand the factors associated with food security status, to cross-reference the food and nutrient consumption data to identify population sub-groups whose nutritional health is potentially compromised because of financial resource constraints, and to explore the food security situation of the particularly vulnerable Aboriginal populations living off-reserve. Such research can also inform policy and program decisions.

Households considered to be food insecure are not homogenous. The specific factors associated with their vulnerability may vary and, therefore, so will the required actions to prevent food insecurity at the household level. However, from a population health perspective, it is clear that tackling income-related food insecurity in a sustainable way will require addressing factors associated with income. Macro-level approaches—such as national, provincial or local level policies and programs aimed at improving access to adequate and affordable housing, education, secure employment and financial support when required—have the potential to profoundly influence the key determinants of income-related food security and to alleviate the burden on those Canadians who are most vulnerable. Collaboration between various government portfolios at all levels and other sectors responsible for health, social and economic policy development will be required for long-term and sustainable solutions that address the complexity of issues that determine income-related food security. The food security data would provide important information to help inform some of these solutions.[30]

III. Canada Helps Launch Global Agriculture and food Security Program:

---

[30]Canadian Community Health Survey Cycle 2.2 Nutrition (2004), Office of the Nutrition Policy and Promotion, Health Products and Food branch, Canada

Minister Jim Flaherty spoke at the launch of the Global Agriculture and Food Security Program (GAFSP):

"Today, it is estimated that more than a billion people go to bed hungry. This new Global Agriculture and Food Security Program can help change that, and I am pleased that Canada is among the first to contribute. I am particularly encouraged that there is a role for the private sector to boost the resources available to combat hunger, and that countries in need will play a leading role in putting these new funds to their best use.

Canada is delivering on its food security and sustainable agricultural development commitments made last year at the G8 L'Aquila Summit. Lack of access to safe and nutritious food is one of the major obstacles to reducing poverty in developing countries. Through its contribution to this initiative, Canada supports developing countries' efforts to increase long-term agricultural development in order to improve the incomes and nutritional status of people in developing countries."

The GAFSP was established by the World Bank in response to calls made at the G8 L'Aquila and the G20 Pittsburgh summits for a multilateral trust fund to boost sustainable agriculture and food security assistance to low-income countries. The GAFSP is an improvement over current initiatives as it is designed to strengthen links to the private sector, provide additional and rapidly available resources for sustainable agriculture development, and ensure country ownership by linking funding to developing countries' identified priorities and strategies.

Canada is providing $230 million to the GAFSP as part of a three-year, $600-million agriculture package, a doubling of Canada's existing spending in this area. It is a further demonstration of Canada's leadership in global food security, where Canada is the third-largest contributor to the World Food Programme, and has fully untied its food aid.

Minister Flaherty noted that the Canadian contribution is another example of Canada's commitment to international financial institutions such as the World Bank and International Monetary Fund (IMF). Over the past year, Canada has boosted its contributions to these multilateral institutions by more than US$22 billion. This includes being the first donor nation to the World Bank's Global Trade Liquidity Program, and the first G20 nation to provide an increased commitment to the IMF's Poverty Reduction and Growth Trust, to support low-income countries facing severe economic challenges.

The Global Agriculture and Food Security Program was launched before the G20 and G7 meetings of finance ministers and central bank governors, and the spring meetings of the IMF and World Bank. Minister Flaherty is also participating in a conference organized by the Bertelsmann Foundation, where he will discuss the changing role of the G20 in the global economy.[31]

IV. Hunger and food Security in Canada

Hunger is the compelling need or desire for food coupled with the physiological, painful sensation or state of weakness caused by the need of food. Many citizens often believe that hunger is not an issue faced by industrialized countries, as these issues are often associated with developing nations; it is not faced by the wealthy. However, this is a perfect example of misinterpretation the issues that surround many of Canadians every day.

---

[31]Department of Finance, Canada; Washington, D. C., April 22, 2010, 2010-030

Hunger does not necessarily refer to poverty-stricken countries, although their issues may be greater, but it can also refer to low/no-income individuals within a society experiencing economic growth. Although their situations are vastly different from those of the poorer countries, they are also entirely the same and connected. Hunger is hunger regardless of nationality, class, age, race, sex, or any other defining characteristic and is an issue, with many daunting aspects, that is in need of immediate and constant attention to obtain its ultimate elimination from our world society (World Food Summit 1996).

Although Canada is one the wealthiest countries in the world, 15 percent or 3.7 million Canadians are considered "food insecure". This means that many Canadians are not sure where their next meal is coming from or if they'll have enough resources to prepare a sufficient and nutritious meal for themselves or their families.

The Canadian Association of Food Banks' *Hunger Count (2006)* reports that food bank use is at a record high, with 753,458 Canadians relying on food banks in one- month period. Of these food bank users, 41 percent are children. This growing group of food bank users includes children, seniors, and persons with disabilities, lone mothers and working poor. The reality is that although food bank use has increased over 99 percent since 1989, 34.5 percent of food banks faced difficulties in meeting the demand. It states that everybody is at risk of becoming food insecure at some point in his or her lives; however, certain groups are more vulnerable. The following groups are more vulnerable to food insecurity:

(a)Income Assistance Recipients - People, who receive income assistance as their main source of income, make up over 50 percent of the clients at food banks. This may suggest that welfare rates in Canada are not enough to ensure food security for low-income Canadians, which, according to the National Council of Welfare, continue to fall below poverty lines.

(b)Working Poor - The second largest group of food bank clients are people with jobs, at about 13.1 percent. Due to low wage incomes, they are unable to meet basic needs for themselves and their families, even with full-time jobs.

(c)Seniors - About 7.1 percent of food bank clients are seniors.

(d)Children: Children under 18 represent approximately 40.7 percent of food bank clients in Canada, and the situation of child poverty has not improved since 1989 when Canada had made an all-party resolution to end child poverty. This representation is directly tied to the level of household income, 50 percent of recipients are families with children.

(e)Lone Mothers: Women head almost one-fourth of Canada's lone parent or single parent families; 41 percent of whom were living below the poverty line in 2001.

Between 1989 and 2004, the number of Canadians using food banks increased by 123 percent, and in 2004 Ontario had the highest provincial food bank use, at 38 percent (Ontario Association of Food Banks, 2006).

What is Food Security?

The definition of food security developed at the World Food Summit in 1996 at which 187 countries pledged to halve the number of hungry people within their respective nations by the year 2015 has been accepted by Dietitians of Canada and adhered to by the Canadian Government:

Food security exists when all people, at all times, have physical and economic access to sufficient, safe, and nutritious food to meet their dietary needs and food preferences for an active and healthy life.

The **Centre for Studies in Food Security** notes five components of food security (1):

(a) **Availability:** Sufficient food for all people at all times;
(b) **Accessibility:** Physical and economic access to food for all at all times;
(c) **Adequacy:** Access to food that is nutritious and safe, and produced in environmentally sustainable ways.
(d) **Acceptability:** Access to culturally acceptable food, which is produced and obtained in ways that do not compromise people's dignity, self-respect or human rights.
(e) **Agency:** The policies and processes that enable the achievement of food security.

In the broadest sense, food security can be boiled down to the surety that individuals have the opportunity to access food, have the availability of reliable food at all times and finally have the ability to utilize safe, nutritious food to meet their daily recommended dietary intakes for a productive, healthy life. Since these terms are so broad, food security can be open for interpretation; however, it is imperative that an individual possess all of these elements, for lacking even one, exacts food insecurity.

A Canadian perspective looks at defining situations of zero hunger, a sustainable food system, and healthy and safe food; they take all steps to reach zero hunger. This means that all people at all times must be able to acquire, in a dignified manner, adequate quantity and quality of culturally and personally acceptable food. A sustainable food system means that food in Canada must be harvested, produced, processed, distributed and consumed in a manner which maintains and enhances the quality of land, air and water for future generations, and in which people are able to earn a living wage in a safe and healthy working environment by harvesting, growing, producing, processing, handling, retailing and serving food. Healthy and safe food ties into a sustainable food system, one does not work without the other.

Healthy and safe food means that nourishing foods must be readily at hand (and less nourishing ones restricted); food (including wild foods) must not be contaminated with pathogens or industrial chemicals; and no novel food can be allowed to enter the environment or food chain without rigorous independent testing and the existence of an on-going tracking and surveillance system, to ensure its safety for human consumption.

Why does Hunger and Food Insecurity Exist?

(a) Unequal distribution of food globally and locally
(b) Societal treatment of food as a commodity
(c) Inadequate resources to produce food in a sustainable way
(d) Limiting trade restrictions and government policies on food exportation and importation
(e) Poverty

The Public Health Agency of Canada lists income/social status as the number one determinant of health, hunger, and food security; and so in our modern world where food is treated as a commodity rather than as a necessity, it is reasonable to assume that the solution to food insecurity would simply be a reduction of financial strain on those persons having a low-income. However, upon closer scrutiny, one would realize that although food and monetary aid indeed superficially addresses the issues of hunger and food insecurity, this approach gives way to more deeply embedded cracks in Canada' social and political structures.

Approaches to Address Food Security Issues

Food Security= Short-Term + Capacity Building + Redesign

The following sections give a closer look at what each level represents, the approaches which have been and are currently being used at each level to address food security, and give a discussion surrounding the pros and cons of each of these approaches.

(1) Short Term:

Short-term relief strategies are the first level on the Food Security continuum. This level represents emergency programs such as charitable food distribution agencies, which intervene to prevent hunger and famine in times of environmental, societal or personal crisis. Food banks first arose in Canada during a period of large scale unemployment and recession in 1981 in Edmonton, AB as an "emergency measure," with the expectation that when the crisis was over, the program would fold. Throughout the rest of the decade it was still unclear as to if and when the food banks would close; the need, however, continued to increase and more food banks opened in response. Today, food banks are virtually embedded as an integral component in the food security network, meanwhile government unemployment and welfare policies are as yet inadequate and unfortunately these charities have the potential to divert the attention away from underlying issues giving politicians an "out".

Example of Short Term Relief Strategies:

(a) Babies First/Steps and Stages – Pregnant women and families with children under 18 months have access to a food cupboard, food vouchers, nutritious snacks and lunch at these CPNP/CAPC drop-in programs at the Ontario Early Years Centre.
(b) Soup Kitchens - Usually held in a church basement or other community building where the community provides free food to people living on the street or who are in need.

(2) Capacity Building:

The second rung along the food security continuum is a capacity building approach. Strategies in this category reflect an effort to bridge gaps between the community and public policy, and to build-up the capacity of individuals to improve or control their own food-provision situation. The Community Food Security Movement combines components of food security with community strategies that ensure all members of the community have an affordable and quality food supply. Community Food Security program promotes collaboration and inclusion while developing sustainable food systems that promote good nutrition and health. In so doing, these programs aim to empower and educate vulnerable community members. Meal Exchange aims to work with youth and communities across the country to promote the community food security movement and address the root causes of hunger to create real social change.

The key point to consider concerning building the capacity of an individual to provide for them, is that there is movement away from a reliance on short-term emergency aid toward self-sustainability and influencing of policy. By equipping persons with the skill set and the tools necessary to survive within their respective societies, we are in a sense fulfilling the age-old saying, which goes:

Give a person a fish, and you feed them for a day; teach a person how to fish, and they can feed themselves for a lifetime.

Other benefits of capacity building strategies include: the development of support networks, increased nutrition and policy knowledge, opportunities to share information about other cultures and stimulation of local economy. The examples of Capacity Building Strategies are:

Community Kitchens (Peer-Led): Collective Kitchen is a place where people can cook food for themselves and/or their families. Prices are kept low as compared to supermarket specials. Community Members may meet twice a month - once to plan and the next time to cook and take 3 to 5 meals to home. Collective Kitchens are often supported by a variety of services for clubs and community organizations but the cost to participants is minimal.

Community Gardens: A Community Garden is a cooperative venture in which families, groups or individuals get together to grow their own vegetables, fruits, herbs, and flowers on public or private land. There are several sites located around the city for this purpose.

Gleaning: The ability to pick fruits and vegetables is free. Farmers donate their extra produce and local churches pay for the bus transportation. Because produce ripens quickly and farmers are never sure when they will have any excess, gleaning trips are usually organized on short notice. Last year tomatoes, corn, strawberries and raspberries were some of the fruits and vegetables gleaned by community members.

This is a fantastic way to ensure that foods will not be wasted that cannot be sold by farmers. It also offers healthy, fresh products for citizens but is limited because it is organized on short notice

Just Food Box: Save up to 25 percent on your grocery bill and receive healthy, nutritious food and a great newsletter. Two kinds of boxes are available each month. The Staple box holds a variety of non-perishable groceries, as well as some fruit and vegetables. It comes in two sizes: regular $15.00 and small $11.00. The Fresh Produce Box is full of just fresh fruit, vegetables and an herb. It comes in two sizes as well: regular $20.00 and small $12.00.

Breakfast for Learning: This community oriented, cross-Canada program is a great way to provide nutritious breakfasts for children who might not have been able to eat otherwise. They provide a way to access food to help youth become informed about issues like food security.

(3) Structural Redesign

The redesign approach is the most effective strategy for attacking the core issues of poverty, food system sustainability, and promoting the connection between health and social environment.

The Canadian government has included several structural redesign commitments within the past 15 years. These are:

(a) The World Declaration on Nutrition and the Plan of Action for Nutrition (1992),
(b) The World Summit for Social Development (1995),
(c) The Declaration on World Food Security (1996),

(d) Canada's Action Plan on Food Security (1998) and
(e) The Declaration on World Food Security - Five Years Later (2002).

All of these target the appropriate issue within the social structure, however they have not yet been fulfilled and a large proportion of Canadian citizen's continue to live marginally.

In 1995 employment insurance (EI) was restructured to reduce the numbers of workers eligible for benefits from 75 percent in 1990 to 38 percent in 2001. Social Assistance eligibility restrictions were also increased alongside decreased provincial funding for the program and the "claw back" of the National Child Benefit. The federal government canceled social housing programs. Minimum wage and social assistance rates are relatively static and remain consistently well below the poverty line in many provinces. The only exception to the general decreases in funding was the Child Tax Benefit which saw significant funding increases during the 1990's, and the only province to address poverty as a health issue, with food security as part of the solution, was Quebec.

Currently there is a rising voice speaking out on behalf of society and the poor, using a "bottom-up" approach, to the Canadian government's policy makers. Organizations backed by research and partnered with health professionals, institutions, the community and even areas of government are forming across Canada and the world to promote and ensure adherence to food security policy change. For example: Ontario Public Health Association, Nova Scotia Nutrition Council, Population Health, Atlantic Health Promotion Research Centre, Health Canada, Public Health Agency of Canada, FAO, and Agriculture and Agri-business Canada.

(d)Farm Production

Canadian agricultural producers are the backbone of a highly competitive sector worth $130 billion a year. Agriculture and Agricultural-Food Canada provides information and programs for those who raise animals or who grow plants for food, feed or industrial use. Agricultural producers will find information about economic forecasts and statistics, policies and acts, incentive programs and other services.

1. Animal producers can find market information on livestock, meat, poultry, egg and dairy products, programs, and links to related producer organizations.

Animal Production: Livestock farmers provide the largest share of Canada's agricultural production. As well as providing traditional varieties of red meat, poultry and eggs, and dairy, producers are expanding into new markets for organic and specialty foods, at home and abroad. Find out more about the three main areas of animal production: red meat, poultry and eggs, and dairy.

Red Meat: beef, pork, and lamb dominate Canada's red meat and meat products industry, the largest sector of the Canadian food manufacturing industry. It is one of the most valuable manufacturing industries overall.

Poultry and Eggs: Canada's annual chicken and turkey meat production totals more than 1 billion kilograms, eviscerated equivalent. The poultry industry exports over 20 million live birds per year to 86 countries, plus more than 1 million kilograms of poultry meat and edible by-products.

Dairy: Canada's dairy sector plays an important role in the Canadian agriculture and agricultural-food economy. Dairy production generates $5.31 billion in total farm cash receipts and $13.1 billion in manufacturing sales. Livestock includes Beef Cattle, Bison, Dairy Cattle, Goats, Sheep, Pigs, Laying Hens, Meat Birds/ Broilers, and Turkey

2. Crop producers can find information on fruits, vegetables, honey, maple, greenhouse, ornamentals, pulses, special crops, grains and oilseeds commodities including: commodity reports, markets information, business incentives, trade data, and links to related associations and government initiatives.

Crop Production: Although Canada has an international reputation as a grain producer; Canadian farms provide a diverse range of crops for domestic and international markets, including fruits, vegetables, cereals, oilseeds, greenhouse, ornamentals, specialty crops and nursery stock. Find out about three crop sectors: grains and oilseeds, horticulture and pulses and special crops.

Grains and Oilseeds: Canada's main grain crops are barley, corn, oats, rye and, of course, wheat. Canadian oilseed production is concentrated in canola, soybean and flaxseed. Explore the grains and oilseeds sectors for economic forecasts, situation reports and historical data.

Horticulture: The Canadian Horticulture sector produces and packages more than including field and greenhouse fruit and vegetables, and thousands of varieties of flowers and ornamental plants, as well as maple and honey products. Canadian fruits and vegetables are exported as fresh and frozen product for retail, foodservice and processed markets. Detailed situation and trends analysis and markets information are among the resources available on Canada's horticultural and ornamental (floriculture, nursery, and Christmas trees) production.

Pulses and Special Crops: Pulses are grain legumes, such as peas, beans, chickpeas and lentils. The term "special crops" is a catch-all for those crops not included in other categories, such as: buckwheat, canary seed, essential oils, forages, ginseng, herbs and spices, industrial hemp, medicinal plants and seeds for consumption.

Crops grown includes Wheat / Durum, Oats, Lentils and dry peas, Barley, Flex, Grains, Soybeans, Rye, Spelt, Corn, Oilseeds, Mustard, Buck Wheat, Hemp, Canola, and Alfa / Grass. The farmers grow forage crops, plow down green pasture and keep some land fallow. Horticultural crops include Potato, Sweet Corn, Fruits and Vegetables, Tree Fruits, Small fruits / Berries, Grapes and Nuts

3. The organic food market is a dynamic and rapidly growing sector of the global food industry. Find statistics about the organic market, information about organic certification and links to the laws and regulations governing organic production in Canada. Organic Production: today industry analysts describe the organic food market as the most dynamic and rapidly growing sector of the global food industry. The global market for organic products, once a small scale niche market, reached a value of over $US 50 billion in 2008 (Source: International Federation of Organic Agricultural Movements). Worldwide, about 35 million hectares of agricultural land are certified according to organic standards, and there are almost 1.4 million organic producers. In Canada, there has been a small but increasing organic agriculture sector since the early 1980s. In recent years, this sector has seen dramatic growth with organic food consumption developing at a faster rate than production.

Canada’s Organic Industry (2008)

Canada's large and varied land base, combined with its cooler climate, makes it an ideal country for producing organic food. The sector is diversifying and expanding into new markets while achieving double digit annual growth in production and retail sales over the past decade. This growth rate is expected to continue increasing in coming years as the organic sector in Canada becomes more organized, trade impediments are reduced or eliminated, and consumer confidence and demand continues to grow due to the implementation of mandatory certification to minimum standards.

(1)**Canadian industry facts:**

(a)Approximately 3,700 producers working on 612 thousand hectares of land produce certified organic products in Canada.

(b)Certified organic farms account for approximately 1.5 percent of the total number of farms in Canada. Organic fruit and vegetable farms lead the way at about 2.3 percent.

(c)Organic livestock is one of the fastest growing sectors.

(d)There are more than 1,200 certified organic processors and handlers in Canada, producing a wide variety of ingredients and consumer-ready products.

(e)Total annual retail sales of certified organic products in Canada are approximately $2 billion, with about 45% moving through mainstream supermarkets.

(f)Fresh vegetables account for 25 percent of all supermarket organic food sales.

(2) **Organic exports**

(a) Canada exports a wide selection of certified organic products, ranging from bulk grains to pre-packaged consumer-ready products in every category.

(b) The largest share of our exports goes to the United States, the European Union and Japan.

(c) As can be expected from the breadbasket of the world, organic wheat is our most popular export. However, exports of oats, flax, barley, lentils, peas, spelt, hemp, soybeans, corn, sunflowers, and other grains and oilseeds are also significant.

(3) **Organic standards:** New Organic Products Regulations make certification in accordance with the National Standard for Organic Agriculture mandatory for all organic products. Canada is pursuing agreements with our trading partners to facilitate the unfettered trade of organic products.

4. **New Farmers**

New farmers are the keys to the revitalization of the agriculture sector. That is why there are a variety of programs and services available to help them get established in agriculture. This website section, therefore targets young and beginning farmers in order to allow them to learn about these tools and find out which programs may meet their needs.

Young and beginning farmers face specific challenges such as access to capital, access to farm assets, and high debt levels. Nevertheless, young people continue to enter the sector with an energetic entrepreneurial spirit, respect for the environment, innovative ideas and new ways of doing business. The YBF section contains a wide range of information that young and beginning farmers will find useful. Be it exploring farming as a potential career or accessing funding opportunities to develop your farm, you will find the information here. This is your one-stop business information site on farming. The government allows facilities to the new farmers in all respects financially, legally and tries to train them for successful farming.

Canadian Health Measures Survey (CHMS)

This survey (2007-2009) will provide biochemical data from blood and urine samples, dietary intake from 24 hour recalls and food frequency questionnaires as well as socioeconomic and demographic data for generalization to the national and provincial levels. When completed, the CHMS will be an extremely valuable tool for furthering the argument against food insecurity and pushing for policy change and restructuring.

Nutritious Food Basket: The National Nutritious Food Basket (NNFB), which is a list of 66 food items that has been validated for use in Nova Scotia to estimate the cost of a basic, nutritious diet, was used to survey 43 randomly selected grocery stores and an additional 14 more under the supervision of the Nova Scotia Nutrition Council. In 2002 it was found that the cost of the NNFB for a family of four was $502.79, a price that many Nova Scotia's cannot afford, especially those living on Income Assistance or earning minimum wage.

Youth and Food Security: Youth play an enormous part in the issue of food security, as they are what keep the awareness and aid continuing for future generations and they will be a significant part of the work behind the complete elimination of hunger, not only on a local community bases, but also on the large global scale. Without their interest in the improvement of the welfare for all mankind, initiatives such as food banks, community relief programs, etc., would not continue and would eventually fade out.

Today's youth are becoming more and more distant from the problems that we all face today as local and global communities, one being hunger. However, without their interest now, the chances for the future are pretty slim. Programs, such as Meal Exchange who work towards engaging youth involvement, are how youth interest in regards to hunger and food insecurity will continue. More organizations need to take on a youth approach, getting them involved where they can and where they are willing. The youth can be, and are in a lot of cases, the drive and energy behind many of the initiatives and changes put forward in today's society, and to the surprise of many, the youth are looking for things they can do to make a difference, they simply need the opportunity and push in the right direction. [32]

Conclusion

All developed countries are not cent percent food secured. The UK and Australia are food secured countries, but the USA and Canada have food insecure families.

Food insecurity was more than 16 percent in New Mexico, Mississippi and Texas during 2003 - 2005. In 2011, about 46 million Americans or 15 percent of population were living on 'food stamps' doled by the government. The Community Food Safety is a program for the food in-secured families. The agriculture-hunger-poverty nexus affects the food in-secured families in USA. But the USA works with developing countries to mitigate the sufferings of food in-secured families. There were 26 net exporting countries of food grains in 2008. The UK is a surplus county and it would continue to be a surplus country for next 50 years. The UK must provide clear leadership; tackle the existing weaknesses in food system that will otherwise prevent it from achieving its long-term objective of securing food supplies.

---

[32]Hunger and food Security in Canada, 2006 Meal Exchange

Australia is food surplus country and would continue for another 100 years as a surplus country. The Australian Government helps developing countries in its region to reduce poverty and address food security by promoting trade liberalization, peace and stability, good governance, security of land tenure, rural development and agricultural research. Australia also provides emergency food aid to developing countries in need. In May 2003, the Australian Government announced a A$1 billion food security pledge for the five years from 1 July 2003 to 30 June 2008 for programs and initiatives that enhance the food security of people in the developing world.

Canada is providing $230 million to the GAFSP as part of a three-year, $600-million agriculture package, a doubling of Canada's existing spending in this area. It is a further demonstration of Canada's leadership in global food security, where Canada is the third-largest contributor to the World Food Programme, and has fully untied its food aid. There are also food-insecure families.

In short, hunger is not confined to developing countries. It is possible in developed countries too. It simple refers to low /no-income individuals. But the state is responsible for hunger related deaths and sufferings.

+++++

Chapter III

FOOD SECURITY IN DEVELOPING COUNTRIES

It is not necessary to advertise food to hungry people, fuel to cold people, or houses to the homeless. -- John Kenneth Galbraith

It is a fact that all low-income countries are agriculture-dominated countries and more than 70 percent of population depends upon agriculture. Hence, these countries should follow pro-poor, pro-rural and pro-agricultural policies to enhance the morale of the peasants and allow them an opportunity to grow crops, livestock, poultry, pigs, goats and fish to enhance their income, living standards, and employment opportunities and to protect their culture. But the developed nations, the World Bank and funding institutions have influenced the governments of these countries for higher borrowed funds, infrastructure development and industrialization for higher GDP growth rate. These low-income counties now follow pro-rich, pro- urban and pro-industrial policies even though the people oppose their policies. This has resulted in mass unemployment, mass rallies, mass resentments and high corruption. All the low-income countries are now infected with Maoism, Naxalism and Terrorism because they are hungry; because they are unemployed; and they search for alternatives.

People go without food because they don't have land, income and assets. Millions of people have been rendered homeless as the governments are forcefully occupying their land for industrialization and special economic zones. The governments remain in power through elections with donated funds of the industrialists and repay their obligations by allotting thousand acres of land, mines and minerals and even permit these big industrial houses to utilize irrigation water for industrial uses. The canal water or water of reservoirs is utilized by the industrialists. Moreover, low price structure of wheat and rice has resulted in 'massive agricultural losses to the farmers. Agriculture has become a loss bearing profession in India and other countries.

Mr. Meles Zenawi, Prime Minister of Ethiopia opined in April 2000 that the agricultural sector remains our Achilles heel and source of vulnerability. Nonetheless, we remain convinced that agricultural based development remains the only source of hope for Ethiopia. Similarly Mr. Mekonnen Manyazewai strongly advocated that perhaps the greatest challenge that the country faces is that of ensuring food security. This is so because of the low technological base of agriculture, limited rural infrastructure and off-farm employment compounded by neglect and inappropriate policies over many years. The food security strategy, whose implementation has begun, is meant to break the complex problems to close the food gap and ensure food security.

In this chapter, problems and prospects of 'Food Security' in Pakistan, Brazil, Ethiopia, Bangladesh and

Malawi have been analyzed for rendering a solution to achieve the target of having a 'world free of starvation' in this twenty-first century. It is felt that food security necessarily means a boost in agricultural production, fair price to the farmers and a mechanism by which the food grains would reach all the consumers.

Food Security in Pakistan

Population – 176, 745, 000- (2011) U N Report

Food is a basic daily need for growth and sustenance of life and access to food is deemed as a basic human right. Whereas, undernourishment and malnutrition reduce the productivity of an individual, undermining national productivity and economic growth, food insecurity breeds crimes and fuels socioeconomic and political instability. On the contrary, food security helps underpin national stability through enhanced productivity and resultant economic growth & development.

Being a basic human need, food has been declared as a fundamental right under the United Nations (UN) Universal Declaration of Human Rights (UDHR) 1948. Scarcity of food can be a potential source of conflicts and incidence of socio-economic and political instability. There is a close nexus among food insecurity, poverty and disease. So food is not only an agricultural and a trade commodity but is also a political and public health issue.

Despite being a complex process, securing food is the only way to honor the right to food and thus international commitments. Food security leads towards healthy lives, a resolve national governments have reiterated through international covenants and declarations such as the UDHR 1948, International Covenant on Economic, Social and Cultural Rights (ICESCR 1966) and World Food Summit (WFS-1996).

Food Production in Pakistan

Pakistan is self-sufficient in food in most of the years, but all regions are not equally benefited. The country gives emphasis on the following variety of foods, of both plant and animal origin. The commodities produced for food purposes are: Buffalo Milk, Wheat, Cow Milk, Rice /Paddy, Sugarcane, Indigenous Cattle Meat, Indigenous Buffalo Meat, Indigenous Goat Meat, Indigenous Chicken Meat, Mangoes, Chick Pea, Hen Eggs, Indigenous Sheep Meat, Dry Onion, Maize, Potatoes, All Spice Pimento, Oranges, fresh Vegetables and Goat Milk. Rural Pakistan is mostly food-insecure. It is caused because of poverty of landless labourers and small farmers. Food security is possible if the government adopts pro-poor, pro-rural and pro-agricultural policies.

Food Security in Rural Pakistan

Food security[33] has international, regional, national and household dimensions. Effective supply and demand and equitable distribution of food are the preconditions to secure food at any of these levels. A minimum level of health standard that can help convert food intake to support a healthy body is an additional requirement to measure effective food security.

For sustainable food security at national and household levels, states need to provide its people an enabling environment by ensuring them an easy access to opportunities of having sufficient food. They need to monitor the state of food security within their respective countries and at household levels. Food Security Analysis (FSA) provides such an opportunity that helps plan and timely intervenes to ensure food security. This however, requires institutional capacity and capability, which many developing countries including Pakistan lack at present.

---

[33]Food Security in Rural Pakistan, sustainable development Policy Institute, 3, UN BD Enclave, Islamabad, Pakistan

World Food Programme (WFP) Pakistan, being cognizant of this deficiency, undertook a preliminary FSA in 1998. Its findings however, could not help ascertain the true food security situation of Pakistan due to limited scope and content of the FSA.

This shortcoming prompted WFP to plan another more comprehensive FSA, both for rural and urban areas. As in case of poverty, there also exists in many countries a rural urban divide in terms of food security. Accordingly, at first place, FSA 2003 for rural Pakistan was undertaken from June 2003 to June 2004. It analyzed, using a set of relevant indicators, available secondary data on the basis of three key determinants of food security namely physical access to food (availability), economic access to food, and effective biological utilization (food absorption). FSA 2003 findings, summarized below, translate into a "State of Food Insecurity" prevailing in Rural Pakistan.

Food availability, the 1st pillar of food security, was assessed on the basis of food production and consumption. Out of 120 district settings in Pakistan, 74 (62 percent) were found to be food deficit in terms of net availability. This deficit varies ranging from low through high to extreme degree. Wheat, a staple, catering for 48 percent of caloric needs in Pakistan, was found deficit in terms of net availability and the shortage was estimated at 3.2 million tons annually. Out of 120 districts, only 48 (40 percent) were producing surplus or enough to cater to the needs of these districts. In other words, 72 districts (60 percent) were deficient in wheat availability.

Among 29 wheat surplus districts, 69 percent were in Punjab, 21 percent in Sindh and 10 percent in Baluchistan. FSA 2003 ranked, in terms of availability, NWFP, Northern Areas and AJK as net food insecure. This state of insecurity, translated into caloric supply at provincial level, revealed that in

NWFP caloric poverty in terms of its incidence was the most prevalent as only 1106 Kcals per capita were available from the provincial resources. This caloric shortfall leads towards hunger, as defined by FAO and discussed elsewhere in this report.

FSA 2003 also indicates that mega cities pitted against mounting population pressure are also being adversely affected. For example, even in wheat surplus province of Punjab, the provincial capital Lahore, home to 81 percent of the district population, was among the net food insecure zones in terms of availability.

In Sindh, 6 out of 17 (35 percent) districts were wheat surplus and only 8 (47 percent) were in self-reliant bracket as against 9 (53 percent) wheat insecure districts. It suggests that even Sindh, the 2nd largest wheat-producing province, was deficit in terms of wheat availability. In Baluchistan, only 3 (12 percent) out of 26 districts were production surplus as against 18 (69 percent) wheat deficit districts. In NWFP, there is no wheat surplus district and only 2 (8 percent) out of 24 districts were self-reliant in wheat production.

In case of rice, the 2nd staple, only 37 (31 percent) out of 120 districts were found to be production surplus. Of these, 57 percent were in Punjab, 19 percent in NWFP, 16 percent in Sindh, 5 percent in Baluchistan and 3 percent in F ATA. In Punjab, 71 percent of districts had either surplus production or had enough rice to meet local needs, and 29 percent of districts experienced varying degree of deficit in rice. In Sindh, out of 17 only 6 (35 percent) districts were surplus, while 65 percent of districts were deficit in rice production, compared to 53 percent deficit in wheat.

In case of NWFP, rice availability was better, as 10 (42 percent) districts out of 24 had surplus production or they were self-reliant, compared to wheat where 22 districts were deficient in wheat.

Cereals meet half of caloric needs in developing countries.

On net cereal availability basis, out of 120 districts, 31 (26 percent) had surplus production. Of these, 23 were in Punjab, 5 in Sindh and 3 in Baluchistan. There were yet another 21 (18 percent) districts that could meet local needs. In sum, 52 (43 percent) of the districts in Pakistan were found self-reliant in net cereal availability and remaining 68 (57 percent) were deficit in cereals.

On overall crop-based food availability (exclusive of livestock products) out of 120 districts, 39 (32 percent) had surplus production, 6 (5 percent) were self-reliant while 35 (29 percent) were extremely insecure and 40 (33 percent) experienced deficit of low to high degree. This suggests that net crop-based food availability, compared to net cereals or wheat/rice availability was better.

Availability of livestock products, contributing 7 to 16 percent in daily diet of rural people, presents altogether different picture compared to crop-based food. In this case, the marginal land areas such as Baluchistan, Northern areas, FATA and part of NWFP, that are otherwise acutely deficient in crop-based food, generate production surplus in case of livestock products. Out of 120 districts 43 (36 percent) have surplus production and another 37 (31 percent) have sufficient livestock-based food production. In total, out of 120 districts, 80 (67 percent) are self-reliant and only 40 (33 percent) encounter some degree of deficit in livestock-based food. FSA 2003 findings suggest that marginal lands of Pakistan have comparative advantage in livestock production, as against fertile belts of Sindh and Punjab that enjoy advantage in crop-based food production.

On net agro-livestock products basis, including both key sources of food availability, 34 (28) out of 120 districts were found surplus. These figures, translated into net food availability, suggest that 74 (62 percent) out of 120 districts faced deficit of varying degree.

In terms of economic access to food, as against the physical access food availability affords, FSA 2003 revealed that income inequality factors especially land, and access to opportunities such as education and employment have led to a wide range of disparities. Consequently, women, labor, landless and small farmers are being adversely affected in terms of access to food, as the above-mentioned inequality factors impact income opportunities. For example, in 57 (48 percent) out of 120 districts literacy rate was in the range of 1130 percent.

Reduced capacity of agriculture sector in terms of gainful employment is another important factor impacting opportunities in rural Pakistan. Further, as majority of holdings were small, such as in 105 (88 percent) out of 120 districts, percentage of marginal cultivators having less than one acre of land was up to 30 percent. The small farmers were thus unable to enhance agricultural productivity beyond a certain limit for want of resources and economy of scale.

The number of landless farmers too was high, for example, in 30 (25 percent) districts; the number of such farmers was above 20 percent. As a result, the low income of (80 percent) districts out of 120 found further plunging into low through very low to extremely low-income bracket, impacted economic access to food. This limited physical and economic access to food, translated into caloric poverty, suggests that out of 120, only 34 (28 percent) districts had surplus, while 12 (10 percent) had enough caloric supply. Whereas, 74 (62 percent) districts were found deficient in terms of caloric supply assessed on the basis of 2350 Kcal per capita per day and as recommended by Planning Commission of Pakistan. Other factors such as rural infrastructure, especially the roads that provide access to local market, also seem to affect the income and thus access to food.

Effective biological utilization or food absorption, the 3rd pillar of food security, was assessed on the basis of parameters including access to safe drinking water, immunization cover and infant mortality, access to medics and paramedics and rural health infrastructure. It revealed that out of 120 only 11 (9 percent) districts of Pakistan performed reasonably well while 45 (38 percent) experienced extremely low rate of food absorption.

Poor food absorption speaks of nutritional insecurity, even if food is available and is also accessible. Achievement of nutritional security implies biological availability of protein, energy, micronutrients and minerals to households. Since ensuring nutritional security of the household in Pakistan remains the exclusive domain of women, responsible for preparing and serving food, they along with their children and other members of the household whom they cater food are adversely affected by this situation.

The contributory factors to this state of affairs include inter alia the poor access to potable water, for example in 113 (94 percent) out of 120 districts, safe drinking water was available to less than 50 percent of the population. It implies that 50 percent of the population drinks unsafe water which contaminates food. The food-borne diseases perhaps are the most widespread health problem in the contemporary world and are important cause of reduced economic activity. Similarly, on disease control front, primarily a function of effective immunization programs, FSA 2003 revealed that 108 (90 percent) out of 120 districts had immunization cover of less than 80 percent. Resultantly, infant mortality rate was above 80 per thousand in 34 (28 percent) districts out of 120.

Overall health security as assessed by rural health infrastructure and access to medics and paramedics was another contributory factor towards poor food absorption. For instance, in 117 (98 percent) out of 120 districts, rural health facilities were less than 51 per million populations. This included Punjab province which otherwise had better performance, on parameters such as food availability and economic access. As ensuring food security for household is not only a function of food availability and economic access but also of whether or not the available and accessible food fulfills nutritional requirements of the household. So, the poor health security and resultant poor absorption impacts the net gains.

The net impact of these factors, assessed on the bases of three aforementioned determinants or three pillars of food security translates into net state of food insecurity, prevailing in 80 percent of the rural Pakistan, ranging from less to extremely insecure levels.

FSA 2003 also came up with substantial evidence that inter and intra provincial disparities exist in terms of food security. For example, majority of food insecure districts 28 percent fall in Baluchistan, followed by 26 percent in NWFP, 14 percent in Sindh, 13 percent in Punjab, 9 percent in FATA, 6 percent in Nas and 5 percent in AJK. In the intra provincial context, 65 percent of food insecure districts were in Sindh, 29 percent in Punjab, and 88 percent in NWFP, 85 percent in Baluchistan, 100 percent each in Nas and FATA.

These findings of FSA 2003 are revealing in many ways, for example they disagree, based on available evidence, with the commonly held opinion that

Pakistan was moderately food secure at macro level. The findings support the argument that hidden hunger is more pronounced in Pakistan than what macro picture of food security presents. In view of growing population pressure and resultant demand of food, FSA findings are enough to ring the alarm bell, as they estimate an annual shortfall of 3.2 million MT of wheat alone, the main staple, on the basis of average annual wheat harvest of 18 million MT.

In view of the foreign exchange required in procuring such a huge quantity of wheat, factors constraining productivity, the changing trade paradigm under the World Trade Organization (WTO), and the huge cost involved in readjustments, challenge is enormous yet it is not insurmountable.

Investment in agriculture and rural development, institutional capacity building, human resource development, integration of gender in development, promotion of equitable distribution, development of material and quality infrastructure inter alias are among some of the recommendations that logically follow FSA 2003.

FSA 2003 underscores the need for well thought of national food security strategies and suggests institutional arrangements needed for orchestration and integration of a strategy with other socio-economic interventions such as food availability and nutritional security at national level. It underlines the need that, to make development process responsive to the needs of the people, initiatives such as poverty alleviation should go hand in hand with those aiming at food security.

In this context, agricultural and rural development needs high priority in development plans which shall help correct the existing mismatch between food availability and the population's nutritional requirements.

Food Security in Brazil

Population - 196, 655, 000 (2011) U N report

Brazil is the largest and most densely inhabited country in South America. Its relative prosperity is US 500 GDP per head. A quarter of the population lives in extreme poverty on a daily income, which is less than US $1.06 a day. A strong political agenda was adopted in Brazil to eradicate food insecurity among the masses. This program would benefit 84 million of people. The budget was only US $ 5.8 million.

Recent studies have revealed that about 90 percent of Brazil's total food production is concentrated in the south, southeast and the southern part of the central western region. However, 60 percent of food insecure populations are located in the north and northeastern regions. Here, local food production is inadequate to satisfy the populations' nutritional requirements. In December 2002, at the request of President Lula, a FAO-led multi-agency mission convened in Brazil to lay the foundations for the implementation of the Zero Hunger Programme.

An FAO Technical Cooperation Programme grant funded 3 projects (with an estimated value of US $1.1 million) in support of the Zero Hunger Programme. These included.

(a) Background studies;
(b) Policy formulation;
(c) Developing a monitoring and evaluation system; and
(d) Working on participatory methodologies for reaching the most vulnerable groups in the northeast of Brazil.

In the light of the promising results attained by these projects, the Government of Brazil and FAO signed a US $5.8 million agreement in December 2003, to bolster cooperation in support of the Zero Hunger Programme.

Food Production in Brazil

Each family of a country can be food insecure if nature is favourable to agricultural production. The land distribution system is another factor that is responsible for poverty and hunger. Hence, all the low-income countries must pay special attention to follow pro-poor, pro-rural and pro-agricultural policies. The inflow of rural youths to towns has made agriculture a loss bearing profession. Brazil produces the following commodities in agriculture and animal husbandry. The commodities are: Indigenous Cattle Meat, Soybeans, Indigenous Chicken Meat, Sugar Cane, Cow Milk, Maize, Indigenous Pig meat, Oranges, Rice / Paddy, Cassava, green Coffey, tobacco Leaves, Hen eggs, Dry Beans, bananas, Wheat, Grapes, Potato, and Fresh vegetables.

The Government of Brazil aims at guaranteeing food Security and eliminating hunger through an integrated set of policies.

The Programme seeks to mobilize different areas of Government (Federal, State, municipal and local) and civil society, NGOs, unions, church groups, private sector, etc. In 2003, the Government of Brazil launched a major conditional cash transfer program known as "Bolsa Familia". This involves transferring about US $20 per month to the poorest families in situations of food insecurity. By the end of 2005, the "Bolsa Familia" program had significant results - it improved the lives and nutritional intake of more than 8 million families.

Another significant initiative was the Food Products Procurement Programme, which aimed to ensure a market (and reasonable price) for products from small-scale farmers. Some of the methods were:

direct procurement of products at harvest for maintaining local food security stocks; advanced procurement of products at planting time; local procurement by local governments to be used in school feeding programs, and a program supporting milk production and consumption, benefiting producers with limited production and bargaining power.

Results

(a) Despite a far from ideal economic situation, the results achieved by the Zero Hunger Programme have been remarkable, and the level of national resources allocated considerable.
(b) The Brazilian experience has been instrumental in encouraging other countries, in both Africa and Latin America, to follow Brazil's example.
(c) FAO encourages food security experiences to be exchanged between countries through a program.[34]

East African Countries

Famine conference focuses on future

The Agriculture Minister of drought-hit Kenya appealed on August 18, 2011 for seeds, irrigation plans and infrastructure to avoid a repetition of famine and food crises in the Horn of Africa "every two years."

Sally Kosgei and other delegates at an emergency conference in Rome voiced what they said was a need to look beyond the starving populations' immediate

---

[34]Special Program for food Security, Food and Agriculture Organization – Success Stories

needs and focus on longer-term solutions for the region.

"It is really very important that the world focus now on how to avoid yet another famine or many more famines," Kosgei told the delegates gathered by the U.N. agency Food and Agriculture Organization.

Tens of thousands of people are feared to have died in the famine, caused by war in Somalia and drought in the Horn of Africa — Kenya, Ethiopia, Djibouti, Eritrea and Somalia. More than 12 million people in the region need food aid, according to the United Nations. An estimated 3.7 million Somalis are at risk of famine today.

Kosgei said that meetings with several delegations from all over the world over the past months have left her with the impression that "long-term solutions we have put on the table have not been taken seriously by those we have met."

"They seem to be more focused on what is to be done now, which is important," she said, "but what to do to avoid a repetition of this every two years to us is very crucial."

The Kenyan official called for drought-resistant crops to be spread across the region, small irrigation plans to be implemented to help small scale farmers, 60 per cent of all farmers in the area, and infrastructure to allow for quicker transportation of foods across the region.

Even those who survive the famine may be unable to support themselves or their families, as their animals are dead and their crop prospects dire, officials said.
Opening the second FAO conference on the famine in East Africa in less than a month, the agency's Director-General, Jacques Diouf, said that "what we

are witnessing now is the unfortunate result of three decades of under-investment in agriculture and rural development."

Given modern technology, resources and expertise, he said, it was "inadmissible" that some 12 million people would be exposed to the risk of starvation. He called for building irrigation systems and providing feed and nutritional supplements to livestock, fertilizers and seeds well into the spring rainy season of 2012.[35]

Food Insecurity in Ethiopia

Population – 84, 734, 000 (2010) –U N Report

Eating is not merely a material pleasure. Eating well gives a spectacular joy to life and contributes immensely to goodwill and happy companionship. It is of great importance to the morale. - Elsa Schiaparelli

Food insecurity[36] incorporates low food intake, variable access to food, and vulnerability – a livelihood strategy that generates adequate food in good times but is not resilient against shocks. These outcomes correspond broadly to chronic, cyclical and transitory food insecurity, and all are endemic in Ethiopia.

The main triggers of transitory food insecurity in Ethiopia are drought and war. Seasonality is a major cause of cyclical food insecurity. Structural factors contributing to chronic food insecurity include poverty (as both cause and consequence), the fragile natural resource base, weak institutions (notably markets and land tenure) and unhelpful or inconsistent government policies.

---

[35]A. P. quoted from The Hindu, Friday, August 19, 2011 (News)

[36]Stephen Devereux (2000), "Food Insecurity in Ethiopia – A discussion Paper for DFID, IDS, Sussex, October 2000.

Ethiopia has been structurally food deficit since at least 1980. The food gap rose from 0.75 million tons in 1979/80 to 5 million tons in 1993/94, falling to 2.6 million tons in 1995/96 despite a record harvest. Even in that year, 240,000 tons of food aids were delivered, suggesting that chronic food insecurity afflicts millions of Ethiopians in the absence of transitory production shocks.

The distinction between transitory and chronic food insecurity is increasingly blurred. A subgroup of virtually asset-less rural Ethiopians is emerging who are subjected to all forms of food insecurity. They cannot meet their food needs even under ideal weather conditions, they suffer seasonal hunger and malnutrition, and they are acutely vulnerable to famine in years of low or erratic rainfall. Less well understood than the immediate impact of drought on rural livelihoods is the impact of repeated droughts on long-term food insecurity. Two vicious cycles are at work: recovery (e.g. of herds) from food crises is cut short by the next drought, and the threat of drought - which occurs frequently but is unpredictable in its timing and severity - inhibits investment in productivity-enhancing agricultural inputs, because the downside risk for marginal farmers is too high.

Current conventional wisdom on food insecurity in Ethiopia asserts that the problem can be simply conceptualized, as follows:

(a) Landholdings are too small - although (or because) unusually evenly distributed - to allow most farming households to achieve food production self-sufficiency;

(b) Population increase reduces landholdings further and places intolerable stress on an already fragile natural resource base;

(c) Soil fertility, already very low, is declining due to intensive cultivation and limited application of yield-enhancing inputs;

(d) Recurrent droughts add food production shocks to abnormally low yields;
(e) Limited off-farm employment opportunities restrict diversification and migration options, leaving people trapped in increasingly unviable agriculture.

The poor performance of Ethiopian agriculture is certainly a large part of the explanation. There occurred extreme variability of agricultural performance during the 1980s and 1990s, ranging from –20 percent to +20 percent growth, with no discernible average or 'normal' year. It also reveals the close correlation between agriculture and GDP. The entire Ethiopian economy is dependent on low productivity rain-fed agriculture, and rainfall is the single most important determinant of Ethiopia's economic success or failure from year to year.

The implications for food security in the longer term are twofold. On the one hand, a structural transformation of agriculture is urgently needed - for instance, through the promotion of technological inputs, or land tenure reform, to increase yields. The inherent vulnerability of agriculture in the economy must eventually be reduced by significantly increasing growth in other sectors.

Yet agricultural failure is only part of the story. Following Chambers (1983), analysts of food insecurity in Ethiopia can be divided into two groups: the 'physical ecology cluster', which focus on population growth, declining soil fertility and drought, and the 'political economy cluster', who blame government policies, weak markets and institutional failure. Both the 'Malthusian' and 'governance' approaches have some merit as partial explanations, but neither is sufficient in itself. A holistic 'livelihoods' analysis is needed.

Food Production in Ethiopia

Cereals, like rice or wheat, which forms the staple food of mankind, supply us only with a fraction of our nutritional requirements. A balanced diet is necessary for all of us. We need to supplement minerals and vitamins for a healthier life. But this doctor's advice is necessary when we have at least assured two square meals per day. The country faces the problem of survival first. The war between Ethiopia and Eritrea has forced these countries into poverty trap and reign of terror, hunger and no-peace. The government must ensure peace to all and food for all. It is reported that donated food materials are snatched away by the military forces from the hungry mouths.

Ethiopia produces the following food commodities. The commodities are: Indigenous Cattle Meat, roots and Tubers, Cow Milk, All Spice Pimento, Maize, wheat, Other Cereals, Sorghum, Green Coffee, Game Meat, Indigenous Sheep Meat, Nuts, Barley, Dry Broad Beans, Fresh Vegetables, Dry Beans, Honey, and Yam.

Incidence of food insecurity

Since food production and population statistics in Ethiopia are notoriously unreliable, all estimates of national food availability and consumption requirements are 'guesstimates' at best. During the late 1980s, 52 percent of Ethiopia's population consumed less than the recommended daily allowance of 2,100 kcal even in the record harvest year of 1995/96.

Poverty in rural Ethiopia is "a result not simply of drought but of an increasing shortage of the barest assets needed for agricultural survival. ... The root factor is common too much of the rest of Ethiopia: ever greater density of the rural population through natural increase". An example of the 'political economy' discourse comes from the World Bank: "Centuries of poor policies and institutional failures are the primary cause of Africa's under-capitalized and uncompetitive agriculture. Adverse resource endowments have also had some direct effects".

Food insecurity in Ethiopia derives directly from dependence on un-diversified livelihoods based on low-input, low-output rain-fed agriculture. Ethiopian farmers do not produce enough food even in good rainfall years to meet consumption requirements. Given the fragile natural resource base and climatic uncertainty, current policy emphases on agricultural intensification are misguided, while institutional constraints such as inflexible land tenure and ethnic federalism perpetuate this unviable livelihood system. Inappropriate food aid interventions by donors add another layer of dependence, at both household and national levels. This paper concludes by proposing a range of options for consideration by donors and government to redress chronic and transitory food insecurity.

Although food insecurity and poverty are conceptually and empirically distinct, in Ethiopia the overlap between the two is greater than in most countries. Real GDP grew at just 1.9 percent during the 1980s, which, given population growth of 3.1 percent produced a negative per capita growth rate of (-) 1.2 percent. Agricultural growth, at 2 percent per annum - negative in four years of drought during the decade - was insufficient to maintain per capita food consumption.

Ethiopia's economic performance has improved since the EPRDF took power from the Derg in 1991. GDP growth rates averaged 4.4 percent between 1991/2 and 1997/8, or 1.3 percent per capita. Agricultural performance was weaker and more variable, however, averaging only 1.6 percent per annum. Ethiopia's growth in the 1990s was driven by industry (7.9 percent p.a.) and services (7.6 percent p.a.) - both starting from a very low base - not by agriculture. The impact of this impressive growth performance on poverty has been limited, and on food security negligible.

Another indicator of the interconnectedness of food insecurity and poverty is that the government calculates poverty lines based on a food consumption norm of 2,200 kcal per adult per day. Using a 'national minimum consumption basket', the Welfare Monitoring Unit finds that 50 percent of the population is living in 'food poverty': 52 percent of rural and 36 percent of urban Ethiopians (Government of Ethiopia 1999:15). Food insecurity is also differentiated by wealth. A survey of food consumption in rural Ethiopian households found that transfers - food aid from government, donors or NGOs, plus gifts from other households plus - were the second most important source of food, after production and ahead of purchases, for all but the wealthiest 25 percent of the sample.[37]

A basic distinction between poverty and food insecurity is the latter's focus on instability. While poverty indices measure headcounts, depth and severity at a point in time, food insecurity incorporates vulnerability as a determinant of ill being. People are food insecure not only because their food consumption level is low, but also because their access to food is variable and unpredictable over time (from one year or season to the next).

In the poorest quartile, 42 percent of food consumption derived from production, 38 percent from transfers and 20 percent from purchases. Even the richest quartile was far from food secure or self-sufficient, deriving 54 percent of its food from the farm, 26 percent from the market and 20 percent from transfers.

---

[37]Tekabe A. (1998), "food Security in Ethiopia", Food Security in ACP countries, Belgium, 26-30 October

Livelihood strategies and food insecurity:

Rural livelihood strategies include agricultural extensive farming (increasing farm size) and intensification (raising farm yields), income diversification (off-farm economic activities), and migration (Scoones 1998). This section examines three dominant livelihood activities in Ethiopia: agriculture, income diversification, and pastoralism.

Agriculture: Even by African standards, Ethiopia's economy is dominated by smallholder agriculture, which employed 89 percent of the labour force and contributed 56 percent of GDP and 67 percent of export earnings in 1997. Rural Ethiopia is also unusually undifferentiated: small farmers account for over 90 percent of total crop area and agricultural output.[38] Food production in Ethiopia is highly variable and unpredictable, due mainly to erratic weather, which has triggered famines for centuries. A 10 percent decline in rainfall below its long-term average reduces national food production by 4.4 percent (von Braun 1991).

Ethiopia witnessed a major famine in 1984/5 and it caused mortality of one million people.

Droughts have affected northern Ethiopia in 1987/8, 1990/2 and 1993/4, and southern Ethiopia since 1998. Some droughts were exacerbated by civil conflict, which undermined food production and inhibited government, trader and donor responses to harvest failure.

Military rule also diverts resources away from support to agriculture and development programs - as recently as 1991, spending on 'defense' amounted to

[38]Bollnger, L.et al (1993), "The Economic Impact of AIDS in Ethiopia, Washington DC

37 percent of GNP. This factor has dissipated since the overthrow of the Derg and the secession of Eritrea in the early 1990s, but the recent conflict between Ethiopia and Eritrea eroded government response capacity and was directly responsible for the sluggish reaction of donors to the ongoing drought in southern Ethiopia.

Ethiopian agriculture appears to be locked into a downward spiral of low and declining productivity, caused by an adverse combination of agro-climatic, demographic, economic and institutional constraints, trends and shocks. Some observers argue that a 'Malthusian crisis' is developing, as rapid population growth (almost 3 percent per annum) is associated with steadily falling landholdings and per capita food production.

Between 1960 and 1990 the population doubled from 23 to 48 million, while per capita landholding shrunk from 0.28 to 0.10 hectare, and per capita food output collapsed by 41 percent from 240 to 142 kg.

As landholdings have declined, farmers allocate smaller proportions of their fields to non-cereal crops, which provide essential dietary diversity and cash incomes. Cereal yields have virtually stagnated, rising by only 0.5 percent per annum between 1980 and 1996 - from 1.19 to 1.26 tons per hectare - not fast enough to compensate for falling farm sizes. Pressures on the physical environment increase inexorably, with forest cover, grazing land, livestock ownership, soil fertility and even rainfall all decreasing in many areas. A survey in Hararghe Region documented a 72 percent decline in barley yields over a 15-year period, due to soil erosion (ICRA 1996:35).[39]

---

[39]Mesfin WM (1999), "The Horn of Africa: Conflict and Poverty", Addis Ababa, commercial Printing Press

Future prospects for food production in Ethiopia are not encouraging. The Horn of Africa has been identified as one of the world's most vulnerable regions to climate change. Alternative models of global warming predict a rise in mean temperature for the Horn of 1-3 degree centigrade by 2030, with consequent reductions in staple cereals yields of up to 30 percent, though precise impacts on agriculture are impossible to predict.[40]

So is focusing policy attention on agriculture the solution to food insecurity or part of the problem? There is a persistent belief in Ethiopia that national self-sufficiency is both necessary and sufficient to achieve household food security. This logic was misguided in 1996. Despite record harvests and food prices 20-40 percent less than their inflation-adjusted average since the 1984 famine, many households remained unable to access adequate food. A government report concluded: "The current situation is therefore one of food abundance co-existing with widespread food insecurity" (MEDAC 1996:1).

Nonetheless, this bumper harvest prompted the government to declare that Ethiopia had "crossed the great divide" from chronic food insecurity and aid dependence to national self-sufficiency.[41] This premature optimism (given the subsequent three years of poor rainfall that resulted in the drought emergency of early 2000) failed to take into account the strong correlation between rainfall and agricultural yields: good rainfall equals good harvests, but the converse is equally inevitable.

Dependence on unreliable and low-productivity rain fed agriculture may well be the primary determinant

---

[40]Parry, M. (1999), Climate change and World agriculture, London: Earth scan Publications

[41]Masefield, A. (1997), "Food Security in Ethiopia: Crossing the Great Devide? Brighton :IDS Sussex

of household food insecurity in Ethiopia. Arguments that center on enhancing access to agricultural inputs - fertilizers, draught oxen - implicitly assume that household food security can be achieved by increasing food production on individual farms. The productivity of Ethiopian agriculture is among the lowest in the world - around 1.2 tons per hectare. Although higher yields are possible through agricultural intensification, the evidence suggests, "average land holdings would be insufficient to feed a family of 5 even if production could be successfully increased three times with the use of improved technology" (Masefield 2000:4).

The government's strategy of Agriculture Development Led Industrialization (ADLI), as formulated in 1994, views agriculture as the driving force of the economy, and argues for investment in agriculture as both a motor for economic growth and a means of ensuring household and national food security. ADLI aims to promote the adoption of improved technological inputs and practices, in order to raise agricultural productivity and generate savings for investment in other sectors. The major components of ADLI include: input provision to peasants, promotion of small-scale irrigation, improved livestock herds, environmental protection and natural resource management, grain marketing efficiency, promotion of farmers' organizations and women's participation in agriculture, expanding rural roads.[42] Like most strategy documents, the ADLI is strong on rhetoric but low on detail, and it has been only partially implemented to date.

Nonetheless, a number of agricultural development programs have been put in place in recent years. These include the Participatory Demonstration and Training Extension System (PADETES), which

---

[42]Holt, J and D. Rahmato (1999), "Sustainable Livelihoods on Wollo and Wag", Addis Ababa

disseminates information on crops and inputs packages on credit, and the Sustainable Agriculture and Environmental Rehabilitation Program (SAERP), which aims to expand small-scale irrigation and watershed management schemes, thereby reversing environmental degradation and stabilizing crop yields. An example of this questionable thinking comes from a draft UN strategy document on 'The Elimination of Food Insecurity in the Horn of Africa' (September 2000):

The fact that 80 percent of the population of the region lives in rural areas means that increasing agricultural productivity and production in various ways, will be the principal approach to solving the problem of long term food insecurity.

Of course, the inherent vulnerability of agriculture suggests that the case for solving food insecurity by diversifying out of agriculture could be argued with equal force.

Farmers' access to fertilizers was undermined by sharp increases in prices during the 1990s, firstly following the devaluation of the Birr in 1993, then by the elimination of fertilizer subsidies and pan-territorial pricing in 1996, and the decontrol of input prices and marketing in 1997.[43]

The Commercial Bank of Ethiopia, the Development Bank and the Bureau of Agriculture all extend input credit to farmers, including in-kind loans through Sasakawa Global 2000. There are reports that agricultural extension workers with quotas to fulfill are coercing farmers into taking inputs packages (models) which many resist, knowing that the seed

---

[43] Ayelegn, F and Shirega M (2000), "Constraints to Agricultural Input Loan Payment', Economic Focus, 3(2): 25-27

varieties and fertilizers delivered require high levels of moisture and are not well adapted to Ethiopia's variable rainfall regime.

No grace periods or debt write-offs are given in drought years, and poor farmers are often forced into selling their food production at low post-harvest prices to repay their loans. Defaults occur for several reasons: inability to repay following drought-triggered crop failure, loan diversion to non-agricultural uses, high fertilizer prices and lack of markets for produce. [44]

A study in Oromiya Region found that repayment was positively correlated with livestock ownership - a proxy for wealth - and negatively correlated with spending on social ceremonies (Belay and Belay 1998:61). Farmers who fail to repay agricultural loans have been imprisoned. Because of chronic poverty, access to informal credit is also limited. Only 29 percent of 300 households in a survey in Wollo had taken a loan during the previous year, though many had tried and failed. Half these loans came from relatives and half from credit associations (FSCO 1999:23).

Clearly, agricultural performance must improve if the food security of the majority of Ethiopians who depend on farming is to be enhanced. But more attention must be given to stabilizing yields - disseminating drought-resistant varieties to farmers in marginal areas, rather than high-yielding but riskier varieties, for example - and access to inputs must be provided on more reasonable terms.

More attention also needs to be given to the needs of the landless and effectively landless - farmers on tiny 'starvation plots' – for whom

---

[44]Carswell, G. et al (1999), "Sustainable Livelihoods in Southern Ethiopia', IDS Research Report 44, Brighton, IDS

agricultural-based livelihoods are less sustainable from year to year.

These people are chronically food insecure and will require recurrent relief until viable alternative livelihood options open up for them. Unpalatable though this may be to policymakers, the long-term solution to food insecurity for the effectively landless may lie in providing an enabling environment for rural differentiation - allowing successful farmers to accumulate land and raise their agricultural productivity, inter alia by hiring labour provided by a class of landless labourers.

Income diversification

Most Ethiopians are 'sub-subsistence farmers' who have been forced to diversify into off-farm incomes to bridge their annual consumption gap, while some are effectively landless and depend entirely on non-agricultural sources of food and income, including food aid. The typical rural livelihood strategy combines crop and livestock agriculture, off-farm income-generating activities (daily labour, petty trading, and seasonal migration) and dependence on food aid (mostly delivered with a work requirement). The main problem with available off-farm economic activities, apart from their low returns, is that most are directly or indirectly affected by rainfall, which limits their risk-spreading potential. In areas where farming is unable to generate viable livelihoods and this cannot be solved.

Ellis (2000)[45] has defined 'off-farm' means off- own-farm activities, while 'non-farm' refers to non-agricultural livelihood activities. Household food security can also be undermined by other threats to off-farm incomes apart from rain failure. For

---

[4545]Ellis, F. (2000), "Rural Livelihoods and diversity in developing Countries", Oxford: oxford University Press

example, thousands of Tigrayans used to travel to Eritrea for several months each year to labour in rural areas or in Asmara town. When the border was closed in 1997 because of political tension and commodity flows were restricted or taxed, these families lost a vital component of their regular livelihoods (Boudreau 1998). Through land redistribution or intensification, the solution is not to focus policy attention on agriculture, but to promote non-covariate non-agricultural livelihood options.

Off-farm employment opportunities in rural Ethiopia are limited in both availability and income-generating potential. Only 44 percent of rural households surveyed by the Ministry of Labour in 1996 reported any non-agricultural sources of income, and these contributed only 10 percent to household income. Another survey in Hararghe Region confirmed that off-farm activities generated only petty incomes: women collect and sell firewood and forage, men and women seek irregular, low-paid work as farm labourers, and some men migrate seasonally (ICRA et al. 1996:28). In an Amhara Region survey, 25 percent of households had one or more members migrate during the dry season in search of work, mostly to nearby rural areas. One in three migrants had difficulty securing employment, while half brought back no food or income for their families (FSCO 1999:24).

Human capital is extremely low in Ethiopia, which is both a cause and a consequence of food insecurity, due to adverse synergies between poor education, health and nutrition status, and labour productivity. Illiteracy constrains access to skilled and semi-skilled off farm employment - literacy rates in Ethiopia are just 36% for males and 17 percent for females (CSA 1999:91) - perpetuating dependence on low-input, low-output agriculture. Ethiopian children display some of the highest malnutrition levels in the world – 55 percent being stunted and 45 percent underweight in 1998, which undoubtedly affect their cognitive development. 'Food economy baseline assessments' conducted by Save the Children UK in rural Ethiopia has consistently identified three critical determinants of relative wealth and household food security status: farm size, availability of family labour and access to draught power. As landholdings and livestock ownership fall, the most food insecure households are:

(a) The labour constrained
(b) Female- and elderly-headed households,
(c) People with disabilities,
(d) Households affected by HIV/AIDS.

One possible solution to unviable livelihoods in rural areas is to move, either to urban areas or to farm in parts of the country where arable land is available. In Ethiopia, both these options are problematic. Employment opportunities in towns are very limited, and there is little investment in job creation by government or by local or foreign investors. Excessive bureaucratic red tape discourages local businesspeople and deters inward investment, which is exacerbated by persistent uncertainty in the policy environment.

There is little spare arable land in rural Ethiopia, and the extent of landlessness or near landlessness is increasing. Land pressure is worse in some areas than others, and many farming households would certainly move if they could. People should be free to settle where they choose, but rigid institutional and administrative barriers - including ethnically based rationalization ('ethnic federalism'), state administered land redistribution and tenure insecurity - all impose severe constraints on mobility.

Anyone who leaves their community for a farming season risks losing their land. Farmers in severely degraded highland areas of Amhara Region have started to request re-settlement and the Amhara

Regional State Food Security Coordination Office recently completed a "reconnaissance".

Not only does HIV/AIDS selectively remove economically active adults from the labour force, the direct costs of the disease often exceed a poor household's annual income. A small survey of 25 AIDS-afflicted rural Ethiopian households in 1993 found that average treatment costs plus funeral expenses totaled 2,494 birr, at a time when net farm income varied between 270 and 620 birr per annum. The death of adult males is associated with an increase in female-headed households and a fall in farm yields. This call for voluntary resettlement should be distinguished from the National Resettlement Campaign implemented by the Derg regime during the 1980s famine, when hundreds of thousands of people were forcibly resettled from northern Ethiopia to the south. This measure was widely perceived as driven more by political motivations than the interests of the resettled, and it certainly resulted in elevated mortality rates.

Survey of potential resettlement sites that identified some possible sites but cautioned that basic infrastructure needs to be in place before people are assisted to move. "In principle, voluntary resettlement from areas of land scarcity to areas of abundance may be the short and long term solution to the problem of landlessness.

However, unless it is absolutely clear that an individual or a group of people has the right and the means to settle and make a living anywhere in the country; this may be nothing more than wishful thinking". [46]

---

[46]Aklilu K and Tadesse A. (1994), " Rapid Population growth and Access to Farmland: Coping Strategies in two Peasant Associations in North Shoa" Addis Ababa University

Pastoralist

Ethiopia's ±3.4 million pastoralists constitute roughly 7 percent of the population. Most live in the lowland areas of Afar (29 percent) and Somali (53 percent) regions, with smaller numbers in Oromiya and SNNPR. Many pastoralist communities have become partially sedentarised in response to recurrent droughts, livestock disease, encroachment by cultivators, rangeland de-vegetation and degradation, and rangeland enclosure for dam construction, state farms or national parks. Livestock income is supplemented with vegetable and cereals production, mainly around springs that provide small-scale irrigation. But adding crop farming to livestock rearing has limited risk diversification advantages, and should therefore be interpreted as distress diversification in the face of an increasingly unviable livelihood strategy.

The shift from nomadic Pastoralism to sedentarised agro-pastoralism accelerated after the succession of droughts and famine that have decimated livestock herds since the 1970s. Including mortality, sales and slaughter, cattle herds were reduced by an estimated 72 percent in Afar region during the 1972/4 drought famine, by 60 percent In Borena during the 1984/5 famine, and by 78 percent in Somali and Borena areas during the 1995/7 drought. [47] The cumulative effect of these shocks was to reduce herd sizes below levels that pastoralists consider viable to meet their food and cash needs and to reconstitute the herd. When the present drought started in southern Ethiopia in early 1998, herds had had no time to recover following the 1995/7 droughts. Southern Somali and northern Oromiya Borena suffered catastrophic losses of cattle (possibly exceeding 70 percent) between May 1999 and May 2000.

---

[47]Standford, S. and Yohannes H. (2000), " Report of the Pastoral Appraisal Team", London DFID

Pastoralism as a livelihood system has been further undermined by adverse terms of trade movements between livestock and cereals, especially in drought years (Ali 1996:204). During the 1984 drought, for instance, cattle prices fell by 70 percent while grain prices rose by 250 percent.

Livelihood diversification also includes salt mining and trading - and migration to the Middle East, both activities having the risk-spreading advantage of being independent of rainfall variability. Remittances are an important source of food security, especially in drought years. On the other hand, women and children left behind are economically and socially vulnerable, since remittances are uncertain and migration became more difficult during the 1990s, as Saudi Arabia expelled illegal immigrants, and pastoralists became increasingly dependent on agriculture and on irregular deliveries of food aid. [48]

During the 1990s, the proportion of Ethiopia's pastoral's population defined as being in need of assistance ranged from 10-22 percent until 1997/9, when it jumped to 40 percent. However, government institutions such as extension services are weakest in arid areas, where actual food aid deliveries are much lower than needs.

Food Aid

This section reviews Ethiopia's experience with food aid, and considers three topical policy issues: market development, access to land, and the role of government policy.

It doesn't matter if it is raining here or it is raining in Canada. - A popular saying in Ethiopia

---

[48]Assefa T. (1996), " Economic Strategies of Diversification" Addis Ababa

Ethiopia is the world's most food aid dependent country. Although food aid is a standard response to transitory food insecurity (e.g. drought emergencies), in Ethiopia it has become an institutionalized response to chronic food insecurity as well. Annual food aid deliveries to Ethiopia since 1980 have varied from 200,000 to 1,200,000 metric tons. The number of 'needy' Ethiopians between 1980 and 1995 ranged from 2.5 million (1987) to 7.85 million (1992), and in the current drought emergency it stands at 7.7 million. Food aid deliveries to Ethiopia averaged 11 percent of national cereals production - or 12 kg per capita - between 1985 and 1995, peaking at 26 percent in famine years.[49]

Paradoxically, food aid may be the most important guarantee of household food security in rural Ethiopia. Food-for-work acts as safety-net that mitigates agricultural risk and stabilize food consumption over time. One impact assessment found that food aid reduced the food deficit of recipients by 60 percent in 1995/6, from 753 kcal to 313 kcal /day. Most food aid is delivered through food-for-work programs such as the Employment Generation Scheme. Although the EGS has been positively evaluated, it does not provide a guaranteed access to food in the Maharashtra sense of 'Employment Guarantee Scheme'. Food deliveries are often late, rations are sometimes cut, and coverage of food insecure communities and households is limited.

Given the importance of food aid in poor households' livelihoods, poor targeting becomes a significant determinant of food insecurity. A recent study found that 78 percent of needy Ethiopian households received no food aid at all. Correlates of poor targeting include inaccurate proxy indicators of need,

---

[49]Clay, J. et al (1999), "Food Aid Targeting in Ethiopia" food Policy, 4(4): 391-409

such as female-headed and elderly-headed households, and institutional rigidity, which orients the food aid pipeline toward historically deficit areas - a powerful determinant of food aid receipts, is whether the recipient received food aid the previous year. This geographical bias can be interpreted in two ways. On the one hand, generous allocations of food aid to historically drought-prone regions have been held responsible for the neglect of the south during the current drought. On the other hand, rectification of historical neglect means that northern Ethiopia is arguably less famine-prone today than at any time in its history.

Ethiopia has not achieved effective 'drought-proofing', despite recognition for decades that this is urgently needed. The National Disaster Prevention and Management Policy includes a National Emergency Food Reserve that aims to maintain a food stock capable of feeding 4.5 million people, but this reserve was not replenished for several months after being drawn down during 1999. Also, despite three years of low rainfall and predictions of imminent famine by early warning systems, donor and government response to the drought emergency in southern Ethiopia was sluggish until the international media brought the situation to world attention. Contributory factors include:

(a) The lack of a food aid pipeline to the south
(b) The sociopolitical marginalization of Ogaden Somalis within Ethiopia
(c) The logistical difficulties of reaching dispersed and mobile pastoralist populations, and
(d) Strained relations between the donor community and the Ethiopian government because of the border war with Eritrea.

Food aid is no solution to chronic food insecurity, as evidenced by declining per capita food production since at least 1970. Nonetheless, Ethiopia remains ready to receive food aid every year, and the donors seem willing to continue providing food indefinitely. WFP's food-for-work program in Ethiopia is the largest and longest running in the world. These reflex responses are allowing the government and donors to ignore the underlying causes of food insecurity. Even worse, a recent analysis found evidence of a disincentive effect on agricultural production, exacerbated by food aid's "continuance during good harvest years and its distribution in non-emergency regions of the country"[50].

Part of the problem is the high volume of non-emergency food aid and food-for-work, which increases food supplies and depresses prices in local markets. To reduce dependency and create incentives for farmers and traders, at least where nascent markets exist, relief programming should shift from food to cash transfers - cash for- work rather than food-for-work, possibly financed by magnetization of food aid.

The restructuring of the Relief and Rehabilitation Commission (RRC) to the Disaster Preparedness and Prevention Commission (DPPC) was associated with a shift towards reducing vulnerability and linking relief and development. For example, food-for-work programs select community projects (such as soil and water conservation activities) that will enhance food production and reduce vulnerability to drought, thereby steadily reducing the numbers of people who are dependent on food aid. Food-for-work has also contributed to developing feeder roads and other physical infrastructure.

Ethiopia has one of the world's lowest ratios of road per person - just 90cm (Webb and von Braun 1994).

---

[50]Teressa and Heidhues (1998), " Explaining the performance of Ethiopian Agriculture", E.J.A.E. 2(2): 117-151

Rural Ethiopia suffers from a demographic paradox - too many people in parts of the country in relation to arable land; but too few people to provide economies of scale in public infrastructure. Almost 90% of the population lives in the highlands (1,500+ meters above sea level), which has the advantage of being a relatively disease-free environment but all the disadvantages of inaccessibility. In this context, carefully designed food-for work activities have great potential to improve opportunities for trade, market integration and drought resilience. To date the ultimate goal of phasing out non-emergency food aid altogether has not been realized, but the intention is correct and should be supported.

Food aid dependency undermines food security in Ethiopia at every level, from the household to the national government. The government produces policy documents such as the National Food Security Strategy and ADLI guidelines, but has little incentive to expend its scarce resources on food security programs as long as the international community remains willing to sink its food surpluses into Ethiopia.

For their part, the primary concern of the donors is to prevent famine, which reduces their food security strategy for Ethiopia to a food aid strategy, and explains why responding to annual food needs assessments dominates over multi-year planning and programming. More creative thinking is needed, together with an operational commitment by all stakeholders to achieve sustainable food security with dignity for all Ethiopians.

Access to land

Land tenure insecurity is a severe constraint to peasant production. Redistribution of land by the state has achieved socially equitable outcomes, but at the cost of household food security. "Radical egalitarian measures, as practiced in Ethiopia and Tanzania in the 1970s and 1980s, probably undermined overall farm production and food security, leading to increased poverty. This was due to the high level of insecurity generated by fears of further redistribution and a consequent unwillingness to invest effort in measures to improve soil conservation and enhance fertility" (Quan 2000:39).

The drive towards market liberalization in Ethiopia has been accompanied by a renewed but unresolved debate around an appropriate land tenure policy. One side argues that private ownership will provide tenure security and improve land use efficiency, by encouraging investment, improved land maintenance and higher yields. The opposing argument is that state ownership combined with state allocation of usufruct rights (through regular equitable redistribution) is the only way of guaranteeing access to land for all Ethiopians. Some writers have proposed intermediate forms of tenure based on community-level land ownership and management.

The National Food Security Strategy of 1996 stated that: "to promote commercialization of agriculture the government will strengthen security of access to land by developing regulations to frame a market-based leasehold system of transferable property rights throughout the country" (Republic of Ethiopia 1996). Subsequently the government has backtracked on this commitment. Land rights can now be transferred by inheritance within families, though the government retains ultimate disposal rights. The government now argues that treating land as a commodity would result in land concentration in the hands of rural elites, who would buy up land at distress prices when the poor face livelihood crises such as drought. This raises the twin specters of mass displacement of rural people with no employment prospects - the urbanization of mass poverty - and a reversion to quasi-feudal social relations in rural communities, with an emerging class of landless labourers who would be deeply vulnerable to exploitation by wealthy landowners.

Since land was redistributed proportional to household size, ownership of land (farm size) is less useful as an indicator of household food security status than access to land, which can be rented from other households. Access to cultivable land is negotiated through various rentals, borrowing and sharecropping arrangements between peasant households. A typical arrangement is to rent in land and pay the owner half the production from this plot.

Market development

Access to productive assets can derive from individualized ownership, but households that do not own key productive assets can also access them through informal sharing arrangements, and markets (leasing land, hiring agricultural labour). Conversely, institutions and social relations can also impose barriers to resource access: for instance, inflexible land tenure systems prevent people from settling and farming where they choose, and patriarchal norms exclude women from lucrative income earning opportunities (gendered labour market segmentation). These institutional rigidities need to be addressed, and input and output markets must be promoted.

Access to food is mediated by market access and price fluctuations. Food price volatility undermines food security for the poor, who by definition are net food purchasers. Since 80 percent of food produced in Ethiopia is consumed on farm, market supplies are limited and prices are highly volatile. The solution lies in more efficient food marketing and trade, both between regions within Ethiopia and between countries in the IGAD region. The 'privatization' argument has been associated most strongly with the

World Bank, though its attitude towards land policy in Africa has softened in recent years (cf. World Bank 2000:197).

The Ethiopian government has made the 'state control' argument most forcefully. The debate is typically characterized as a trade-off between economic efficiency and social equity. The statement of Prime Minister Meles Zenawi (2000) is as follows:

We agree that peasants need to know that their access to land is secure in the long term. We feel that we have achieved the necessary levels of security by making it clear that access is a permanent right passed on through inheritance. How more secure can you get? This is security in perpetuity! However, we reserve the right to redistribute if necessary.

We do not see the land, as a commodity is economically rational at this point. We do not have the necessary levels of economic growth to allow for productive peasant displacement. Major social disruption would undoubtedly occur as a result of land sales. A significant unemployed and unemployable sector would result.

The Derg banned inter-regional trade for many years, though agricultural marketing was liberalized during the 1990s. The Government of Ethiopia with USAID has established a grain market stabilization program "designed to stabilize grain prices, stimulate domestic production incentives and increase food security" (Tekabe 1998:2). Some improvements have been observed: for instance, grain price volatility fell during the 1990s, and food prices are gradually falling in deficit regions.

Inter-annual variability in food production is exacerbated by sluggish movement of produce between surplus and deficit regions within Ethiopia. This is due to both logistical constraints (which inhibits trader responses) and rural poverty (limited effective demand). Agricultural reforms during the 1990s have reduced the monopoly power of parastatals such as the AMC, but "the expected level of competition and private sector participation has not developed" (World Bank 1999: ix). Private traders have been discouraged by limited access to capital and storage facilities, and high transactions costs due to poorly developed road networks and the inaccessibility of food deficit communities.

During the record harvest year of 1996 the European Union implemented a local grain purchase program in Ethiopia, buying wheat, maize and sorghum in surplus regions in order to provide food aid to food insecure households, without undermining farmers and traders by importing food and depressing prices (MEDAC 1996). Similar interventions should be implemented even in years when Ethiopia is not nationally self-sufficient, to facilitate inter-regional trade and promote the private sector in agricultural marketing. Future interventions must provide both opportunities to traders (e.g. improving roads and marketing infrastructure) and incentives to traders (by raising rural incomes, and by generating confidence that traders will not be adversely affected by policy reversals).

Government policy

A crucial factor for food security is policy stability and continuity. Uncertainty over the nature and extent of future state interventionism in the economy inhibits investment and contributes to risk-averse behaviour by farmers. Quite apart from the recurrent droughts and conflicts that have devastated rural Ethiopia for centuries - and continue to do so in the year 2000 - agriculture in Ethiopia has undergone three radical transformations in the past three decades alone. The overthrow of Haile Selassie following the 1974 famine was followed by the replacement of a landowner-dominated semi-feudal agrarian system with a "socialist transformation of agriculture" by the Derg. The Land Reform proclamation of 1975 nationalized all land, abolished landlordism and tenancy, and redistributed land to farmers on the basis of household size. This was followed by the formation of Peasant Associations and service cooperatives, state and cooperative farms, and a marketing parastatal.

Village Unit and forced resettlement programs were initiated to support the establishment of large-scale Soviet-style mechanized farms, but succeeded only in creating social and economic upheaval in the Ethiopian countryside.

In 1990 the Derg government took Ethiopia's first steps towards agricultural liberalization, reversing its policies of the 1980s.The twin goals of the Transitional Government of Ethiopia, which followed the overthrow of the Derg in 1991, were improved food security and market-led economic growth.

The EPRDF-led government after its election in 1995 made a transition from command economy to an economic system driven by market forces. Implementing these objectives has included market liberalization, decentralization to a federation of 9 autonomous regions, and measures to raise agricultural production through yield-enhancing technologies. These policy shifts can be seen positively, as removing the constraints on peasant farming that heavy state. Peasants were declared the legal owners of the crops they produced - quota deliveries were abolished - and hereditary usufruct rights over farmland were established. Grain market restrictions were relaxed and the Agricultural Marketing Corporation was exposed to competition on open markets for the first time. Interventionism brought with it, or negatively, as dismantling the state institutions that had provided vital inputs and services to farmers. The removal of constraints and impositions on peasants has been associated with the phasing out of fertiliser subsidies (under World Bank pressure) and restricted access to agricultural credit except on un-favourable terms.

One current initiative that has great potential if sufficiently supported by government and donors is the establishment of a regional state Food Security Coordination Office (FSCO) in each region. Activities implemented or planned by the FSCOs in support of their overall objective - enhanced food security at the regional level - include small-scale irrigation, micro-finance, employment generating food-and-cash-for-work projects, environmental rehabilitation, and improved rural infrastructure and marketing.

This brief historical digression is intended to illustrate two points. The first is that various alternative models of agricultural policy - crudely, semi-feudalism, state socialism, and market liberalization - have failed to bring food security to rural Ethiopians or even to halt the steady decline of agricultural production per capita in recent decades. The second point is that rural Ethiopians have confronted an extraordinary amount of radical change in the policy environment within a single generation, all of which has contributed to a climate of uncertainty that is arguably as severe - in terms of undermining incentives to invest in agriculture - as the climatic uncertainty that farmers face each year. Excessive state interference in rural lives and livelihoods has bred a deep and lasting distrust of government institutions in many parts of the country.

Governance - related initiatives - notably rationalization and decentralization – are continuing to mediate the degree of state interventionism in the rural economy and to transform state-farmer relations. Though these are important steps in the right direction, policy-making in Ethiopia - both by government and donors or NGOs - remains induced and top-down. Current debates around land reform options, for instance, are largely confined to workshops in Addis Ababa, with little attempt to involved farmers themselves. There has been too little consultation with communities, too little building on indigenous knowledge and practices (e.g. small-scale water management and irrigation techniques).

Subsistence peasants know best for themselves what they need, and will be motivated most thoroughly to productive effort if they participate actively in decisions regarding their own development. (Pausewanget al. 1990:11)

A role for donors

Vulnerability to food insecurity in Ethiopia is a complex product of shocks (drought, war) plus low resilience (due to poverty, weak infrastructure and institutions, a constraining rather than enabling policy environment). Donors and federal and regional governments should adopt locally differentiated strategies, reflecting the differentiated nature and distribution of chronic and transitory food insecurity in Ethiopia. The government persists in seeing agricultural intensification as "the only source of hope", while donors in Addis Ababa are beginning to argue for an institutionalized safety net programme for the millions of Ethiopians who depend on food aid every year. However, intensification has limited potential on **"starvation plots"** and provides no immunity against drought, while safety nets risk perpetuating dependency on two levels: beneficiaries will remain trapped in unviable livelihoods and dependent on relief indefinitely, and governments and donors will have little incentive to invest in agriculture and other sectors.

The following recommendations recognize the need for a strategy that is differentiated over time. In the immediate future, continued shipments of food aid are unavoidable, but in the medium- and long-term more creative solutions to food insecurity must be found. Recommendations for immediate action include improved food aid targeting and safety nets programming. Medium-term interventions focus on recapitalization of asset-less households, plus agricultural yield stabilization. Long-term strategies must involve diversification away from rainfall-dependent livelihoods.

Short term:

Donors should make a multi-year commitment of food assistance to Ethiopia, rather than reacting belatedly to annual needs assessment exercises.

For the growing numbers of chronically food insecure Ethiopians, who are unable to meet their subsistence needs even in good rainfall years, an institutionalized safety net, linked to a realistic exit strategy, is urgently needed.

The preoccupation with national food availability risks neglecting household access to food. Targeting of food aid must be sharpened to improve efficiency and minimize dependency and disincentives.

To stimulate market development and provide choice to recipients, local purchases must be preferred to food imports, where surpluses are available, and food-for-work should be phased out in favour of cash-for-work, where market conditions permit.

Medium-term:

Especially in drought-affected areas, recapitalization is essential. This might include support to livestock restocking in the pastoralist regions, and restoring access to productive assets - notably land and draught power - to asset-fewer households in crop farming regions. (Note that access does not necessarily imply individual ownership.)

Given Ethiopia's extreme climatic variability, stabilizing agricultural production is as important as raising yields. Policy focus should shift away from yield-enhancing technological inputs packages, towards interventions such as investing in indigenous, small-scale irrigation technologies to stabilize crop yields in drought years.

Long-term:

Disincentives and barriers that prevent people from pursuing sustainable livelihoods exacerbate food insecurity in Ethiopia. A policy dialogue should be initiated around policies and practices that (1) constrain agricultural productivity (e.g. rigid land tenure systems and insecurity caused by repeated land redistribution); (2) undermine alternative economic activities (e.g. regulations that inhibit investment).

Support to diversification away from precarious livelihood systems (agriculture and pastoralism) towards sustainable alternatives whose returns are not correlated with rainfall - possibly agro-industry, or services such as community-based tourism.

To conclude, a switch from annual 'emergency' response to multi-year planning and programming by donors is strongly recommended, together with enhanced coordination of government, donor and NGO activities and strategies around the priority objective of achieving sustainable food security for all Ethiopians.

An exit strategy is equally essential, to reverse the present institutionalization of food aid dependency. Safety nets for the 'working poor' represent a failure of the economy and of policy; the only sustainable solution lies with economic growth and policy corrections that will ultimately make safety nets redundant. The key to long-run food security in Ethiopia is to identify and invest in alternative employment opportunities to rain fed agriculture.

Food Security in Bangladesh

Population – 150, 494,000 (2010) –U N Report

The United States Government (USG), as represented by the U.S. Agency for International Development (USAID), Bureau for Democracy, Conflict and Humanitarian Assistance (DCHA), Office of U.S. Food For Peace (FFP), through USAID/Bangladesh implemented food security programs in Bangladesh.[51]

This was complementary to the approved food security strategy of the USAID/Bangladesh Mission. This general description provides:

(a) A background of food insecurity and program history in Bangladesh;
(b) Desirable food security program strategies and types of activities which are encouraged by the Mission;
(c) Identification of important considerations and criteria which are expected to be used by the Mission in reviewing and evaluating subsequent and/or parallel proposals for development assistance;
(d) Mission programming priorities and expectations, and
(e) Reference to useful materials available on the Internet

Food Production in Bangladesh

[51]New Title II Development Programs in Bangladesh FY 2005, see Section E, Reference Sources.

Human diet is not restricted to any special category of food. The likes and dislikes of taste of food vary from one state to another. The people of Bangladesh prefer rice and fish curry in their diets. The land is fertile but is associated with vagaries of monsoon. Moreover, the country is thickly populated and most of them are poor, laborious and landless. The fertile land of Bangladesh is suitable for paddy, jute and sugarcane. The landless peasants of Bangladesh are migrating to Orissa coast (India) through sea route for fishing, dairying and paddy cultivation.

The farmers of Bangladesh grow: Rice / Paddy, Potatoes, Goat Milk, All Spice Pimento, Jute, Cow Milk, Indigenous Goat Milk, wheat, Fresh Vegetables, Sugarcane, Hen Eggs, Indigenous Chicken Meat, Bananas, Tobacco Leaves, Rapeseed, Spices, Tea, Mangoes and Garlic.

Food Aid and Food Security Policy

Bangladesh had a per capita income of $360 in 2005. Poverty alleviation is a core challenge for Bangladesh. Poverty, malnutrition is a fundamental problem in the country. To reduce poverty in Bangladesh, it is crucial to develop and improve the capacities of its most vulnerable populations and regions. For this, Bangladesh needs to accelerate the growth and productivity of its agriculture and non-farm sectors, improve the quality of social services, ensure proper functioning of its community and rural institutions and expand the rural support infrastructures.

Over the last three decades food grain production in Bangladesh has more than doubled – rice and wheat production has increased from around 10 million metric tons in the early 1970s to 25 million metric tons by the early 2000s. However, nearly half of the population still cannot afford an adequate diet. Also, as much of the countryside lies in disaster-prone, largely flood plain areas, annual flooding, together with periodic other natural disasters, often cause crop damage and food shortages for the vulnerable population.

Poverty and lack of social services leave a significant portion of the Bangladesh population hungry and malnourished. To alleviate these problems, USAID focuses its resources on long-term sustainable development. Within a framework of law and USG policy and interests, USAID invests in people and processes, and promotes policies and institutional environments which attack the primary basic cause of food insecurity and hunger – namely, poverty, especially in rural areas. Agency priorities for Title II development programs as set forth in the 1995 Food Security Policy Paper focus on improving household nutrition and health status, especially for children and mothers, and on increasing agricultural productivity, including field production, post-harvest handling, transportation and marketing.

Program foci for improving food availability, access, and utilization include closing the seasonal food gap through improved storage, small-scale post-harvest transportation, crop diversification, expanded market opportunities, and on overcoming household cash flow and liquidity constraints. The focus on food utilization places a major emphasis on changing critical nutrition (diet, care and feeding) and health enhancing behaviors. In addition, improved food utilization includes such areas as basic education, maternal and child health, control of infectious diseases, crop and food diversification activities and improvements in water and sanitation.

The Gender Dimensions of Food security

Gender relates to the socially assigned position and behavior of men and women. It affects the allocation of resources and work, decision-making and power, and the enjoyment of rights and entitlements within the family as well as in public life. Men and women have different roles and responsibilities in their individual lives, in their families and households, and in their communities. Both men and women are income earners and agricultural producers. Within the family, the women' responsibilities often involve care provision for their families and intra-household food distribution. Women also play a vital role in the processing and preparation of food, and frequently use their own earned income in support of their children. Women seeking to make these significant family contributions frequently have only limited access to the necessary resources, or to the related decision-making processes of family resource allocation and use.

Individual and household food security is affected by individual actions and choices men and women make in producing food, earning income or acquiring assets, and feeding and caring for family members. Thus, it is critical to ensure equitable access to and control over the resources needed to meet their respective roles and responsibilities. Overcoming gender-based inequities in resource access and decision-making could very much enhance women's contributions to food security and ultimately result in significant nutritional benefits to the family. Furthermore, by improving women's health and nutrition, and their access to education and training opportunities, overall human capital is enhanced as an input to ensuring individual and household food security.

Title II Programs in Bangladesh

Bangladesh, being one of the most food insecure countries of the world, has received Public Law 480 Title II food assistance since 1972. During the first three years (1972-74) of the Title II program in Bangladesh, food aid was almost exclusively emergency assistance, helping the GOB feed people displaced by the nine-month war of independence. The subsequent programs, implemented by CARE into the mid-nineties, consisted of food for work programs, primarily earth moving for road and canal rehabilitation. CARE's Integrated Food for Development Program (1994-99) reflected a shift towards development on the relief-to-development continuum.

It utilized 70 percent of about 70 percent of the Title II resources undergoing monetization to fund larger scale in higher quality rural infrastructure. The current CARE program (1999-2004) is fully monetized, which enabled CARE to implement a wide array of developmental activities such as low cost paved rural roads, flood proofing, urban slum development, local government capacity building and training, and disaster management.

The other ongoing five-year program with World Vision began in FY 2000 and focused on improvement of food security in 16 of the country's 466 sub-districts. The World Vision activities are in water and sanitation, agriculture, rural roads and other infrastructure, and disaster management. The program also included a direct distribution component utilizing approximately 20 percent of the approved program commodities. Both programs monetize commodities through the Government of Bangladesh. Although the monetization process itself is relatively simple, to transfer the local currency to the Cooperating Sponsor's account, at which time it becomes available to support program activities, is commonly a lengthy, tedious process.

Prospective Program Strategies

Although Bangladesh appears to be approaching aggregate national cereals self-sufficiency, an estimated 32 million plus people cannot afford a daily intake of more than 1800 kilocalories. Due to the frequency of disasters, primarily annual flooding and occasional cyclones typically accompanied by high tidal surges, people in many rural areas remain ultra poor and are trapped by their poverty. Related contributing factors include the lack of reliable and regular income sources, with the majority of the rural population landless and reliant upon income from unpredictable employment. Insignificant economic activity in most areas further contributes to poverty and thereby affects community livelihoods and food security. The domain of vulnerability in this group encompasses exposure to risk, hazards, shocks and stress, difficulty in coping with contingencies, and access to assets.

The goal of the Title II Program in Bangladesh is to reduce poverty and achieve long-term food security for the poor and malnourished, helping them to graduate to a more decent level of living. Future Title II programs need to address the living conditions of the poor people in the above cited areas.

Activities proposed in new DAPs should be in conformity with Bangladesh government and multilateral food security assessments and strategies. Conformance with both the Agency and USAID Mission food security strategy and related development priorities is highly desirable, as program and resource integration is encouraged. It is recognized that no proposal may be disapproved solely because it is not in such conformance with the latter.

The DCHA/FFP policy is to encourage an appropriate mix of direct distribution and monetization activities. The Bangladesh Mission is encouraging proposals, which rely less on monetization to sustain proposed program interventions. Proposals to implement Title II programs in Bangladesh may reflect a combination of direct distribution, cash for work, and monetized program elements. Activities should be implemented in geographic areas where food insecurity is acute and where interventions can be expected to have a significant economic impact. Innovative approaches that require initial pilot phases should, nevertheless, be structured to eventually address the needs of the poor people within the overall project scope and activity duration of the approved DAP.

Overcoming food insecurity requires attention to specific factors that promote food availability (e.g. productivity-enhancing technology, infrastructure, and markets), food access (income, prices, employment, control of assets and resources) and food utilization (health care, clean water, sanitation, and improved diets). Given the relative recent success of the Government of Bangladesh in achieving national cereals self-sufficiency, the Bangladesh Mission encourages DAPs, which focus primarily on the food security components of access and utilization. Some possible interventions are listed below. Note that the list is by no means exhaustive.

Important Considerations in Programming: The Mission strongly encourages monetization through private channels rather than the existing procedure through the government. Experience has shown that monetization through the Government of Bangladesh is a lengthy, time consuming, and often frustrating process which hinders the timely transfer of sales proceeds to project accounts.

In countries where multiple DAPs are anticipated, joint monetization by cooperating sponsors is encouraged to minimize workload and accrue program efficiencies.

We encourage the programming of value added commodities. The DCHA/FFP policy encourages programs to utilize value-added commodities. Wherever feasible, monetization of value-added commodities is preferable to the monetization of bulk commodities.

Each DAP should include a disaster component which would include the capacity building of local NGOs, governmental bodies and local communities.

The Bangladesh Mission believes that PVO cost sharing is an important element and demonstrates a partner's commitment to the program in Bangladesh. USAID expects applicants to demonstrate a commitment to program success by proposing an appropriate and meaningful level of cost sharing.

Effective partnering can increase efficiency and effectiveness, scale of coverage, transparency, sustainability of service delivery, and programming scope. Partnering with other organizations such as local NGOs, GOB Ministries, research institutions, governmental bodies and universities expands community participation, ownership and control and improves the development process. Therefore, partnering with local indigenous NGOs, local elected bodies, and relevant government agencies is strongly encouraged.

Promoting stakeholder participation in the design and implementation of the program activities is encouraged. Use of Participatory Learning and Action techniques are important to bring together residents and leaders from the community, government officials, and representatives of local entities, local NGOs to expand stakeholder participation, foster ownership, promote long-term maintenance assurances, and promote sustainability.

The proposal must reflect gender considerations in all activities. In recognition of the relative imbalance of women vis-à-vis men in economic and social arenas, wage disparities, and widely variable degree and scope of economic and social independence, the DAPs should make special efforts to ensure that women are given optimum opportunity as program participants and beneficiaries in all activities.

The Title II program should be designed to help achieve the Mission's goal of improving the food security of the most vulnerable groups. The geographic strategy used in programming should allow for the targeting of the neediest beneficiary groups. It needs as follows:

To achieve a tangible program result a holistic approach is necessary. It is recommended that programs consider a carefully focused range of complementary activities to accelerate improvements to the food security of the target population.

Appropriate food utilization is critical to the achievement of improved food security in Bangladesh. The direct food distribution component(s) of the DAP should reflect a balanced diet package as opposed to the sole distribution of food grains.

Linkages with other USAID funded projects and partners implemented by Louis Berger, is encouraged.

Mission Priorities and Expectations: In future DAPs, USAID/Bangladesh envisions having multiple Title II Cooperating Sponsor development food aid partners, with smaller individual programs and a strong programmatic and geographic focus within each program.

The USAID Bangladesh Mission expects to make a currently undetermined amount of DA resources available to support DAPs which are approved in the FY 2005 DAP review cycle. Priority points in the Mission evaluation of grant proposals for the use of DA resources will be awarded to those approved DAPs that most appropriately and thoroughly meet the following criteria. These are:

(a) Mission Program Priorities
(b) Linkages with other elements of the Mission program;
(c) Inclusion of direct distribution components;
(d) Monetization through private channels;
(e) Inclusion of value-added commodities;
(f) Significant partner cost-share in the budget;
(g) Gender considerations adequately reflected and included in program activities;
(h) Creative, innovative and effective approaches to food security in Bangladesh, including disaster preparedness and mitigation, utilized.
(i) Contextual Knowledge
(j) Demonstration of a clear understanding of the political, cultural, social, and institutional norms in targeted areas;
(k) Incorporation of "lessons learned" from past food aid programs in Bangladesh;
(l) Clear understanding of local capacities and demonstrates inclusion of the vulnerable populations in program planning;
(m) Clear understanding of the community dynamics and incorporate appropriate steps for gender integration and balance in activities at all levels.
(n) Institutional Capability/Past Performance
(o) Demonstrated previous successful Title II program implementation in Asi
(p) (p)Demonstrated internal technical capacity to address food insecurity issues;
(q) Demonstrated strong and productive relationships with former and current partners and beneficiaries;
(r) Appropriate targeting of vulnerable communities.

Personnel

(a) Key personnel have relevant experience in managing international development programs and working collaboratively with Asian governments and disaster-related organizations
(b) Key personnel have relevant experience in working with community organizations and/or regional organizations
(c) Program operational personnel have demonstrated sector-specific technical capability in their skill areas and appropriate language skills.

Cost Effectiveness: percentage of the overall budget going as direct assistance to beneficiaries; significance of program impact in terms of number of beneficiaries and cost per beneficiary;

Cost Realism: likelihood that the program can be accomplished within the stated budget and within the projected operational period;

Cost-Sharing: Extent to which the applicant intends to use its own funds, and/or those of other non-USG donors. [52]

USAID's Response in Bangladesh: Food Security

Food security is defined as the condition in which all people at all times have both physical and economic access to sufficient food to meet their dietary needs for a productive and healthy life. It is a multi-dimensional development topic that requires cross-sectoral integrated interventions and is dependent upon factors such as: agricultural production, food imports and aid, intra-household decision making, resource allocation, employment opportunities and income earnings. Due to the high level of poverty in

[52]US AID, Bangladesh

Bangladesh, roughly half its people are unable to meet this basic need.

Donating Food for Local Development: The United States of America donates food through P.L. 480 (under Title II program). A part of the food aid, including wheat, vegetable oil, and lentils are programmed for direct distribution through Food for Work (FFW) and Maternal and Child Health (MCH) activities. The bulk of the Title II food is sold to the Bangladesh government for local currency. The funds raised go to USAID's implementing partners to support local development activities. The Government of Bangladesh uses the food grain to support its social safety-net activities. Government programs include relief following a disaster, open market sales to the poor to stabilize prices, need-based targeting, and feeding the poorest people. US Aid's implementing partners, CARE and Save the Children USA; also distribute grain directly through food-for-work programs.

Working for Food or Income: Food aid programs give men and women living in areas with chronic food shortages the opportunity to work for a wage and/or food. These programs build environmentally sound, all-season roads that allow people to get to markets. A second project area is tree planting (to prevent soil erosion) where poor women are then employed to care for the trees. USAID assists communities with flood proofing to protect their villages while also helping prepare at-risk areas in case disaster strikes. Disaster shelters are built in villages to protect the local population from cyclones and floods. The shelters also serve as schools for local communities. Other efforts include:

(a) Improving access to safe water and adequate sanitation;

(b) Implementing seed distribution programs as well as providing homestead garden training; and,

(c) Expanding agricultural productivity and increasing the incomes of the poor.

Improving Nutrition: A varied, healthy diet is important for good nutrition. The International Maize and Wheat Improvement Center supported by USAID, works with poor farmers to plant wheat and corn in the dry seasons and increase the productivity of their land. Wheat and corn are excellent dry season crops, since they require much less water than rice. They provide families variety in their diets and a new source of income.

Improving Food Security: USAID also works with the Government of Bangladesh to improve food management and food security policies. Past programs helped ensure public food programs and supplies reached those most in need. Current efforts are focused on improving food security policy development and implementation.

More Facts about Food Security

(a) Women eat last and eat less. They are the most malnourished group in Bangladesh.
(b) Fifty percent of all Bangladeshi babies are born underweight.
(c) Frequent floods, cyclones and other natural disasters pose special problems for assuring food security.
(d) The Government relies increasingly on the private sector to assist in food security.[53]

The people of Bangladesh encounter two threats in most of the years. These are: military rule and poverty. The government should adopt pro-poor, pro-rural and pro-agricultural policies. The price of agricultural commodities is also un-remunerative. Peace in Bangladesh is marred for food-insecurity.

---

[53]World Development Indicators, World Bank, 2004

Food Security in Malawi

Population – 15, 381, 000 (2010) U N Report

Poverty causes food insecurity. Vulnerability to poverty in Malawi is highly associated with risk. Households face multiple shocks, most of which threaten their livelihoods and impact negatively on their welfare. Among the important risks that rural households face is drought, which is exacerbated by environmental change. This study analyses the impact of drought on household's vulnerability using a two-period panel dataset of 259 rural households in Malawi.[54]

The results show that recurrent drought makes households more vulnerable to the extent that households that were affected by drought in both periods were twice as vulnerable as those who experienced drought in only one period. Policies that are aimed at building poor households' resilience to recurrent drought hold more promise of enabling the households cope with this livelihood-threatening hazard.

Other key findings include: Rural households depend on safety net programs to cope with drought - targeted direct welfare transfers, especially in the form of direct food transfer, should be promoted as a short-term intervention to help poor households to be able to smooth their consumption in the face of drought.

Social protection interventions should, however, go beyond direct welfare transfers to incorporate productivity-enhancing safety nets the agricultural input subsidy program that the Government of Malawi

---

[54]Makoka, D. (2008), "The impact of drought on household vulnerability: the case of rural Malawi, Munich Personal RePEc Archive, Quoted from Eldis Poverty reporter June 11, 2009

has been running since 2005 should therefore be encouraged as a short-term strategy. In the longer-term, small and medium scale irrigation schemes need to be promoted in order to enhance food crop production - irrigation should continue to be promoted, especially among poor communities where the impact of drought is most severe.

The Department of Disaster Management Affairs[55] is likely to get all of the maize required for the humanitarian response from the Strategic Grain Reserves (SGR) but has not yet secured government or donor funding for moving the humanitarian maize to the affected areas. The delayed commencement of humanitarian assistance in the affected districts will result in affected households beginning to adopt coping mechanisms with damaging consequences. The Malawi Vulnerability Assessment Committee (MVAC) identified 718,000 people between March and June in eight districts in southern Malawi that are currently food insecure due to failed harvests as a result of prolonged dry spells in the 2009/2010 agricultural year. All 718,000 food insecure people have not yet started receiving humanitarian food assistance. The number of food insecure people is projected to increase to 1.1 million by October 2010.

The food security situation in northern and central Malawi remains favorable. National maize production figures project yet another national maize production surplus in the 2009/2010 agricultural year of about 800,000 MT. National maize grain stocks are also favorable at about 150,000 MT, significantly above the SGR level of 60,000 MT that the Malawi government and their development partners agreed to some years back. Additionally, the Agricultural

---

[55] Malawi Food Security Outlook, Famine Early Warning Systems Network, USAID, From the American People, June 2010

Development and Marketing Corporation (ADMARC) have about 40,000 MT in its stocks. Retail prices for maize in all markets across the country are dropping as is expected at harvest time. However, the failed/reduced crop production in the south is translating into minimal price drops at harvest time. There is a need to promote competition in the affected areas as well to ensure maize is available for the households who have some cash to access food at favorable prices.

Food Production in Malawi: The commodities are: Potatoes, Maize, Cassava, Tobacco Leaves, Plantains, Tea, Bananas, Sugar Cane, Pigeon Pea, Indigenous Cattle Meat, Fresh Vegetables, Fresh Fruits, Indigenous Pig Meat, Indigenous Chicken Meat, Hen eggs, Dry Cow Peas, Chick Pea, and Rice/ Paddy.

Updated food security: Prolonged dry spells experienced during the main production months of the 2009/2010 seasons have resulted in maize production falling in all 13 southern region districts. Eight districts experienced a drop in rain fed maize production of more than 40 percent. As result of the crop failures, there are about 718,000 people in June that are food insecure in the eight southern districts of Balaka, Chikhwawa, Mwanza, Neno, Nsanje, Phalombe, Thyolo, and Zomba. The crop failure has come about as a result of prolonged dry spells that affected parts of the country with particularly devastating effects on crop production in the southern Malawi. MVAC analysis has projected that the number of food insecure people will reach 1.1 million people by September. The Ministry of Agriculture and Food Security (MoAFS) reports show that in the districts of Neno, Mwanza, Chiradzulu, Blantyre, Thyolo, Mulanje and Phalombe, Chikhwawa and Nsanje; the food insecure households are coping through petty trading, fish selling, selling crafts, excessive sale of charcoal and firewood, and casual labor. In the districts of Balaka, Mangochi, Machinga and Zomba, households are relying on firewood sales, vegetable sales, fishing and fish selling, and casual labor. The situation is expected to worsen as more households deplete meager harvests and start using more desperate coping mechanisms, for example, whole families spending entire days in the Shire River harvesting water lilies, locally known as interventions should not undermine the efforts of private traders who are moving food from high production to deficit districts at low prices because of competition.

May 2010 retail maize prices in all local markets are decreasing as expected during harvest time. The favorable prices mean that more people in the food insecure areas in the south will be able to access food through markets if they have the income. However, a detailed analysis shows a telling pattern that is linked to the food security situation but not necessarily future price prediction. Maize prices in March and May were compared mainly because March is the month when maize prices are usually at their highest in most markets and just beginning to drop due to the harvest that normally starts in April, and May 2010 is just one month into harvest when farmers start selling their produce and maize prices are normally at the lowest.

It is evident that retail maize prices between March 2010 and May 2010 have fallen by more than 50 percent in most (75 percent) markets in northern Malawi. The prices have fallen by more than 50 percent in about half of the markets in central Malawi. The maize prices have fallen by less than 50 percent in most (72 percent) of the markets in southern Malawi. Therefore more price reductions between March and May have been recorded in the surplus maize production in the northern region during the same period. The significant retail maize price drops in the southern Malawi may signify that prices are likely going to rise significantly within the consumption year. It is however unlikely that the maize prices are going to exceed MK60 /kg because maize prices will remain low in the central and northern regions where there is surplus maize production.

There are widespread anecdotal reports of farm gate prices being as low as MK20/kg in central region of Malawi against the government recommended minimum farm gate maize price of MK35/kg. It was also observed last year that private traders managed to supply maize into southern region from central region at lower prices compared to the maximum selling price of MK60/kg that the government allowed ADMARC to sell its maize at. Using cash transfers as a humanitarian response mechanism is also viewed by some stakeholders a tool that would induce more competition among private traders and lead to low prices, to the benefit of the food insecure population and private traders as well.

In short, agriculture becomes a successful enterprise when all factors of production such as fertile land, hybrid seeds, manures and fertilizers, pesticides, irrigation facility, adequate manpower and technical know-how are available. The rich farmers can use all recommended inputs and arrange irrigation facility. But in hilly tracts and degraded soil conditions, a poor peasant may not be able to follow package of practices for higher yield. The low yield of crops, low bargain power for sale of food grains or other produce and natural calamities make unbearable loss to agriculture. The developing countries face the following problems in farming. These are:

(a) In all developing countries there are economic disparities between irrigated and rain-fed areas
(b) The sale value of homegrown agricultural commodities is less than imported commodities as developed countries give higher subsidy to agriculture. So local crop output cannot compete with the substitute

(c) The World Trade Center appeases the rich countries
(d) Un-organized local markets and lack of market intelligence
(e) The Government tries to keep market prices of cereals low for the benefits of government employees and urban people
(f) Vagaries of monsoon like flood, cyclone, drought and torrential rain
(g) Poverty and hunger

The farmers should possess land rights, remunerative prices for homegrown agricultural commodities. The government must undertake pro-poor policies including free education, free healthcare, free insurance and pension to all farmers after 60 years of age. Unless the peasants and labourers are assured food security and government assistance, permanent peace would not be possible. In short, higher prices of cereals (Paddy / Rice and Wheat) to the farmers could save the world from hunger. The actual hungry people could be supplied free cereals of two quintals once a year. This would induce the hungry people to search for other necessities.

Let us study the suggestions of other specialists that are necessary for drawing conclusions for a world free of hunger, where an individual can live a decent life. The world is divided into different countries politically; nature has divided into different climatic zones; but the world would survive if all are food secured. Let us act as the family members of the whole world.

Conclusion

Food security has posed the greatest challenge to all the developing countries. These countries are in the grips of poverty, disease, illiteracy, inequality, population explosion, war, famine, climate change, lawlessness and insurgency. The political leaders are more worried for foreign funding. Hence, ensuring 'food to all' would take many years if suitable policies issues are not implemented at the earliest possible time.

The governments of these developing countries should ask poverty economists of their countries to formulate policy prescriptions for justice to all. All problems could be solved provided there is a sincere effort to solve the problems. The situation of Pakistan, Brazil, Ethiopia, Bangladesh, Kenya, Djibouti, Somalia and Eritrea is alarming. But we feel that their problems could be solved. Some of the problems are described here for discussion and suggestions from intelligentsia around the globe.

Tens of thousands of people are feared to have died in the famine, caused by war in Somalia and drought in the Horn of Africa — Kenya, Ethiopia, Djibouti, Eritrea and Somalia. More than 12 million people in the region need food aid. An estimated 3.7 million Somalis are at risk of famine today. Ethiopia witnessed a major famine in 1984/5 and it caused mortality of one million people. Between 1960 and 1990 the population doubled from 23 to 48 million, while per capita landholding shrunk from 0.28 to 0.10 hectare, and per capita food output collapsed by 41 percent from 240 to 142 kg.

Human capital is extremely low in Ethiopia, which is both a cause and a consequence of food insecurity due to adverse synergies between poor education, health and nutrition status, and labour productivity. Illiteracy constrains access to skilled and semi-skilled off farm employment - literacy rates in Ethiopia are just 36 percent for males and 17 percent for females - perpetuating dependence on low-input, low-output agriculture. In 2004, the socio-economic condition in Bangladesh was as follows:

(a) Women eat last and eat less. They are the most malnourished group in Bangladesh.

(b) Fifty percent of all Bangladeshi babies are born underweight.
(c) Frequent floods, cyclones and other natural disasters pose special problems for assuring food security.
(d) The Government relies increasingly on the private sector to assist in food security.

In short, the developing countries must ensure pro-poor, pro-agricultural and pro-rural policies in budget formulation. Each country must include Pensioners' benefits to senior citizens; grow cereals to meet their local demands, take up horticulture, social forestry, dairy, poultry, and goat rearing for generation of income and employment. Government must ensure each farmer, peasant, sharecroppers, and agricultural labourers to own land, bank account, education and health care facility.

Subsidy in agriculture should be replaced by direct payment to farmers. Government must take steps to meet requirement of cereals in the country and there should be free flow of rice and wheat through length and breadth of the country.

Each country should not wage war against the neighbor country / countries. Each country should fight against poverty. As a result, each country would enjoy peace, food security and prosperity. And it is possible.

+++++

Chapter IV

FOOD SECURITY IN INDIA

God comes to the hungry in the form of food.
---- Mahatma M.K. Gandhi

Prof. Amartya Sen expressed his concerns over the widespread prevalence of hunger and undernourishment in the world in general and in India in particular. There are problems of inclusion and exclusion errors while targeting the below poverty line (BPL) population. Some of the African countries are performing better than India in reducing the levels of malnutrition. India has escaped the global economic crisis and it is good to find that the Government has not dismantled all the schemes and programs. He said that there was a time when the country was terminated by communal riots and violence, which is mentioned in his newly released book titled: The Idea of Justice. Public scrutiny and action is must for the proper functioning of the Right to Food Act. There is need for good provisions within the Act. One of the problems of undernourishment is that it is invisible. Poverty and food insecurity exists due to lack of access to gainful employment, education and health care. Without food, children cannot perform well in their classrooms. There are complementarities between hunger and education. Accountability of primary school teachers is essential. There is a need for a range of interventions, to address different aspects of the problem. Programs such as NREGA, ICDS and the Public Distribution System (PDS) have much to contribute, but no single program is the panacea – "we need them all."

Professor Sen[56] highlighted the complementarities between different interventions, and the correlation between malnutrition, poor health, illiteracy, and other deprivations. He explained life cycle approach to inter-generational malnutrition, where nutritional status of mothers determines the nutritional and health status of the children (even when they grow up). He mentioned about the World Health Organization's (WHO) Commission on Social Determinants of Health.

He asked not to go for premature privatization of the health system. The extent of gender inequality is quite large. Among other neglected aspects of the nutrition situation is the lack of health care. He strongly criticized India's "ghastly premature privatization" of health care. Asked about his views on "targeting versus all" of the PDS, Professor Sen said that there were strong arguments for all beneficiaries. For instance, a universal system is less divisive, and helps to create a strong public demand for quality services. A targeted system, on the other hand, always involves exclusion errors. These arguments for all beneficiaries are "not dismissible",

---

[56]A face-to-face interaction of Prof. Amartya Sen with reporters and journalists from media on the issues related to the newly drafted National Food Security Bill that took place in the Press Club of India, New Delhi on 8 August 2009.

but may need to be weighed against the possible costs. The universal PDS allows for better public provision because even the better-off groups with more political voice have a stake in ensuring it works well.

There are limitations pertaining to the voucher system since it can neither stop corruption nor prevent gender inequality. He found merit in the universal Public Distribution System (PDS). When questioned on privatization, he said that privatization of the Indian Airlines/ Air India is a different thing than allowing private contractors to supply ready-to-eat food at schools. Things must be judged within a particular context. The success of the Integrated Child Development Scheme (ICDS) is extremely important.

In this chapter discussions are presented on India, the second most populous country, which can solve its food problems, provided the country invests less on military equipments and military research. Indians are naturally peace-loving by birth where Hinduism, Buddhism, Jainism, Sikhism and many other religions are born and practiced. But the governments shift away from the people to remain in power by preparing for war.

India can achieve food security when the government would try to uplift the peasants and farmers. The country should follow pro-poor, pro-rural and pro-agricultural policies to save the vast majority of hungry people and save the farmers which commit suicides more often by changing their mindsets and economic standards.

The United Nations estimated that India's population was 1,241,492,000 in 2011. So food security to all assumes the greatest and urgent need of the government. But does the country marches to achieve the goal?

Hidden Hunger

Despite several programs to tackle malnutrition, India is home to 40 per cent of the world's malnourished population. According to the report, "Children in India 2012", of the Ministry of Statistics and Programme Implementation, 48 per cent of children under the age of five are stunted. This indicates that half of the country's children are chronically malnourished. The number of 'wasted' ~- acutely malnourished and stunted ~ children has been put at 19 per cent, which would mean that one out every five children under five is not receiving adequate nutrition. The worst-affected states with underweight children under five years of age are: Madhya Pradesh (60 per cent), Jharkhand (56.5 per cent) and Bihar (55.9 per cent). Similarly, the prevalence of anaemia among children (6-59 months) is more than 70 per cent in Bihar, MP, UP, Haryana, Chhattisgarh, Andhra Pradesh, Karnataka and Jharkhand. Malnutrition is the primary cause of child mortality. The rate of under-five mortality decreased from about 150 per 1000 live births in 1990 to 74 per 1000 live births in 2005-06. At the present rate of decline, India will hardly be able to achieve the Millennium Development Goal ~ 4 (MDGs) target by 2015.

The term 'malnutrition' is often loosely used by laymen without paying much attention to its actual meaning. Even among biologists and nutritionists there is no consensus on the basic question of how malnutrition should be defined and by which yardstick it should be measured. There is no universally accepted terminology to distinguish between various nutritional deficiencies. However, the term malnutrition is used in relation to under-nutrition (protein-energy malnutrition-PEM), over-nutrition (consumption of excessive calories) and also micronutrient deficiency (hidden hunger).

The most important and lethal form of malnutrition is PEM which is referred to when world hunger is discussed. The micronutrient malnutrition does not necessarily create a feeling of hunger. Hence it is referred to as hidden or silent hunger, but it undermines the child's growth and development, intelligence, and education. It predominantly affects adult women and men. The consequences of malnutrition transcends generations. The risk of malnutrition is higher among children whose mothers suffer from chronic malnutrition. The mother's present nutritional status in turn depends on her childhood nutritional status. Thus a vicious circle (mother-child-mother) of malnutrition seems to have set in for generations.

The factsheet of women's malnutrition reveals that India has the highest number of malnourished women among developing countries. Every second Indian woman is reported to be anaemic and more than one-third suffer from chronic energy deficiency (CED). The adverse effects of maternal malnutrition extend beyond maternal mortality to intra-uterine growth retardation, child malnutrition and an increasing prevalence of chronic diseases.

At critical periods of development of the womb, maternal malnutrition can trigger an adaptive redistribution of the foetal resources in such a way that such adaptations and metabolism expose individuals to cardiac-vascular and endocrinal diseases. The foetus of the malnourished mother protects its brain by directing the blood-flow from the other organs. The changes in the flow patterns also weaken blood vessels and make the individuals more prone to strokes and heart-attacks. This vulnerability is not restricted to one person; it may be passed on for generations. Moreover, if the foetus receives limited nutrients in the womb, its cells may use nutrients sparingly, and the trait gets ingrained in the growing organism. Malnutrition in the womb leads the foetus to conserve fat and calories. This may place the child at a high risk of obesity during adolescence. Similarly, malnourished foetus produces fewer insulin producing cells and heightens the chances of Type-11 diabetes. Therefore, diseases blamed on lifestyle can often start before birth.

The standard method to measure the nourishment status of adults is by the Body Mass Index (BMI) ~ the ratio of the body weight (in kg) to the height squared (m2). The international cut-off is a BMI of 18.5, with 18.5 to 25 being the normal range; beyond 25 is considered obese; below 18.5 is said to be living in famine conditions. In India, the National Family Health Survey ~ 3 (NFHS-3), conducted in 2005-06, reports that in rural India 38.4 per cent of men and 40.6 per cent of women have a BMI of less than 18.5. This is suggestive of endemic near-famine conditions. However, the sanctity of BMI has of late been questioned.

The World Health Organization and the Food and Agriculture Organization have advanced two alternative approaches for measuring the extent of malnutrition. But the global picture is somewhat contradictory. WHO's approach is based on the condition of the human body and the basic functioning - the so-called 'anthropometric' measures. On the other hand, FAO measures nutritional status through per capita food availability statistics. The FAO estimates suggest that the incidence of malnutrition in sub-Saharan Africa is about twice as high as that in South Asia. An indicator used by WHO reveal quite the reverse picture - the prevalence of malnutrition among children is twice as high in South Asia as in sub-Saharan Africa.

Anthropometric measures adopted by WHO for ascertaining malnutrition are stunting (low height for age), wasting (low weight for height) and underweight (low weight for age). Stunting is an indicator of chronic malnutrition, attributable to prolonged food deprivation, and/or disease or illness; wasting indicates an acute stage of malnutrition caused by more recent food deprivation or illness; underweight is an indicator of both acute and chronic malnutrition. Children whose measurements fall below a certain threshold of the reference population, based on WHO standards, are marked as undernourished: stunted, wasted or underweight. By this measure, the NFHS-3 reports that roughly half of the children fewer than five are stunted, about one in five children under three is wasted. But WHO's methodology does not take into account race, culture, geographical locations etc. Moreover, overlapping amongst the measures is also a puzzling feature. Some children who are stunted will be wasting and/or overweight. Those who are wasting will also be stunted and/or underweight. A more comprehensive measurement of child malnutrition is, therefore, imperative.

India is now passing through a phase that nutrition experts describe as a 'dietary transition'. Dietary preference is shifting from cheap calories (cereals) to more expensive non-cereal foods like meat, fish, milk, milk products, fruit and vegetables. Clearly, India is eating less and the choice of food is unhealthy. The diet is more "energy-dense" ~ rich in saturated fat and sugar but deficient in complex carbohydrates (main sources of dietary fibre) and micronutrients, iron etc. Dietary transition is the major factor behind under-nutrition and over-nutrition. As per NFHS-3 data around 25 per cent children below three in the wealthiest 20 per cent families are stunted and 20 per cent are chronically underweight in India.

Economic growth is positively influenced by improved nutrition.

In the short run, the best way to break the vicious cycle of malnutrition is the direct intervention policy and feeding programmes like ICDS / MDM, availability of safe drinking water etc. Hopefully, lessons can be drawn from the success of Kerala, Tamil Nadu and Sri Lanka. Malnutrition should be viewed as an important issue of human development, rather than as a health-specific issue. We have the wherewithal to eradicate malnutrition; what we lack is the leadership to carry out the essential task.[57]

In short, economic growth is positively influenced by improved nutrition... Malnutrition should be viewed as an important issue of human development, rather than as a health-specific issue.

Justice to the Poor

Kalyani Shankar analyses the future prospects of the food security bill. She opines that the consensus seems to be eluding the proposed Food Security Bill for a variety of reasons. While the Advisory Council (NAC) led by All-India Congress Committee president Sonia Gandhi was able to push through two important legislations, the Right to Information Act and the National Rural Employment Guarantee Act, during the previous government from 2004 – 2009. But the Food Security Bill is still being drafted even in 2010.

While the idea of providing food security to all is laudable, there is a tug of war between the National Advisory Council (NAC) and the Government regarding the Bill. The NAC, which is perceived as a super-Government in many respects, is battling issues like dual pricing at INR 3 a kg for below-poverty-line families and a rate close to the minimum support price for the rest.

---

[57]Jaydev Jana (2013), " Hidden Hunger", The Statesman, September 16, 2013

The Arjun Sengupta Committee, Saxena Committee and Tendulkar Committee have made poverty estimates for the requirement of food grains. But the Planning Commission studies the requirement of subsidy amount on the basis of survey method. Even within the Congress, opinion is divided on whether food security should be universal or only for BPL families. Other political parties also have a say when the Bill is brought to Parliament. The Left is insisting on the PDS for all.

If one goes by last year's UN World Food Programme report, more than 27 per cent of the world's undernourished people live in India. About 43 per cent of children in India are underweight, which is more than the corresponding figure in the Sub-Saharan region. At present, it is a bizarre scenario where the poor are denied food while huge amounts of food grains are rotting in some States.

According to the Supreme Court commissioners, 50,000 metric tonnes of food grains have already gone bad. Another 2738 thousand tonnes are lying in the open in Punjab. In Haryana, too, 31,574 tonnes of grain have been lying in the open since 2008-09.

India's food security is worsening by the year. The cost of food items is increasing rapidly. There is also a short supply of pulses and edible oils, which are being imported at present. It is quite alarming that by 2050 the country's population is going to double, crossing two billion. While the population is on the rise, the food production is falling and the gap will become increasingly larger. Unless the population growth is contained, it will be a serious problem. Still, procurement is not so much a problem as is the distribution of food grains. The focus should be on a successful delivery mechanism and a good Public Distribution System.

Thirdly, with declining productivity and growing population, the future looks bleak. There is need for a second green revolution. Fourthly, preservation of the acquired food grains is yet another problem. The Government must ensure that storage space is adequate and there is no wastage. Fifthly, unless proper distribution of food grains is ensured, passing any number of laws is not going to help the poor. Corruption and leakage in the PDS is widespread. The efficiency of the PDS is good in the southern States while the northern States have much to improve.

In March, the Empowered Group of Ministers cleared the de-linking of food security from nutritional security. It recommended a blanket definition of BPL families and suggested a monthly quota of 25 kg of rice or wheat without fixing the price. It also introduced the concept of a food security allowance in cash if grains are unavailable. With rethinking on both sides, the NAC and the Government must meet each other halfway on the matter. The biggest worry would be how to find the funds to finance food security.

Food Insecurity is caused by the following factors:

(a) Less production
(b) Water crisis
(c) Land degradation
(d) Land deals
(e) Climate change
(f) Agricultural production
(g) Wheat stem rust
(h) Large family members
(i) Lack of market facility for saleable surplus
(j) Less availability of per capita aerable land
(k) Political Corruption
(l) Court cases
(m) Lack of earning members in family
(n) Absence of source of income in family

(o) Natural Calamities like flood, cyclone and earthquakes etc.[58]

Climate threat to food security

Suman sahai[59] opines that independent India has not faced large-scale famines, yet widespread hunger prevails and is growing.

According to official data, almost 87 per cent of rural India gets less than the minimum calorie requirement.

The decline in agricultural productivity, the diversion of food grains to feed poultry and livestock, policies that focus on export products and cash crops, as also inflationary food prices are contributing to a growing food crisis in the country. In addition, there is the proposed diversion of land and water to the production of Jatropha-based bio-fuels, the rapidly changing land use policy and the government's support for special economic zones even when they encroach on prime agricultural land.

Economic reforms in India have led to disinvestment in the agriculture sector. This has adversely affected more than two-thirds of the population that is dependent on agriculture for its livelihood. Farmers themselves face hunger due to rising input costs and non-remunerative prices of farm products. There is no effective crop and livestock insurance to cover damage and credit is not available at reasonable rates.

[58]Kalyani Shankar, "The Long Road to Food Security", The Pioneer, Bhubaneswar, September 3, 2010 and September 14, 2010

[59]Suman Sahai (2012), "Climate of threat to food security", Asian Age, October 15, 2012

Food availability has declined. Immediately after Independence, from the 1950s to 1964, it ranged between 140 and 170 kg per capita per annum. Between 1979 and 1994, it went up to 180 kg per capita per annum. After the reform period, food grain availability declined sharply to 150 kg per annum. There is a considerable shortfall in the actual requirement and availability of food grains. In the context of the current agrarian crisis, this trend poses a grave danger to communities already afflicted with hunger.

Adding to this already grim scenario is the new challenge of climate change. This year's see-saw with the monsoon is a pre-runner of what awaits us ahead. According to climate estimates, agriculture in the productive areas of South Asia will be among the most adversely affected. As temperatures rise, the growing season is expected to shorten with decreases in agricultural productivity of up to 40 per cent. The worst brunt of climate change on food production will be borne by farmers in rain-fed areas.

Coping with the impact of climate change on agriculture will require careful management of resources like land, water and biodiversity. A large-scale public education and training program is necessary to help farmers cope with the changes coming from global warming. Nothing in their experience has prepared them for the rapidly evolving, anthropogenic climate turbulence.

The disbanded extension service in the agriculture sector must be resumed urgently. Training and capacity building programs must help to increase sensitivity to the problems that agriculture will face and understand its causes. At present, there is little understanding among rural communities about global warming and they are facing difficulties adjusting to the unpredictable changes that are throwing their long-held cropping patterns out of gear. The new extension service must be geared to teaching farmers how to adapt their agriculture to the new weather conditions that will negatively impact their food and livelihood security.

Not just farmers, it will be necessary to provide education and training to a range of actors. This would include policymakers, Panchayati Raj institutions, the banking sector, civil society groups, corporate executives and others, in the theory and practice of adapting agriculture to climate turbulence. Such capacity building will enable the successful adoption of adaptation strategies at policy and implementation levels.

There will have to be a fundamental strategy change in food production. Practices in agriculture will need to shift from intensive, mechanized, water-demanding agriculture to a more sustainable, conservative agriculture that grows crops using less water. "More crops per drop of water" is a strategy recommended to tackle drought. The same approach is applicable in a wider sense when addressing the challenges posed by global warming.

The first step in adapting agriculture to cope with climate change will be to diversify the farm production model to minimize risk and obtain the most benefits from available resources. Such sustainable models will have to include crops, livestock, poultry and where possible, fisheries and agro forestry.

As the monsoon rainfall gets reduced and more uncertain and receding glaciers reduce water flows in rivers, farmers must learn to make maximum use of available water. Rainwater harvesting and traditional water storage structures such as farm ponds, wells and tanks will have to be revived. Watershed development and catchment area recharge treatments to allow for aquifer replenishment will have to be undertaken on priority basis in all ecosystems. As rainfall becomes less reliable, water conserved in tanks, ponds and wells will provide life-saving irrigation to crops.

Soil management will need to focus on increasing organic matter to improve soil nutrition and water retention capacity, thus increasing crop productivity. The eco-system approach to agricultural production using crop rotation, maintaining an appropriate balance of soil nutrients and using an integrative and bio-organic approach to pest management will be effective in coping with rapidly changing farm conditions.

Contour bonding will be useful, especially in the hill areas, to increase water retention in terraced fields and improve crop productivity. It was a central component in regenerating degraded soils in Burkina Faso in West Africa and is credited with as much as a 40 per cent increase in agricultural production the first year after its implementation. Planting hedgerows of leguminous plants, especially in poor soils, which constitute the bulk of the soil in India, is important to fix nitrogen, prevent soil erosion and conserve soil moisture.

Mulching and other types of soil cover is helpful in arresting soil erosion and extending the availability of soil moisture. Mulching has the added benefit of reducing weed populations by up to 60 per cent, saving on weeding costs. None of these are rocket science but they are neglected in our policy and implementation plans. India's strategy to deal with climate change, encapsulated in the National Action Plan on Climate Change lacks vision and offers no realistic solutions. We need urgently to come up with a policy and framework to protect our agriculture and food production from the onslaught of global warming.

Food Security, then and now

Huen Tsang, in his travelogue, has given a vivid picture of how the Indian society ran and conducted its business on the issue of food security.

For at least two centuries, India has suffered scarcity of food grains. After independence, nearly half the country suffered from food scarcity and semi-starvation. During this period, under PL480, substandard wheat was imported from the US. During those years, the international market of food grains increased drastically.

From 1950 to 1960, semi-starvation reigned in the country. The Government then put all its strength to overcome this severe situation and, as a result, the Green Revolution came in spearheaded by agricultural scientists. At that time, even the rain Gods smiled and food scarcity became less and less ferocious.

Once former Prime Minister Atal Bihari Vajpayee, describing the situation, said, "Today, the problem is of plenty and not scarcity. We have scarcity of storage capacity and not production capacity. When sacks are stacked in the open field, it indicates that we do not have enough space to store food grains produced by the hard labour of our farmers and, as a result, they are rendered prone to all types of rotting." He then announced construction of certain silos for storing food grains. Otherwise, billions of rats enjoy free lunch on those food grains. Today, rats without any hindrance are consuming food grains in warehouses throughout India. The loss of food grains by rats and other animals is a matter of great concern. The same types of stories are appearing frequently nowadays and losses are multiplying. Voices of concern are becoming louder and louder each passing day.

On August 31, 2010, the Supreme Court of India suggested free distribution of food grains rotting in the Food Corporation of India storage houses to the poorest of the poor. It wanted the Government to work over the loopholes in the Public Distribution System. The suggestion was aimed at giving food grains to the poorest of the poor for free rather than being wasted in FCI storage houses. But the Government remains unperturbed on this issue and shamelessly believes that rotting of food grains is inevitable. The National Advisory Council headed by Sonia Gandhi roars on the Food Security Act but do nothing in reality. The Supreme Court also suggested doing away with ration cards for Above Poverty Line (APL) families as there is no point in giving subsidized wheat and rice to those who could afford to buy it from the open market when the poor were not getting food grains. But, in counter-argument, the Government believes that APL families were being given food grains only after meeting the needs of Antyodaya Anna Yojana (AAY) and BPL families.

The Supreme Court had also suggested the Government not to procure food grains beyond the storage capacity. But the Government again counter-argues that it is not possible to limit procurement as by doing this it will hurt the policy to give attractive prices to farmers and encourage them to increase their productivity. By doing this, farmers would be left at the mercy of traders who would not pay remunerative prices. If the Government had exerted time and effort in increasing the storage capacity, it would have been far more beneficial to the Indian masses.[60]

Jitendra Bajaj and MD Srinivas (1996) thoroughly studied the storage and distribution system of food grains in different erstwhile kingdoms of India. In

---

[60]Dina Nath Mishra, "Food Security, then and now" Sunday Pioneer, Bhubaneswar, September 12, 2010

those days, the society guaranteed that no person would starve in any situation. Farming lands were donated to temples. Society took several measures to ensure that temples got enough food to run the system. Even today, one can see the living example of that system in gurudwaras in the form of langars by the Sikh community and in temples in the form of Bhandara by the Hindus. Anybody can go there to have food and there is no dearth of food for all. In this way, the society sustained and maintained its food security without an iota of corruption. Now, in contrast, examine the PDS of food grains. Even the Mid-day Meal Scheme run by the Government has generating stinking stories at regular intervals. It requires cultural spirit to inculcate this practice.

Even today, food aid to the hungry is treated as the best form of gift in all the religions throughout world.

The Directive Principles of State Policy – Para IV- of the Indian Constitution explicitly mentions that there should be no concentration of wealth in a few hands. The State shall strive to promote the welfare of the people by promoting a social order in which social, economic and political justice is informed in all institutions of life. The State shall work towards reducing economic inequality as well as inequalities in status and opportunities, not only among individuals, but also among groups of people residing in different areas or engaged in different vocations.

The State shall aim for securing right to an adequate means of livelihood for all citizens --- men and women as well as equal pay for equal work --- the State shall work to prevent concentration of wealth and means of production in a few hands, and try to ensure that ownership and control of the material resources is distributed to best serve the common good.

Farmers' Suicides in India

A report of the Reserve Bank of India says that as against RBI norms, only seven out of 27 PSU banks could achieve the stipulated target of distributing 18 per cent of the net bank credit to the agriculture sector as on November 2008. Hence, the percentage of agriculture in the GDP declined to 30.5 percent in 1988 to 17.5 percent in 2008, and growth in agriculture declined from 3.1 percent to 1.6 percent during 1988 - 2008.

The paradox is that even farmers in apparently prosperous states like Punjab, Andhra, and Maharashtra, are committing suicides.

About 250,000 farmers committed suicide due to indebtedness following crop shifting from traditional crop to cash crops and slapdash trade liberalization and corporate globalization agenda of the government from 1997 – 2012.

The World Bank led structural adjustment policies have brought new imperialism in the farm sector forcing poor Indian peasants to buy new seeds for every planting season from the global corporate. Perhaps there may be a link between farmers' deaths and the 'reform' agenda.

The highest level of farmers' suicide in India is the Virdharbha region in Maharashtra state; it faces 4000 suicides per year or 10 suicides per day.

And this is the reason with the highest acreage of Monsanto's GMO Bt. Cotton.

In Orissa state 126 farmers have committed suicides in 2010 for crop failure and loans over dues from banks and moneylenders. All of them have committed suicides by consuming insecticides and the

Directorate of Agriculture, Government of Orissa issues press notes that the farmers committed suicides because of family disturbances.

Are the officials of Directorate of Agriculture authorized to study family problems of the farmers? How could the press note was circulated? No government official has been punished so far.

Food Security is worsening

The state of India's food security is worsening by the year. The cost of food items is increasing rapidly, making them unaffordable to a majority of the people. Added to these woes is the short supply of pulses and edible oils, which forces the Central government to import them.

Pulses play a critical role in the diet of the people of India, where large sections are vegetarians. Protein plays a key role in the human diet. It is the body-building nutrient that develops muscles and is responsible for body strength, endurance and productivity at the workplace. A solution to the pulses and edible oils crisis is entirely within reach.

It is established that a human body requires a daily intake of about 50 gm of protein. While people in the developed countries and most of the developing countries have a satisfactory intake of protein, in India the per capita daily intake is only about 10 gm. This endangers health and work performance.

Proteins are amino acids. Out of the 22 amino acids required in the human diet, the body supplies 14. The remaining eight have to come from food. If all the eight amino acids are present in a single food item, it is called a complete protein food.

Since all proteins from animal sources are complete proteins, it is easy to meet the dietary protein requirements of non-vegetarians. However, the main sources of protein for vegetarians are leguminous plants — to which pulses belong. In general, pulses have lower concentrations of protein than animal sources. Besides, none of the pulses — except soybeans — are complete proteins. Therefore, combinations of two or more pulses are needed in a vegetarian diet. Dairy products, which are complete proteins, may also be used to supplement pulse proteins in vegetarian diets.

Given the important role that pulses play in the human diet, their availability needs to be increased indigenously. The common belief that without new high-yielding varieties the country will have to continue importing pulses and edible oils to meet the requirements is not true.

The possibility of improving productivity per acre by an order of two to three times using existing varieties has been demonstrated time and again in grower-fields in India. However, it is not done just by following current production practices but through the adoption of entirely new but simple and farmer-friendly technologies and tools that are now not available to Indian farmers.

The underlying problem of Indian agriculture that threatens food security is extremely low productivity. For example, in the case of rice it is only a third of what has been achieved elsewhere. Cotton productivity is only a sixth of what has been achieved in developed countries. The situation is no different in the case of other crops. In order to progress, the mindset with regard to the following two factors needs to change:

It is not the farmer who makes the food: he is only a facilitator. Food is actually made by plants. Therefore it is important to understand the requirements of plants and supply them without restrictions in order for plants to deliver food. Since plants do not talk, their needs are understood through research and experimentation. As indicated by Dr. R.S. Paroda, a former Director-General of the Indian Council of Agricultural Research (ICAR), our agriculture scientists will not by themselves be able to cope with the food security challenges that face the country.

The current policy of pampering farmers with subsidies will get us nowhere in terms of improving productivity. This is well understood not only in developed countries but also in developing African countries like Malawi. Malawi was a basket case of poverty, malnutrition and food shortage. Crop productivity improvements have taken it to the point where the country now exports its surplus food to neighboring poor countries.

In India, subsidy amount is misappropriated by industries such as fertilizer, pesticide or agricultural implements and corporations, dealers and government officials.

The mindset that breeding is the solution to all maladies has to change. Nurturing of plants is several times more important in crop productivity improvement than hybrid seeds per se. A hybrid variety will not produce if planted in non-fertile beach soil. But it will produce several times more if planted in fertile soil.

Brazil learnt this lesson years ago and stopped financing breeding for new varieties. Instead, it scours countries around the world and selects promising varieties to test their adaptability to Brazilian climatic conditions and then provides funding just to do that. It has taken stem cuttings of black pepper varieties from Kerala and spent money and effort on crop production practices. Now Brazil's pepper yield is 1,500 kg an acre compared to India's average of 350 kg an acre, the lowest among all pepper-producing countries.

India has about 50 million acres of irrigated land and is second only to the United States with 60 million acres. In the U.S. it is possible to raise only one crop a year due to weather constraints. However, many areas in India have the potential to raise three crops a year, provided we learn how to sustain the fertility of the soil. This will be equal to 150 million acres of irrigated land. At the present time our system of monitoring soil fertility and maintaining it is flawed and needs urgent attention. We cannot just bury our heads in soil as ostriches may do.

Finally, we have facilities now in place in Tamil Nadu to adopt new crop production technologies and tools, where crop productivity is routinely maintained at 300 per cent to 500 per cent more per acre than the average in India. We are now in the process of developing infrastructure for the rapid propagation of these highly cost- effective crop production technologies across the country.[61]

Vandana Shiva[62] says that the high cost of wheat import makes no political sense, because it threatens our food sovereignty. It makes no economic sense because there is no domestic scarcity and the imported wheat is more costly than domestic wheat. And it makes no sense in terms of health and nutrition because the imported wheat is of inferior quality. Instead of importing high-cost, low-quality wheat the Government should be procuring wheat domestically to secure farmers' livelihood, national

---

[61]Dr. Lux Lakshmanan, CPAg. CPCS, CPSS, is Director, California Agriculture Consulting Service, Davis, California. quoted from *The Hindu January 4, 2010*

[62]The Hindu July 20, 2007

food security and the food rights of the poor to safe and affordable food.

The Government was importing wheat at $ 317 - $330 per ton in July 2007, while Indian farmers were paid 8500 INR per ton, which is less than $200 per ton. And it is not the case that Indian farmers are not growing enough wheat to feed the people of India. This is a decision that will aggravate the food insecurity of the poor in India and undermine the country's food sovereignty. Still then, the Government's declaration that it will continue to import is a blatant violation of food sovereignty. International prices will continue to rise as it exports to India and because more and more food grains are being diverted to bio-fuels. The Government of India should protect the national interest and public interest and procure wheat from the farmers only.

The Right to Food Campaign

The Right to Food Campaign has formulated a set of common "**essential demands**" relating to the forthcoming National Food Security Act after a series of consultations within the campaign, culminating in a day–long National convention held in Delhi on 17th September 2009.

The campaign's "essential demands" sets the Act in the context of the nutritional emergency in India and the need to address the structural roots of hunger. In concrete terms, the campaign demands a comprehensive "Food Entitlements Act", going well beyond the limited promise in the UPA manifesto of 25 kg of grain at Rs 3/kg for BPL households. Aside from an overarching obligation to protect everyone from hunger, as well as to promote sustainable and equitable food production, essential provisions of the proposed Act include:

(a) A universal Public Distribution System (providing at least 50 kg of grain per family with 5.25 kg of pulses and 2.8 kg of edible oils);
(b) Special food entitlements for destitute households (including an expanded Antyodaya programme);
(c) Consolidation of all entitlements created by recent Supreme Court orders (e.g. cooked mid-day meals in primary schools and facilities of ICDS);
(d) Support for effective breastfeeding (including maternity entitlements and crèches);
(e) Safeguards against the invasion of corporate interests in food policy; and
(f) Elimination of all social discrimination in food–related matters

Further, says the campaign, the Act must include strong accountability and grievance redressed provisions, including mandatory penalties for any violation of the Act and compensation for those whose entitlements have been denied.

Preliminary Note of the Right to Food Campaign:

(a)Noting that the UPA Government has announced that it intends to enact a Right to Food Act;

(b)And whereas the Right to Food Campaign is anxious that any statute enacted ought to, at the very minimum, protect existing legal entitlements created by the Supreme Court orders passed in PUCL Versus UOI currently pending in the Supreme Court, and preferably go beyond;

(c)Whereas the Right to Food Campaign envisages a food security and sovereignty system in accordance with Article 39 of the Constitution of India where the ownership and control of the material resources of the community are so distributed as best to subserve the common good and everyone has a right to an adequate mean of livelihood;

(d)And whereas the RTF Campaign understands that a comprehensive RTF Act would require a fundamental realignment of the manner in which society and the state uses its resources today.

(e)Recognizing that there is a considered view within the country to the effect that the WTO system of laws, agreements and practices and particularly the Agreement on Agriculture could fundamentally undermine food security and sovereignty in the country;

(f)Further realizing that what appears possible at this moment is a limited statute that will take the first step towards a more comprehensive approach.

(g)Stressing however, that the Right to Food Campaign is committed towards the immediate drafting of a Right to Food Act, 2009 in collaboration with other organisations and networks having expertise in the issue;

The full realization of the 'Right to Food' to all Indians is in the process. The first step is the promulgation of the Food Entitlement Act, 2009 by the Government of India in 2009.

Statement of Objects and Reasons:

The Supreme Court of India in Chameli Singh Vs State of UP (1996) 2 SCC 549 has held that the fundamental right to life under article 21 of the Constitution necessarily incorporates the right to food. In PUCL vs. Union of India and others (Writ Petition Civil 196 of 2001), the Supreme Court has further held that the state's obligations in this regard include ensuring "that the poor and the destitute and the weaker sections of the society do not suffer from hunger and starvation". It is therefore imperative to create and enforce legal entitlements and obligations to ensure that every person is assured physical, economic and social access to adequate food with dignity as is necessary to lead an active and healthy life. It is also imperative that no man, woman or child sleeps hungry or is malnourished.

As the **Food Entitlements Act, 2009** is in Draft stage and needs the Parliament approval, the details could be available only when it becomes a Statutory Law. However, it would see light within a short period. Because India is the second most populous country in the world and houses nearly 430 millions of hungry people, it would be the most costly budgetary burden on the government. This endeavour could save people from hunger and starvation but it would also encourage corruption through subsidy and infuse idleness among the vulnerable. The country would face: stagnation in agricultural production, budget deficits, inflation and increase in public borrowings including foreign debt. Indian democracy suffers from political corruption, false promises, and black money. Politics has become a profession, an industry for generation of quick money and a platform for image building through press and media.

This Food Entitlements Act 2009 advocates to ensure dignified economic and social access to adequate food and other requirements of good nutrition for all residents of the country, at all times, in pursuance of their fundamental right to be free from hunger, malnutrition and other deprivations associated with the lack of food.

Food Entitlements Act, 2009

(Draft, 12th September 2009)

WHEREAS the Right to Food envisages a food security and sovereignty system in accordance with Article 39 of the Constitution of India where the ownership and control of the material resources of the community are so distributed as best to sub serve the common good and everyone has a right to an adequate mean of livelihood;

AND WHEREAS, Article 21 of the Constitution of India guarantees a fundamental right to life and personal liberty and includes the right to food,

AND WHEREAS, Article 39 (a) of the Constitution of India obliges the State to direct its policy towards ensuring that the citizens, men and women, equally, have the right to an adequate means of livelihood;

RECALLING that Article 47 mandates that the state shall regard the raising of the level of nutrition and the standard of living of its people as among its primary duties,

AND WHEREAS, Article 25 of the Universal Declaration of Human Rights (1949) recognizes the right of everyone to adequate food;

AND WHEREAS, Article 11 of the International Covenant on Economic, Social and Cultural Rights (1966) and the General Comment 12 of the Committee on Economic, Social and Cultural Rights further elaborate the responsibilities of all State Parties to recognize the right of everyone to be free from hunger;

AND WHEREAS further responsibilities in this regard, particularly with reference to children and women, derive from the Convention of the Rights of the Child (Articles 27.1 and 27.3) and the Convention on the Elimination of All Forms of Discrimination against Women (Article 12);

RECALLING that in 1996, at the World Food Summit, Government of India affirmed "the right of everyone to have access to safe and nutritious food, consistent with the right to adequate food and the fundamental right of everyone to be free from hunger";

The draft includes: availability and access to food, elimination of destitution and vulnerability, urban destitution, starvation deaths, emergencies, and disaster situations, children's right to food, infant and young child feeding, school health service, public distribution system, Fisher's rights, pension-based social assistance, maternity entitlements, micronutrient supplements and Nutrition education etc. There are 8 chapters and 35 sub-heads in the draft. The Chapter II deals with 'Availability of and access to Food and Access to Food'. This is as follows:

Availability of and Access to Food

(a) All persons have a fundamental right to be free from hunger and to have access to safe and adequate food.

(b) It is the duty of the state to encourage food production through sustainable and equitable means and ensure adequate food availability at affordable prices in all locations at all times.

(c) It shall be the duty of the state to support and expand local and indigenous food production in the country and prevent the forcible diversion and acquisition of agricultural lands, water and forests for non-agricultural purposes.

(d) It shall be the duty of the State to protect the existing livelihood rights, and the traditional and indigenous knowledge systems of local communities (including but not restricted to, fishers, artisans and forest dwellers), particularly with respect to intrusive commercial and corporate interests.

(e) It shall be the duty of the state to support and assist farming communities so that indigenous agricultural production may thrive in the country. The state shall promote food sovereignty and place community centered and pro-people processes at the heart of its food production and distribution programs in order to ensure food security for all.

(f) The state shall develop and implement a policy to progressively reduce the use of chemical pesticides and chemicals in agriculture, and to move towards the expansion of organic agriculture.

(g) The state shall adopt policies to impose incentives for the production of coarse food grains.

(h) The state shall immediately introduce a moratorium on the import, production and use of genetically modified organisms in food.

(i) It shall be the obligation of the state to in a timely fashion declare the minimum support price two months prior to the sowing season and to procure adequate quantities of agricultural produce from the farmer community at such minimum support prices as will ensure a living wage for farmers and agricultural labourers. In so doing the state will give adequate attention to decentralized procurement of millets, coarse grain, bajra, makki, ragi, jawar, pulses and oil seeds.

(j) The state shall not export staple food grains until malnutrition is overcome in the country.

(k) The state shall not permit the importation of food save by public institutions on a temporary basis in a situation of grave emergency and shall maintain the right to impose quantitative restrictions on food.

(l) The state shall not permit any agreement or arrangement international or otherwise to displace or adversely affect farming communities in India. In particular no Free Trade Agreement shall be entered into by the state if the agreement will have the effect of allowing trans-national's to capture seed, agro-chemicals, food and agricultural markets or weakens the goal of national self sufficiency in food security or increases vulnerability to volatility of global prices and volumes of trade, rising costs of farm inputs, threatens bio-diversity and resilience of local farming systems or threatens nutritious and healthy food.

(m) The state shall take urgent steps to eliminate speculation, hoarding and future commodity trading and excess profiteering in trade in food.

(n) The state shall introduce substantial incentives for the conversion of lands to food production.

(o) Under no circumstances shall the state introduce food coupons or cash transfers in the food programs.

(p) Contract farming and other existing measures that promote agri-businesses to the detriment of the small and medium farmers shall be phased out.

(q) It shall be the duty of the state to protect the rights of the farmers to freely grow exchange and preserve traditional varieties of seeds without any impediment legal or otherwise and to prevent the patenting of seeds.

(r) The state shall prevent bio piracy and stealing of traditional knowledge having particular regard to the attempts to patent basmati rice and neem.

(s) It shall be the duty of the state to reverse the decline in state credit to the agricultural sector and particularly to ensure that small and medium farmers get increased amounts of credit at favourable rates together with subsidized technological and other inputs so as to ensure the long term viability of the food producing agricultural sector in the country.[63]

---

[63] Note: - Chapter 2 is still being debated, especially sections on food production systems and trade.

Food Security Bill 2011

800 million people in India are likely to get legal entitlement to subsidized food grain by April 1, 2011 under the proposed Food Security Bill, which is aimed at tackling hunger and malnutrition. It would cover 90 per cent people in rural areas and 50 per cent in urban areas for subsidized food grain under the Bill. The Bill is likely to come in Parliament during 2011.

The "priority household", comprising most poor 46 per cent households in rural areas and 28 per cent in urban areas, would get 35 kg food grain per month at the rate of 3 INR (Indian rupees) per kg for rice, 2 INR per kg for wheat and 1 INR per kg for millets. The "general households", which would have 44 per cent in rural and 22 per cent in urban areas, are likely to get a monthly entitlement of 20 kg food grain at a price not exceeding 50 per cent of the current minimum support price for wheat, rice and millets.

This categorization appears to be the compromise formula as NAC had earlier favored 35 kg food grain per household while Planning Commission was insisting that legal guarantee should be just for 20 kg subsidized food grain in view of uncertainty over procurement.

Under the Bill, food security would be provided in two phases. In the first phase, 85 per cent rural and 40 per cent urban population would be provided subsided food grain from next financial year while in the final phase, 90 per cent of rural and 50 per cent of urban population would be covered by March 31, 2014. This means 75 percent of people would be covered.

For providing food security to this vast population, 57.36 million tons food grain would be required in the first phase of which 49.36 million tons would be distributed under PDS while 8 million tons would be distributed under ICDS, mid-day meal and other schemes. The food grain requirement would increase to 63.59 million tons. The Planning Commission's 2004-05 poverty estimates would be used for identifying beneficiaries. If the cabinet accepts NAC recommendations, the food subsidy burden for the Government is likely to increase from the present 560 billion INR to 710 billion INR by next year, which means an increase of 150 billion. This would be further raised by 232 billion INR by March 31, 2014. Legal entitlements for children and maternal nutrition, including for pre-school children, Pregnant and nursing mothers, maternity benefits and mid day meals for school children, would be made. Community kitchen and programs for feeding destitute and vulnerable groups would also be incorporated in the Bill.

To avoid pilferage of food grain under PDS, NAC has suggested introducing smart cards And biometrics so that while people could get subsidized food grain the Government would send the differential amount directly into the account of PDS dealer so that he has no incentive to sell food grain in black market.[64]

A Bill to feed 800 Million People

The National Food Security Bill, drafted by Congress President Sonia Gandhi's National Advisory Council (NAC) and cleared by the Union Cabinet despite misgivings expressed by no less than Prime Minister Manmohan Singh himself, was introduced in Parliament in 2011 and, in all likelihood, would have become law. But experts and even officials within the Food ministry remain divided over its consequences.

---

[64]Annapurna Jha, 'Soon, subsidized grain for 90 percent of Rural India' The Sunday Pioneer, Bhubaneswar, October 24, 2010

As always, the devil is in the details. The fine print in the draft legislation, say many, gives enough cause for alarm, both for the central food and finance ministries as well as for the state governments. Government officials apprehensive about the Bill said that implementing it could lead to a food grains price rise worldwide and, what's worse, hit the Indian middle and upper middle class.

Total food grain production (rice and wheat) in 2011-12 is expected to be about 187.52 million tonnes, of which the government is expected to procure 61.41 million tonnes. Indeed, that figure matches the amount of grain that the government will need to send through the extremely porous Public Distribution System (PDS) and ensure that all of it reaches the intended beneficiaries — 60 per cent of India's population, or about 720million people. Meanwhile, this year, the government allowed export of 30 million tonnes of rice and 20 million tonnes of wheat. So, going by figures for 2011-12, 111 million tonnes of food grain will be taken up between exports and the implementation of the food security law. In effect then, some 77 million tonnes of grain will be available for the other nearly 500 million middle and upper middle class people.

Those figures imply that open market grain prices will go up for the latter group, while the grain allowances under the food security bill will only partly fill the stomachs of the hungry poor.

Food minister K.V. Thomas estimates that the food grain subsidy burden will go up from the current 650 billion INR (I billion= 1000 million) to about 950 billion INR (INR=Indian rupees). New expenses will also be incurred on additional storage as the current capacity of 63 million tonnes would be scaled up to 92 million tonnes in the next three years. Add to this over 1.1 trillion INR in agricultural investments needed to ensure the sustainability of the food bill. In all, Finance minister Pranab Mukherjee will be left with a bill of over 3 trillion INR for schemes run by two ministries alone, Food and Rural Development. That's enough to burst the government's already ballooning fiscal deficit.

A number of states, especially Tamil Nadu, Bihar and West Bengal have severely criticized the NFS Bill. The states are concerned that the Bill seeks to cover only 162.7 million families under Priority (7 kg of food grain per person per month at Rs 3 a kg rice, Rs 2 a kg wheat and Rs 1 a kg millet) and General Households (3 kg per person per month at 50 per cent of the government's minimum support price, or around Rs 7 a kg this year), while they have issued more than 240 million ration cards under BPL and APL categories. That will mean that Tamil Nadu, for instance, will need to spend an additional 18 billion INR (Rs 1,800 crore) for those poor that the food bill will leave uncovered. Such expenses will hit the states' financial health.

While the NFS Bill seeks to cover at least 46 per cent of the population under Priority and 28 per cent under General Households, the Bill is silent on how it will identify those eligible under these groups. The Centre will apparently take data from the ongoing Socio-Economic and Caste Survey, with a pre-determined poverty cap decided by the Planning Commission, to decide who the beneficiaries should be. The states protest that by their reckoning there are more poor people than what the Centre decides based on Planning Commission criteria.

A number of chief ministers, such as Uttar Pradesh's Mayawati, have alleged that the populist Bill is being pushed by Congress with an eye on the forthcoming elections in the states. But NAC member N.C. Saxena has answers to these concerns:

(a) The food bill is essential because India is the only country that has failed to reduce the absolute number of poor despite high economic growth in the last two decades.
(b) If the government is concerned that it could result in lower grain availability and higher prices for the middle class, it should simply stop exporting food grain.
(c) If the government is worried about its fiscal health, Mr. Saxena says, just tax high-earners more — specifically impose a surcharge on income tax paid by those earning over 1 million INR (Indian rupees) a year — to fund the food bill.

Critics such as Kirit Parikh, chairman of the Delhi think-tank Integrated Research and Action for Development and a former member of the Planning Commission, have, however, more fundamental concerns. Parikh criticizes the food bill, not for its intent but for its method of reaching out to the poor. He prefers to give 600 billion INR in direct cash transfers to every poor household, covering some 70 per cent of the population, rather than trying to push millions of tonnes of grain through an unprepared, inefficient and corrupt system and burdening the Food Corporation of India and the PDS to the point of collapse in what could ultimately prove to be a futile attempt to feed the poor. Underestimating the dangers of the current food bill, Parikh has warned, could result in a grave 'grain drain'.[65]

Who is poor? Who is hungry?

Indian policymakers have for long been unable to define who is 'poor'. In the absence of an uncontested poverty scale, India takes the World Bank definition (currently, $1.25 a day earning) or a

---

[65]Manish Anand (2011), "A Bill to feed 800 million people", Deccan Chronicle, Sunday, December 25, 2011

variety of domestically-produced numbers to define who should or should not benefit from a particular welfare scheme.

The N.C. Saxena report said 50 per cent of Indians live below poverty line. The Arjun Sengupta report said 77 per cent of Indians do not earn enough to eat. The government of India accepted the Tendulkar report, which said 35 per cent Indians are BPL families.

The debate over how large a section of the population must be covered under the Food Security Bill is an unsettled one. Several members of the NAC, which drafted the Bill, have said they would prefer universal coverage, meaning the whole population, but the Cabinet-approved draft says 75 per cent of rural poor and 50 per cent of urban poor will be covered.

The Plan: The Bill envisages providing 7 kg of food grains per person in BPL (Priority) households and 3 kg per person in APL (General) households a month, against the current entitlement of 35 kg per household, at Rs 3 a kilo of rice and Rs 2 a kilo of wheat. The WHO prescribes a norm of at least 11 kg per person per month.

The Criticism: The Bill is a "more dangerous and rehashed version" of the current Targeted Public Distribution System, that proved to be an "utter failure" in view of the manner in which it eroded the food security of the majority of the poor, the dalits (un-privileged Scheduled caste), the tribal people and women, by excluding them from its ambit.

The Bill proposes to provide wheat at 2 INR and rice at 3 INR per kg at a time when several State governments have on their own accord increased the number of households entitled to BPL status and was providing them with food grains at 1 or 2 INR per kg.

Facts:

(a) Expected Grain Yield: 187.52 million tonnes
(b) Grain required to implement food security bill: 61 million tonnes
(c) Total expected coverage: 60 per cent of population
(d) Estimated cost: 270 billion of Indian Rupees (INR). But estimates as high as 3 trillion of INR is expected including infrastructure spending
(e) Scheme for Below Poverty Line (BPL) families: 3 INR per kilo of Rice, 2 INR per kilo of wheat and 1 INR per kilo of coarse grain
(f) The World Bank reports that 41.6 per cent of Indians live on Below $1.25 per day
(g) Planning Commission estimates that per day rural spending is 26 Indian rupees (INR) for BPL families.

Homestead Gardens for food security

On my recent visit to Kochi, Mr. Suman Sahai looked out of his hotel window and saw that adjoining the hotel boundary was a modest house with a yard, the way traditional houses in villages have and small towns used to have till the real estate mania began to destroy the ecology and beauty of such spaces.

His observation was as follows: My neighbours in the middle of Kochi city were obviously a traditional family with sound values. Their yard had one jackfruit tree in the corner, near the boundary wall, two breadfruit trees (breadfruits are similar to jackfruits although the trees look very different), three areca nut palms with pepper vines climbing up their trunks, two coconut palms, one guava tree, one drumstick tree, two hibiscus bushes, the flowers of which are used to make chutney, a couple of yam bushes and about 10 dwarf banana plants. There was chilly and tomato planted in the space between the trees and one or two other plants I could not identify. The total area of the yard would have been about 300 square yards.

I was thrilled to see this working model of what was a sophisticated homestead garden which obviously gave the family food (including condiments and spices) and incomes (areca nut, surplus banana) throughout the year. Breadfruit is a prolific bearer and yields fruits over several months. It is eaten as a vegetable in much the same way as jackfruit but also as a staple like yam. Tubers continue to be a staple in Kerala cuisine and one can spot tempos (no hand carts here, this is Kerala!) parked in the city selling a variety of tubers.

Such gardens, they may be of differing complexities, are one of the key strategies for household food security as well as nutritional enhancement. Some or the other food comes to the household all year round to supplement the standard rice-based diets that come either from the farmer's field or from the market. Kochi is the constituency of minister of state for agriculture K.V. Thomas, who is aggressively promoting the Food Security Bill, which is high profile priority legislation since it is backed by Congress president Sonia Gandhi.

The bill has been widely criticized for its superficial approach to food security, merely rehashing the existing public distribution system and Integrated Child Development Services programs. Not surprisingly, it has been termed a political gimmick by some. Mr. Thomas could have brought in excellent initiatives, like the homestead garden from his home state to enrich the Food Security Bill, introducing elements of dietary diversity and self-reliance in a bill that has received adverse comments for its "dole" approach. The homestead garden described here is something Mr. Thomas must know about.

The composition of a homestead garden will obviously vary from location to location, depending on what grows in the area and what the food preferences of the local people are. In many parts of north India, for instance, such a homestead garden could contain drumstick, the pods and leaves of which are highly nutritious and available all year round, bananas, papaya, lemon, sweet potato and other tubers, pumpkins, which are rich in Vitamin A, some legumes like cowpea, beans and green gram, perhaps a mulberry tree and one of jackfruit. Availability of space and food preferences will determine what is planted in the garden but whatever is in it will enrich the family's food basket and improve its nutritional intake. The great advantage of homestead gardens is that the food comes directly to the woman of the house since it is she who would normally tend such gardens. This food is likely to be used optimally in her kitchen to the benefit of the entire family.

Another excellent initiative promoted by the horticulture department of the state government in Kerala is the Terrace Garden program, locally known as the Harita Nagari (Green City) program. In this program, largely undertaken by housewives, the government encourages cultivation of vegetables in pots using terraces, verandahs and other spaces available in flats and housing in densely populated urban centers where there are no yards or spaces around the dwelling area. The horticulture department provides (and does this without making you run around 20 times) seed, fertilizer, pots and even implements to start the terrace or verandah garden. This is backed up by information how to get the best results from such potted gardens.

The result of this initiative, which is wildly popular, is a steady supply of some or the other vegetable for the cooking pot year round. The vegetables are clean, often organic and easily available on demand. The lady of the house cooks whatever happens to be available in her pots that day. The nutrition of the family is ensured as is its dietary diversity. When there is a surplus, the housewife can sell this to outlets established by the horticulture department. During festivals, like Onam when there is a big demand for vegetables, a not insignificant supply of vegetables is contributed from within the city by such terrace gardens. Everyone is a winner, the supply of fresh vegetables in the city is augmented and the housewife makes a little profit.

This interesting enterprise can be replicated across the country in dense urban and semi-urban centres. Not every state is blessed with Kerala's balmy weather which is supportive of easy cultivation year round but state specific packages can be worked to accommodate local weather conditions. Here is another idea Mr. Thomas should carry from his constituency into the Food Security Bill.[66]

To the hungry, God is bread

The National Food Security Bill, 2011, designed to make access to food a legal right, is the last chance to convert Gandhiji's vision of a hunger-free India into reality.

What Mahatma Gandhi said of the role of food in a human being's life in a 1946 speech at Noakhali, now in Bangladesh, remains the most powerful expression of the importance of making access to food a basic human right. Gandhiji also wanted that the pathway to ending hunger should involve opportunities for everyone to earn their daily bread, since the process of ending hunger should not lead to the erosion of human dignity.

---

[66]Suman Sahai (2012), " Homestead gardens for food security", Deccan Chronicle , April 02, 2012

Unfortunately, this message was forgotten after Independence, and government departments started referring to those being provided any form of social support as "beneficiaries." The "beneficiary" tag is also being applied to the women and men who toil for eight hours under the Mahatma Gandhi National Rural Employment Guarantee Scheme (MGNREGS).

Sixty-five years after Gandhiji's Noakhali speech, India is still a home to the largest number of under-nourished and malnourished children, women and men as compared to any country. The number of people going to bed partially hungry in 2013 is more than the entire population of India of 1947.

Recent articles by P. Sainath in The Hindu (September 26 and 27, 2011) brought out vividly the extent of deprivation and destitution prevalent in rural India. Rural deprivation and agrarian distress lead to the growth of urban slums and suffering. The Planning Commission's submission before the Supreme Court on the amount of money needed per day per person in urban and rural India to meet needs in the areas of nutrition, education and health care (Rs.35 a day in urban India, and Rs.26 in rural India) showed how divorced this important body has become from real life.

At least there is a ray of hope in the draft National Food Security Bill, 2011 put on the website of the Ministry of Consumer Affairs, Food and Public Distribution, now under the charge of the humanist, Professor K.V. Thomas. This draft will go through a Select Committee of Parliament. I hope that the final version — designed to make access to food a legal right rather than remaining a token of political patronage — will help erase India's image as the land of the malnourished.

The stated aim of the draft Bill is "to provide for food and nutritional security, in human life cycle approach, by ensuring access to adequate quantity of quality food at affordable prices, for people to live a life with dignity." To realize this, we must ensure that every child, woman and man has physical, economic and social (in gender terms) access to a balanced diet (that is, the needed calories and protein), micronutrients (iron, iodine, zinc, Vitamin A, Vitamin B12 and so on), as well as clean drinking water, sanitation and primary health care.

A life cycle approach to food security will imply attention to the nutritional needs of a human being from conception to cremation. The most vulnerable but neglected segment is the first 1,000 days in a child's life — the period from conception to the age of two, when much of the brain development takes place.

Obviously the child during this period can be reached only through the mother. Therefore, the life cycle approach to food security starts with pregnant women. The high incidence of children with low birth weight (less than 2.5 kg) is the result of maternal and foetal under-nutrition. Such children suffer from handicaps in later life, including impaired cognitive ability. Denying a child even at birth an opportunity for the full expression of its innate genetic potential for physical and mental development is the cruelest form of inequity. The Integrated Child Development Services (ICDS) will have to be redesigned and implemented in two time frames (0-2 and three to six years).

From the legal rights viewpoint, the draft Bill addresses the issue of economic access to food. The other two components of food security — namely, availability of food, which is a function of production, and absorption of food in the body, which is a function of clean drinking water, sanitation and primary health care — cannot easily be made legal entitlements. To make food-for-all a legal right, it is necessary to adopt a Universal Public Distribution System (PDS) with common but differentiated entitlements with reference to the cost and quantity of food grain. The draft Bill adopts the nomenclature suggested by the National Advisory Council (NAC) and divides the population into priority, that is, those who need adequate social support, and general, that is, those who can afford to pay a higher price for food grain. The initial prices proposed are Rs.3, 2 and 1 a kg for rice, wheat and millet respectively for the priority group, and 50 per cent of the Minimum Support Price (MSP) for the general group. In a Universal PDS system, both self-selection and well-defined exclusion criteria operated by elected local bodies will help eliminate those who are not in need of social support for their daily bread. In fact, it is the general group that should support financially the provision of highly subsidized food to the economically and socially underprivileged sections. In the case of the well-to-do, the aim of Universal PDS should be to ensure physical access to food.

The widening of the food basket by including a range of nutri-cereals (normally referred to as "coarse cereals"), along with wheat and rice is an important feature of the Food Security Bill. Nutri-cereals such as bajra, ragi, jowar, maize, constitute "health foods," and their inclusion in the PDS, along with wheat and rice, will encourage their production by farmers. Nutri-cereals are usually cultivated in rain-fed areas and are more climate-resilient. Hence, in an era of climate change, they will play an increasingly important role in human nutrition security. During 2010-11, India's farmers produced 86 million tonnes of wheat, 95 million tonnes of rice and 42 million tonnes of nutri-cereals. The production of nutri-cereals, grown in dry farming areas, will go up if procurement and consumption go up. Thus, the addition of these food grains will help strengthen food grain availability and nutrition security.

The other components of the Bill that do not involve legal commitments refer to agricultural production, procurement and safe storage of grain, clean drinking water and sanitation. The temptation to provide cash instead of grain to the 'priority' group should be avoided. Currency notes can be printed, but grain can be produced only by farmers, who constitute nearly two-thirds of India's population. Giving cash will reduce interest in procurement and safe storage. This in turn will affect production. The "crop holiday" declared by farmers in East Godavari district of Andhra Pradesh is a wake-up call.

A committee set up by the Government of Andhra Pradesh and chaired by Dr. Mohan Kanda, pointed to the following factors behind the decision of a large number of farm families not to grow rice during this kharif season. First, the MSP on offer does not cover the cost of production; the MSP fixed by the Government of India was Rs.1, 080 a quintal for common varieties, while the cost of production was Rs.1, 270. Second, procurement is sluggish since it is largely being done by rice mills. Third, the late release of canal water, non-availability of credit and other essential inputs, and delayed settlement of crop insurance dues, are affecting the morale and level of interest of farm families. Thus, farmers are facing serious economic, ecological and farm management difficulties. The government should consider adopting as a general policy the formula suggested by the National Commission on Farmers (NCF), that MSP should be C2 plus 50 per cent (total cost of production plus 50 per cent).

Finally, the Bill provides for the creation of Food Security Commissions at the State and Central levels. The two essential ingredients of implementing the legal right to food are political will and farmers' skill. Hence, State-level Food Security Commissions should be chaired by farmers with an outstanding record of successful farming. They will then help ensure adequate food supply to feed the PDS. At the national level, the composition proposed by the NCF in its final report submitted in October 2006 will help ensure adequate political will and oversight. The suggestion was to set up a National Food Security and Sovereignty Board at the Central level, with the Prime Minister chairing it. The other members could be the Union Ministers concerned, political party leaders in Parliament, a few Chief Ministers of grain-surplus and grain-deficit States, and leading farmers and experts.

Unless we develop and introduce methods to ensure effective political and farmer participation in implementing the Food Security Bill, we will not be able to overcome the problems faced by the PDS in some places arising from corruption in the distribution of entitlements.

The National Food Security Bill, 2011, provides the last chance to launch a frontal attack on poverty-induced hunger and to realize Mahatma Gandhi's desire that the God of Bread should be present in every home and hut in India. We should not miss this opportunity.[67]

Food roulette

As the debate over the Food Security Bill sharpens the focus on securing essential food grains for India's poor at affordable prices, it makes sense to look at what has been happening elsewhere in the globe. After the sub-prime fiasco, the next act in the drama of glee and greed was the global food crisis, a result of the reckless speculation of global investors led by Wall Street's casino bankers. To make their billions it mattered little to them if their machinations brought a billion people to the brink of starvation.

---

[67]Swaminathan, MS (2011), "To the hungry, God is bread", the Hindu, October 1, 2011

Commodities–futures- trading is just gambling aimed at booking profits between sell and buy orders and has little to do with the commodities being sold and bought. It could be petroleum crude or soybean oil, it didn't matter. Just as collateralized debt obligations (CDOs) combined all kinds of debts, in the case of food-based derivatives too complex multi-commodity indices were created. Even institutional investors like pension funds and banks started investing in these commodity index funds. This speculative investment had devastating effects. At least 30 countries around the world saw food riots and Haiti was a poignant example. Arab Spring's origins too go back to the food riots in Tunisia. Before we get to the food crisis of 2008 and the volatile and precarious world food price situation through 2010 and 2011, we need to look at some previous acts in this play of avarice.

Traditionally, in the developed world, in the wake of the last big depression in the 1930s, a limited amount of hedging or risk mitigation was permitted under a regulatory umbrella. This was because agriculture faced so many vagaries that spot prices, when the farmers' produce reached the market, were always riddled with uncertainties. Thus future price agreements, which involved millers or traders or food processors and farmers, were entered into and risks were shared, resulting in some stability. This was confined to actors from the food sector.

However, in 1999, following aggressive lobbying by investment bankers, serious deregulation took place in the US Commodities Futures Trading Commission that opened the flood gates of speculative investments involving food and agricultural products. In 2000 the burst of the dotcom bubble brought several stocks crashing and investment bankers led their herds to the housing market till eventually that bubble burst, too. With avenues drying up, greedy hedge fund managers and Wall Street analysts turned to food and commodities. No longer satisfied with reasonable returns, the game was now to chase windfalls. So you had futures contracts that were bought and sold several times speculatively with little intention of taking delivery of the end agricultural products themselves. Studies indicate in the case of transactions that involved food/agricultural derivatives, only two per cent pertained to actual delivery whilst the rest were speculative. Food prices went upwards. An UNCTAD study points out that between 2005 and 2008, world maize prices tripled, wheat prices went up by 127 per cent and rice prices by 170 per cent.

In our globalised and liberalized world, everybody got caught in the chilling aftermath of this drama — people in the developed countries who spend 13-15 per cent of their income on food, and people in the poorer parts of the world who spend anywhere from 50 to 70 per cent of their income on food. Some have argued that food prices have been going up on account of other reasons, such as global warming, drought, diversion of land to bio-fuels, increased consumption in populous countries where income levels have been rising etc.

Fredrick Kaufman, who wrote the article The Food Bubble: How Wall Street Starved Millions and Got Away With It in Harper's, points out that price of hard red spring wheat that had been stable for a hundred years in America, trading between $3 and $6 per 60 pound bushel, suddenly started to rise. And on February 25, 2008, it rose to a ridiculous high of $25 per bushel. This is ironic, given that 2008 saw record wheat productions. Clearly, unbridled speculation was the cause here. For all the controversy surrounding bio-fuels, they currently account for only six per cent of the total grain production.

And finally, coming to the story that food prices could be going up because Indians and Chinese were eating more because of a growing middle-class. A July 2011 report of the Food and Agriculture Organization of the UN, titled "Price Volatility and Food Security," sets the record straight. Olivier de Schutter, the UN special rapporteur on the right to food, cites FAO data and points to the fact that India and China are seeing falling per capita food grain consumption. Thus, there is a clear case for reining in this mindless speculation.

A number of recommendations have come from concerned quarters across the globe. Knowledge imbalance has to be corrected first. Some of these derivatives and transactions are so complex that regulatory bodies and law makers need to acquire the required expertise, only then can they regulate effectively. Currently, most of the knowledge resides with the financial business sector.

There is an urgent need to regulate over-the-counter trading (OTCs) which are bilateral agreements on derivatives executed, sold and transacted upon, away from the purview of established exchanges. That makes monitoring OTCs difficult. The need to have transparent information is essential as these will establish price visibility of essential food items. International co-operation on harmonizing regulations is a must; otherwise speculators would flock to countries with lax regulations.

Even the setting up of an international fund has been recommended, that can intervene to stabilize prices of essential food items, along with national level buffer stocks.

Instead of focalizing agriculture it needs to get localized, with farmers incentivized to produce for local populations.

As India's planners continue to mull over allowing a larger presence for global giants in the retail sector, regulators need to do their homework first. Contracts involving food supply designed for facilitating supply should not end up in a speculative spiral. Further, as India negotiates more Free Trade Agreements (FTAs), which invariably involve liberalizing the financial sector, these considerations assume special significance. Speculation in food and rising food prices is the last thing we should have to contend with, given our realities and inequalities.[68]

The Hunger Games

Hunger and malnutrition are man-made. They are hardwired in the design of the industrial, chemical model of agriculture. But just as hunger is created by design, healthy and nutritious food for all can also be designed, through food democracy.

We are repeatedly told that we will starve without chemical fertilizers. However, chemical fertilizers, which are essentially poison, undermine food security by destroying the fertility of soil by killing the biodiversity of soil organisms, friendly insects that control pests and pollinators like bees and butterflies necessary for plant reproduction and food production.

Industrial production has led to a severe ecological and social crisis. To ensure the supply of healthy food, we must move towards agro-ecological and sustainable systems of food production that work with nature and not against her. That is what movements that promote biodiversity conservation, like our NGO Navdanya, are designing on the ground.

Industrialization of agriculture creates hunger and malnutrition, and yet further industrialization of food systems are offered as solution to the crisis. In the Indian context, agriculture, food and nutrition are seen independent of each other, even though what food is grown and how it is grown determines its

---

68 A Rangarajan (2012), " Food roulette", The Asian Age, April 01, 2012

nutritional value. It also determines distribution patterns and entitlements. If we grow millets and pulses, we will have more nutrition per capita. If we grow food by using chemicals, we are growing monocultures — this means that we will have less nutrition per acre, per capita. If we grow food ecologically, with internal inputs, more food will stay with the farming households and there will be less malnutrition among rural children.

Our agriculture policy focuses on increasing yields of individual crops and not on the output of the food system and its nutritional value. The food security system — based on the public distribution system — does not address issues of nutrition and quality of food, and nutritional programs are divorced from both agriculture and food security.

The agrarian crisis, the food crisis and the nutrition and health crisis are intimately connected. They need to be addressed together. The objective of agriculture policy cannot be based on promoting industrial processing of food. The chemical application of agriculture and food are recipes for "de-nitrification". They cannot solve the problem of hunger and malnutrition. The solution to malnutrition begins with the soil.

Industrial agriculture, sold as the Green Revolution and the second Green Revolution to Third World countries, is chemical-intensive, capital-intensive and fossil fuel-intensive. It must, by its very structure, push farmers into debt and indebted farmers off the land. In poor countries, farmers trapped in debt for buying costly chemicals and non-renewable seeds, sell the food they grow to pay back debt. That is why hunger today is a rural phenomenon. Wherever chemicals and commercial seeds have spread, farmers are in debt. They lose entitlement to their own produce and hence get trapped in poverty and hunger.

Industrial chemical agriculture also creates hunger by displacing and destroying the biodiversity, which provides nutrition. The Green Revolution displaced pulses, an important source of proteins, as well as oilseeds, thus reducing nutrition per acre. Monocultures do not produce more food and nutrition. They take up more chemicals and fossil fuels, and hence are profitable for agrochemical companies and oil companies. They produce higher yields of individual commodities but a lower output of food and nutrition.

Industrial chemical agriculture's measures of productivity focus on labour as the major input while externalizing many energy and resource inputs. This biased productivity pushes farmers off the land and replaces them with chemicals and machines, which in turn contribute to greenhouse gases and climate change. Further, industrial agriculture focuses on producing a single crop that can be globally traded as a commodity. The focus on "yield" of individual commodities creates what I call a "monoculture of the mind". The promotion of so-called high-yield crops leads to the destruction of biodiversity.

Bio-diverse systems have higher output than monocultures that is why organic farming is more beneficial for farmers and the earth than chemical farming. Industrial chemical agriculture also causes hunger and malnutrition by robbing crops of nutrients. Industrially produced food is nutritionally empty but loaded with chemicals and toxins. Nutrition in food comes from the nutrients in the soil. Industrial agriculture, based on the NPK mentality of synthetic nitrogen, phosphorous and potassium-based fertilizers, lead to depletion of vital micro-nutrients and trace elements such as magnesium, zinc, calcium, iron.

The increase in yields does not translate into more nutrition. In fact, it is leading to malnutrition. To get the required amount of nutrition people need to eat much more food. The most effective and low-cost strategy for addressing hunger and malnutrition is through bio-diverse organic farming. It enriches the soil and nutrient-rich soils give us nutrient-rich food.

Earthworm castings, which can amount to four to 36 tons per acre per year, contain five times more nitrogen, seven times more phosphorus, three times more exchangeable magnesium, 11 times more potash and one-and-a-half times more calcium than soil. Their work on the soil promotes the microbial activity essential to the fertility of most soils. Soils rich in micro organisms and earthworms are soils rich in nutrients. Their products, too, are rich in nutrients. On an average, organic food has been found to have 21 per cent more iron, 14 per cent more phosphorous, 78 per cent more chromium, 390 per cent more selenium, 63 per cent more calcium, 70 per cent more boron, 138 per cent more magnesium, 27 per cent more vitamin C and 10-50 per cent more vitamin E and beta-carotene. And the more biodiversity on our farms, the more is the nutrition per acre, at little cost.

Plants, people and the soil are part of one food web, which is the web of life. The test of good farming is how well it works to increase the health and resilience of the food web.[69]

Rights to Seeds

Genetically engineered seeds and crops (GMOs) have unleashed seed wars and knowledge wars.

The only reason crops have been genetically engineered is to take patents on seeds and collect royalties. If during colonialism the concept of Terra Nullius (empty land or land belonging to no one)

---

[69]Vandana Shiva (2012), "The Hunger Games", Deccan Chronicle, August 15, 2012

allowed the takeover of land and territories by the colonizer, a new concept of Bio Nullius (empty life) is being used to claim "intellectual property rights" on seeds, biodiversity and life forms. But life is not empty.

Seeds are not an invention. They embody millions of years of biological evolution and thousands of years of cultural evolution and farmers' breeding.

When corporations claim patents, they basically "pirate" traits that nature and farmers have evolved. They pirate and patent the aroma of Basmati, the low gluten qualities of our native wheat, the salt tolerant, and drought tolerant, flood tolerant traits of climate resilience our farmers have bred. This is not innovation and invention; it is bio-piracy.

The only traits that the corporations have introduced into plants through genetic engineering are the toxic traits of Bt. toxin and herbicide resistance. Besides being toxic, these traits have not reduced chemical use as has been repeatedly claimed. Navdanya's studies in Vidarbha show a 13-fold increase in pesticide use since Bt. cotton was introduced.

A report published in the journal Environmental Sciences Europe shows that genetically engineered crops have led to a 404 million-pound increase in overall pesticide use from the time they were introduced in 1996 through 2011. This amounts to an increase of about seven per cent over the last 16 years. The data on increased chemical use shows that the claim — that Bt. toxin crops will reduce pesticide use and herbicide resistant crops will reduce herbicide use — is false.

The Navdanya report, The GMO Emperor has no Clothes, shows that genetically modified crops have led to resistance, both in weeds and pests, demanding higher use of pesticides and herbicides.

More than two dozen weed species are now resistant to glyco-phosphate — the primary ingredient in Monsanto's broad-spectrum herbicide Roundup and farmers are being asked to spray Agent Orange, which was used in the Vietnam War.

The only way corporations can push GMO seeds on farmers is by destroying alternatives. They do this by blocking public breeding. India's premier cotton research institute in Nagpur has not released a single variety in Vidarbha since Monsanto entered the cotton seed market.

The second strategy is to lock local companies into licensing arrangements. Sixty Indian seed companies only sell Monsanto's Bt. cotton.

The third strategy is to make local seeds illegal through compulsory licensing and registration laws. This was attempted in 2004 with the Seed Act. It took a seed satyagraha organized by us across the country and a parliamentary committee to prevent it from coming into force.

But in Europe, seed laws are already criminalizing biodiversity and farmers' breeding. This is why we have joined together as a Global Citizens Alliance for Seed Freedom to call for no patents on seeds and no to seed laws that promote industrial seeds and make local, open pollinated varieties illegal.

The Global Citizens' Report on Seed Freedom (www.seedfreedom.in) written jointly by more than 120 groups and individuals was released on October 1, 2012 in New Delhi.

Need is the first link in the food chain. And seed wars are leading to food wars. The California ballot initiative on labeling of GMO foods is the most current contest between citizens' right to know and choose and corporate rights to force feed GMOs.

Seed wars and food wars are becoming knowledge wars. Just before the California initiative, an article was planted in the media across the world arguing that organic foods have no health benefit. It turns out that the so-called scientists from Stanford had done similar work for Big Tobacco during the debate on smoking.

While fraud science is used to promote GMOs, independent public scientists — who do high-quality research on bio-safety and health and environmental impact of GMOs — are attacked by an organized mafia working for the industry that often masquerades as scientists.

Dr. Arpad Putzai of the UK was driven out of his job when the results of his study commissioned by the UK government showed that the brains of the rats in his feeding study had shrunk, the pancreas had expanded and the immunity had collapsed. More recently, a study published by Dr. Seralini in the journal Food and Chemical Toxicology showed:

(a) Death rates in rats fed the Roundup-Ready GM maize were 2-5 times that of the control group.
(b) Female rats had a shockingly high incidence of mammary tumours.
(c) Male rats suffered significant levels of liver and kidney damage.
(d) Tumours were huge and many animals had three tumours by the time they died.

India's Supreme Court set up a Technical Expert Committee to advise it on the gaps in the scientific bio-safety assessment of GMOs. The committee recommended a moratorium on field trials of all GMO Bt. crops, an assessment of the special problems of herbicide-tolerant crops and a ban on all trials of GMO crops, of which India is the centre of diversity.

The Supreme Court is supposed to ensure that the executive and the government functions constitutionally. The GMO lobby has written to the Prime Minister to try and undo the work of the Supreme Court and its technical committee. This is a subversion of our Constitution.

In August 2012, the parliamentary standing committee on agriculture tabled a report titled Cultivation of Genetically Modified Food Crops: Prospects and Effects. Releasing the report at a press conference, the chairperson of the committee, Basudeb Acharia said:

The committee has come to the conclusion that since concerns on the potential and actual impacts of GM crops to our food, farming, health and environment are valid, GM crops are just not the right solution for our country.

Again the GMO lobby wrote to the Prime Minister to undo the recommendations of the parliamentary committee. Since GMOs can only spread via seed monopolies and by destroying our democracy and integrity of science and knowledge, we are better off without them.[70]

Starved of ideas

Expanding the leaky public distribution system won't deliver food security

Perhaps the most powerful argument used by the proponents of the so-called Food Security Bill to further expand the highly inefficient, corrupt and leaky public distribution system (PDS) is adult hunger and malnutrition. Serious flaws exist, however, in both the diagnosis and prescription the proponents offer.

---

[70]Vandana Shiva (2012), "Rights to Seeds", Deccan chronicle, October 29, 2012

Civil society groups and international organizations such as the World Health Organization, Food and Agricultural Organization and World Bank contend that one-fifth or more Indians suffer from hunger and many more from malnutrition. But this contention is principally based on the steadily declining trend in calorie consumption in India during the last two decades. The trend has been observed among all classes of consumers whether rich or poor, rural or urban.

But when asked in the nationwide expenditure surveys whether they have had enough to eat throughout the year, the responses of Indians have shown exactly the opposite trend. Those replying in the negative to the question were 17.3 percent in 1983 but fell to 5.2 percent in 1993-94, 3.6 percent in 1999-2000 and just 2.5 percent in 2004-05.

Some, who reject these numbers as implausible, argue that the household heads answering the question in the survey are too proud to admit hunger in their families. Quite apart from the fact that the same household heads have rarely let their pride come in the way when applying for below-poverty-line or BPL cards and associated benefits, this argument cannot explain the declining proportion of households reporting hunger. Surely, households in the 1980s could not have been any less proud than those in the 2000s!

Several factors have been at work to reduce the need for calorie consumption and hence decline in it among all income classes. In the rural areas, farming has been getting progressively mechanized. Fewer and fewer people rely on long walks or bicycles and more and more on motorbikes and buses to get from one point to another. The proportion of population engaged in farming has been declining as well. With more and more children in school, midday meals are providing calories that do not get counted in the household expenditure data from which the above-mentioned calorie consumption trend is derived.

Similar factors have been at work in urban areas. Improved means of transportation, both private and public, have reduced the need for more physically challenging modes of transportation. Heavy machinery has reduced the need for physical labour in activities such as construction. Workers have increasingly shifted to desk jobs.

Finally, better absorption of calories due to improved epidemiological environment and access to healthcare has reduced the need for actual calorie consumption. Increased access to piped water combined with water purification systems in urban households and proliferation of hand pumps and tube wells in the rural areas have greatly improved the access to safe drinking water. In turn, this has helped reduce the incidence of diarrhoea, a common cause of poor absorption of food. Greater availability of medicines has further helped calorie absorption.

The height and weight trends and improvements in vital statistics further contradict the inference that the decline in calorie consumption represents increased malnourishment. The National Nutrition Monitoring Bureau surveys reveal that the proportion of those having below normal Body Mass Index fell from 56 to 33 percent for men and from 52 to 36 percent for women between 1975-79 and 2004-05. Data also show both men and women steadily gaining in height. Vital statistics such as life expectancy, death rates, infant, child and maternal mortality rates have steadily improved.

For these reasons, the focus on the decline in calorie consumption when the real problem may be a lack of balanced diet that goes well beyond cereal consumption is misguided. But even accepting increased calorie consumption as the goal, an expanded PDS is not the answer. If individuals are choosing to consume less food grains despite rising incomes, making food grain available in larger quantity at lower prices will not change the outcome. Households will pick their share of subsidized grain and simply sell the portion not consumed for a higher price on the market.

Recent work by economist Nisha Malhotra on child malnutrition in India shows that informing mothers on proper feeding practices rather than just access to food is what helps improve child nutrition. The same prescription is bound to apply to adult nutrition that requires a balanced diet.

This evidence and analysis notwithstanding, the proponents of the Food Security Bill insist that universalizing the PDS will ensure that the poor receive more food grain, consume it and become better nourished.

While I have already questioned the second and third links in the argument, the available evidence brings into question even the first link. In a recent article, economist Peter Svedberg makes the point thus: "The evidence in support of universality as an efficient method for eliminating, or even notably reducing, exclusion errors is not altogether convincing. Before 1997, the PDS was in principle universal, but large proportions of poor households were either effectively excluded or purchased very small amounts of subsidized grains."[71]

It is disappointing that having decided to move to cash transfers while also facing severe pressure to cut fiscal deficit, the cabinet has cleared an entirely flawed Bill in the name of food security. Genuine

---

[71] Arvind Panagariya (2012), "Starved of ideas: Expanding the leaky public distribution system won't deliver food security", The Times of India, October 19, 2012

reform requires a shift to cash transfers, public-information campaigns on balanced diet and reforms in agriculture and food safety and health instead. Massive food distribution is neither the comparative advantage of the government nor promises to raise calorie consumption, let alone promote a balanced diet.

Dream or nightmare?

National Food Security Bill

AFTER much waffling and hand-wringing by the ruling dispensation, its pet project the National Food Security Bill got approved of the Lower House late on August 26 with the Congress president, Sonia Gandhi having made an impassioned pitch, posing "the question is not how and whether we can do it, we have to do it". Lest the monsoon session not be another washout, the landmark legislation was taken up in a single day for debate and discussion to be eventually passed before the day was past. But what a flutter ensued in the bourses the next day with manic sell-off of shares and panic reaction in the external value of the rupee which plunged to its nadir touching a new intra-day low at Rs 66.30 against the US dollar.

While other political parties do not want to be seen opposing the so-called poor-friendly strategy of food security, the far-flung repercussions of this bill of fiscal largesse when the economy is in a slowdown mode are too glaring to be gainsaid. Already, a majority of the people in the country are being pummeled by a triple whammy. Income of the legions working in the unorganised and agricultural sectors is inert, but their cost of living is increasing. Even the small and medium enterprises and self-employed can only access credit by paying punitive interest rates. Without being overly concerned over what could be done about falling income, rising prices and the unaffordable cost of credit, the UPA government in its last lap of governance has given the Indian economy the luxury of rights-based entitlements ranging from information, employment, education to the Forest Rights Act for tribals and by putting irremovable impediments on the wheels of industry and big projects and mining operations by rendering land acquisition a Sisyphean task.

It is nobody's case that the welfare State is an anachronism when the hidden hands of markets determine the value of everything. This has been demonstrated even in the capitalist citadel ~ the USA ~ where the Obama Administration found it expedient to bail out investment banks on the pretext that they were too big to fail and rationalised the cost of healthcare system by attacking head-on the excrescence and excesses of health insurance companies. But welfare measures and doles exact a cost and to make them affordable, the smooth growth of the economy is a pre-requisite. In the absence of heady or even normal growth, or when the economy is cruising at a slow speed, enlarging the kitty of doles by rhetorically asking the authorities to find resources come what may only betrays a mindset that is not grounded in reality or modernity.

It is small wonder the country's central bank just a few days ahead of the passage of the National Food Security Bill in the Lok Sabha rightly cautioned in its Annual Report that while its impact on food subsidies is manageable for 2013-14, "in the years to come it will add to fiscal pressures". In fact the key concern, the RBI said, is that it is difficult to contain food subsidies within the budgeted amount even in 2013-14 when the Act will just begin to get implemented. Over the next few years, the growing subsidies could circumscribe investment opportunities, including those in the agricultural sector, where both public and private investment in recent years had not been on any scale commensurate with the need to maintain high foodgrains output.

Still, the UPA went ahead in its self-styled role as a saviour of the poor by passing the food security bill. Which entails giving 800 million out of the country's 1.2 billion people access to rice, wheat and coarse grains at least cost, besides committing one-third of aggregate output of home-grown wheat, rice and nutria-millets to fulfill legal entitlements. It makes provision for the right to receive foodgrains at subsidised prices by persons belonging to priority households and general households under the targeted public distribution system (TPDS), nutritional support to pregnant women and lactating mothers. Besides, it covers children as well as special groups such as destitute persons, homeless, emergency and disaster-affected persons and those living in starvation.

The Bill has been criticised across the country by economists, apex industry bodies such as the CII, and public policy analysts. While there is inherently nothing wrong with a plan to eliminate malnutrition that saps the very energy and drive of individuals to be productive agents of the economy, the new plan is ineptly designed and badly targeted so much so that it might escalate the cost of food subsidies at a time when the food, fuel and fertiliser subsidies scarcely show any sign of let-up despite belated bids to prune them. With the rupee sinking, the cost of imported items such as crude oil and potassium is prohibitive, though the contracted quantity has not shown any spurt. The move proposing procurement of 61 million tonnes of foodgrains with rickety storage facilities would only aggravate food inflation, the bugbear of the common man when imported inputs feed into inflation to make it inexorable.

The dependence of the food security system on the faulty public distribution system (PDS) is also questionable, though there is no dearth of sensible proposals such as the issue of food-stamps to the deserving with the unique identification number in place to confirm that the benefits reach the targeted group. But all these measures would only succeed if the delivery mechanism is tamper-proof and the governance issue really gets the much-needed impetus at every level of administration beginning from the top to the last-mile lower official administering such a massive programme.

Interestingly, the country's supreme policy-making body, the Planning Commission, has a different take when it argues in a facile fashion that the issue of food security is perhaps "the easiest to resolve". Noting that over the past decade there has been a decline in net sown area of approximately two million hectares, the Approach to the 12th Five Year Plan (2012-17) said that this is only 0.6 per cent of the total net sown area. It further noted that given that agricultural productivity is currently half of what it is in many other countries, the solution for food productivity lies not in stopping diversion of agricultural land in all circumstances but in increasing food production through higher land productivity. Though this may look simple, a reality check reveals glitches that continue to dog productivity-enhancement programmes despite the ongoing move to mesh technology with extension services in the farm front.

Interestingly the Plan panel said that efforts can and should be made to preclude diversion of highly productive agricultural land, but this cannot be a rigid criterion to be applied in all cases. Thus in the interest of food security, it called for "reasonable restrictions on acquisition of multi-crop irrigated land, without making it impossible, for instance, to acquire land for security purposes or construction of highways or railway lines". So this sort of wishy-washy land management strategy being advocated by the Plan panel to make exceptions would only compound the problem. With the middle-class populace and the affluent rich constituting a microscopic minority and a vast swathe of the population in penury, the government has to revisit its priorities for a balanced growth paradigm. The least it could do is to help modernise the primary sector that still remains mired in the primitive stage, such as fragmentation of holdings and lamentable lack of modern farm practices and no institutional financial support for farmers, other than tokenism like loan-waivers and grain doles! [72]

Conclusion:

In short, India is a vast country with a load of 1.25 billion of people with at least 430 million of people under poverty line. If the government would promulgate 'Food Security Act' with right earnest to make everybody to live with dignity through right food, good health and enjoy human rights; the country has to solve hunger and malnutrition.

The government should emphasize more on the causes of food insecurity rather than the effects of food insecurity to solve the problems of poverty, hunger and food insecurity to award peace to all.

As 87 percent of rural people in India get less than the minimum calorie requirement of food, the government must try to award more employment and income opportunities to them. All the farmers which committed suicides were living in rural areas. Food security is possible when the farmers stop committing suicides.

It is irony of facts that urban people are staging road shows for price rise of essential commodities such as hike in petrol price, diesel price, bus fare, train fare,

---

[72]Srinivasan, G. (2013), "Dream or nightmare? National Food Security Bill", The Statesman, September 01, 2013

corruption, higher salary, promotional facility, regularization of services, and even for rape and murder cases, but no city dwellers have staged strikes for the poor farmers who committed suicides and committing suicides almost regularly.

A rural house-hold earns one sixteenth (1/16th) income of an urban household in India.

Indian population constitutes 70 percent of farmers. But all farmers complain that agriculture is not a profit generating profession.

To our greatest shock, about 230 thousands of farmers have committed suicides within the last 13 years in India.

They have no security in profession and life. The government grabs their land for industrial houses with police forces; offers less procurement prices for cereals like wheat and rice; delays in procurement programs; engages the millers in procurement with delayed payments; offers no insurance facility to all farmers and peasants.

The Government of India should compare the Base Year 1961 or 1971 and with that of 2011 in relation to salary of government employees / salary structure, gold price, and wholesale prices of rice and wheat. The government can realize that farmers have been deprived off their rights. As a result, they opt either for to leave the profession or commit suicides or neglect agriculture.

Food security is possible if the farmers get profit in agriculture. Therefore, we suggest that Minimum Support Prices of cereals should be fixed in comparison with rise of consumers' Price Index; pay scale of government employees; and gold prices.

India faces the problems of Maoism, Naxalites, and Terrorism; it is perhaps because most of them are poor, hungry and could not get employment.

We feel that these anti-establishment activities can be lessened or put into dormancy if the government or licensed traders procures paddy and wheat from the rural India in raw form and distribute 25 percent of the procured stock (printed with government emblem in the new gunny bags) in the same village or neighboring village free of cost to the real needy and hungry people. These quantities of food stock would incur no transportation cost, no storage cost, no milling cost, no distribution costs or no storage loss. This practice would definitely pave the way for a hunger-free society and the country would be free of Naxalites and Terrorists. We feel that Food Security can make the country an ideal country and a peaceful country.

A number of schemes for poverty eradication programs are being operated by the central government, state government and foreign governments through non-government organizations in India.

But the number of hungry people in India in 2013 has surpassed the total population of India of 1947, the year of independence.

These organizations simply siphoned off 'funds earmarked for the poor' to their personal accounts. These programs should be immediately closed for all time to come.

Free gifts in kind for the poor never reach the poor by the government agencies or NGOs. It is simply misplaced or wasted.

Food security should aim at availability of total requirement of cereals in the country and

farmers should produce more than the country needs. It is possible when the farmers feel that agriculture is a profitable enterprise.

Let thousands of traders be involved in the free flow of rice and wheat in the country which have been denied through state legislation as per Essential Commodities Act, 1956.There should not be inter-state or intra-state barriers for movement of rice or wheat. Rice and wheat should be decontrolled. But the government would declare minimum support prices before 1stOctober each year.

All the inhabitants in the country including the farmers should be offered insurance coverage and there should be Pensioner's benefit for all senior citizens in the country for a living.

The Government of India should make Food Laws for the benefits of country men; implement the laws and evaluate its efficacy in the field.

Food Security is possible by:

(a) Declaring higher procurement price for paddy, rice and wheat by the government to award justice to the farmers;

(b) Free flow of cereals anywhere in India by suspending the movement control orders for paddy, rice and wheat. It would be available throughout the country from Kolkata to Kashmir to Kanyakumari through traders.

(c) Farmers should take up horticulture, fishery, poultry, and goat rearing etc for the market.

The Food Corporation of India needs to be squeezed to support to the hungry victims for four months during natural hazards or wars. More procurement leads to pilferage, wastage, and corruption, and recycling, shortage of storage space, black marketing and financial loss of FCI.

The Food Corporation of India should be authorized to procure and store to the extent of 10 million quintals of food grains in a year. The procured stocks must be utilized or sold before the arrival of new crop.

The State agencies may act as traders or millers or stockiest and sell to the consumers without any loss to the government. The loss-bearing agencies should be closed.

This practice would decrease wastage of food grains during transit, storage and rotting of food grains in open space. The rotten cereals or pulses cause health hazards of school children. The wasted PDS rice is sold as cattle feeds in India. It amounts to loss of billions of Indian rupees. It is estimated that food wastage value in India is as much as 440 billion of INR per year. (1 billion = 1000 million)

The Public Distribution System, Fair Price Shops, and Free mid-day meals should be closed as these are creating problems rather than solving the problems. Free meals, free bi-cycles, free mobiles or free blankets would make the people beggars and corrupt. Political parties offer free commodities on political grounds rather than economic consideration.

The Public Distribution System of food grains and its availability @ 2 INR / Kg has caused shortage of agricultural workers in the rural areas. This has caused squeezing of the area under rice or wheat cultivation. The total yield has come down extremely. It acts as political propaganda.

The government may allow state supply corporations, cooperatives, NGOs, unemployed youths, or traders or dealers to deal in cereals without any financial involvement to the government.

All markets should be barred to collect market fees from the dealers or consumers of paddy, rice or wheat. A minimum of four millions of rural youths could be engaged in marketing of rice or wheat or agricultural commodities and earn their livelihoods.

Food security is a welfare measure for the hungry people. Pension to all senior citizens, and widows would award food security to all families.

Procurement of Rice with husk (paddy) and wheat in the villages and distribution of these stocks in the same village would assure food security for women headed families and unemployed youths.

Storage of food grains could minimize the storage loss in the country. Quality of paddy deteriorates, when farmers stag hundreds of paddy bags on the road because paddy is not procured by the FCI or state agencies on the same day. They must be paid their dues immediately by cheques. Wheat procurement suffers for the negligence of the procurement agencies.

Government of India should undertake sector-wise analyses on food, cash crops, livestock, fisheries, horticulture, and social forestry to study the policy impact on the farmers of the country by professional economists.

All corporations, government departments in developing countries assigned for the welfare of farmers are infected with corruption; hence these organizations should be cleansed by the Central Bureau of Investigation before the Food Security Act is passed by the Parliament.

+++++

Chapter V

COMMITTEE REPORTS ON FOOD SECURITY

Persistent poverty and oppression can lead to helplessness and despair. When governments fail to meet the most basic needs of these people, these failed States can become havens of terror. - Mr. George W. Bush,
Former U.S. President: Speech delivered at the Inter-American Development Bank in 2002.

The world is facing a sharp increase of population in all counties. The US Census Bureau International Data Base has reported that it has crossed a population load of 7 billion in 2011. The natural increase of population is 76, 229, 701 per year; 6, 352,475 per month; 206, 848 per day and 8, 702 per hour. It is predicted that world population would be 9.54 billion by 2050. So food security would be the greatest problem in future and we have to face the emerging challenges by increasing the output in agriculture, horticulture, and animal resources. Food security is the first step to award WORLD PEACE. All countries, world organizations, and research institutes should take proper step for this noble cause.

Why do the rich people try sincerely to control and punish the poor? A starved family accepts all conditionality just for survival. Why the rich countries and the World Bank fail always to uplift the poor people and poor countries? Perhaps the economic theories propounded by rich countries act negatively in poor countries. It may be a fact that these developed countries are again trying to rule the poor countries with economics as weapons such as massive debt, massive interests, high defense purchase and high corruption in the deals. The funding institutions are controlling the governments of all most all low-income countries through money deals. Democracy has failed because people are hungry. So food security could be the best device to protect and enrich democracy. But the tactic policies adopted by western power could again prove dangerous to the starving people. The answer is to empower the poor and hungry people.

Let the peasants of all developing countries own and cultivate their own land; grow crops as per their choices and be engaged in a profitable agriculture. The governments should provide only the market facilities for their produce. The price of agricultural commodities must be indexed and should be weighed with comparative advantages against income of government employees and gold prices. It is a fact that the governments always try to reduce the sale price of rice and wheat because it could prove their ability and efficiency in administration; and the governments take up some populist measures such as construction of village roads or culverts to mobilize the people who are hungry. The politicians know the technique to capture the village head, which would be utilized in praising all actions of the government.

This state policy has landed them in a fear psychosis and it has landed them in poverty zone. The fate of all peasants is limited, as they do not have the capacity to speak their thoughts or problems to the leaders or officers.

These attitudes of the governments and funding institutions would force most of the peasants to commit suicides in future. In India, two hundred thousands of farmers have committed suicides during the last 13 years.

They do not need subsidies because all subsidies of the governments enrich the politicians, government employees and the business houses. It creates black markets and high corruption. Subsidy is more political rather than economic. But agriculture has become a loss bearing enterprise. Why the farmers would be awarded subsidies in seeds, fertilizers and pump sets? Why they would borrow bank credit with less interest rate? Why they are treated as poor people? Simply, allow them to be rich and lead safer life with prestige and live in peace.

Farmers simply need to avail human rights and right prices for their saleable commodities.

Land tillers of the developing countries regard 'land' as their mother, God and permanent Bank Account, which would be transferred to their children after death. It is a security for him and his family members for generations. The government should not take away land from the peasants as land is attached to them for generations. He gets maximum satisfaction when he says others that this land is mine.

Anuradha Mittal says that agricultural system has failed in all low-income countries. As we know, it's totally upside down and backwards. And instead of fixing it, we are now sending it overseas, creating these large-scale corporate plantations, all in the name of development and improving food security in poor countries. But instead we are importing a failed model, and that is causing great threats to food security internationally.

Since 2008, over a billion people, one-sixth of total population is going hungry. And a majority of them are small-scale farmers. And instead of improving their livelihoods, the governments of developing countries are snatching their right to seeds, rights to water and right to land in name of development process. The government is assisting the industrialists to snatch away their rights on land, water and seeds. The industrialists of all countries have the capacity to mobilize the governments of all developing countries with bribe. They snatch away land from the peasants, which are poor and food insecure and hungry.

Even investors, such as Goldman Sachs, for instance, and hedge funds and sovereign wealth funds, looking for new soft commodities market to invest in, and they're buying up land instead of ensuring agrarian reform and land reform in poor nations so people have land to grow food for their families and communities.

The crash of the housing market is that investors have looked for new opportunities in the soft commodities market to invest. And with the price increase of food in 2008—it was almost 83 percent increased between 2005 and 2008—they have decided that agriculture is the next hot commodity. So you have hedge funds, you have sovereign wealth funds, which are buying up and leasing land. And we're talking about unbelievable deals. These are, you know, not just a few hundred acres. We're talking about thousands and thousands of hectares being bought up for ninety-nine years, leases, for one dollar per year lease. In some cases, you know, 70 percent of the financing has been provided by the host country. No taxes have to be paid, and nothing has to be paid for the first four years. So if you look at some of the prospectus of these hedge funds, they're promising 15, 20 percent returns, some are promising 30 percent returns, whereas agricultural land in the United States has usually returned of five to six percent.

In the name of promoting food security, we have dumped in third world countries, where majority of the people are employed in agriculture. And when there is hunger in a place like Haiti or in a place elsewhere, say in Africa, it is because the farmers are too poor to buy food. And instead of creating markets, we have dumped subsidized foods. This whole farm bill in the United States, which subsidizes huge, big corporate giants, such as Cargill, they can go sell below the cost of production. They can take over markets in poor countries, as was done in Haiti in the case of rice. And when a calamity strikes, instead of building up markets again for the local population, we again send more food aid, destroying the capacity of people to be able to grow for them, destroying the markets for the local farmers, and they become dependent on food aid.

It is a shocking trend that international financial institutions, including the World Bank, Food and Agriculture Organization, are claiming that agricultural land and sale and lease of agricultural land is a development opportunity for third world countries; it's a win-win situation; food insecure countries will have access to land to grow food, whereas cash-strapped countries like Ethiopia, Sudan will have cash. The problem is that it is going to increase inequities that the local benefits and the benefits do not accrue to the local population. And that is why we have been forced to call it a new form of colonization. We have to look at plantations in Latin America that did not bring development to these countries. They created banana republics. And now this trend is spreading across the globe in the name of development, and it needs to be challenged. There are no good case studies of how this foreign direct investment in agriculture can promote development in third world countries. In fact, we have to fight back and ensure land reform is back on the agenda and people have access and control over their land, water and seeds, which is the basis of food security and food sovereignty of any country, any community, and of all peoples.

There is struggle at the grassroots level. The local communities in Orissa are fighting back against the South Korean steel company POSCO, which has been trying to take over forest land, denying communities who depend on the forest products for their livelihoods. We know in Madagascar, it was the grassroots revolt which toppled the government, which was selling off half of the country's arable land to a South Korean company, Daewoo. So, on one hand, we have to support these grassroots struggles, which might not be known internationally, but which are fighting back, because it is a matter of life and death. It is about livelihoods.

The peasants practice agriculture for generations. They need technology and markets. At the same time, we have to challenge institutions such as the World Bank, that are once again coming forward with a paradigm, which is going to promote development, which we know is a completely false model and in fact will create these huge, big plantations with small-holder farmers who will become sharecroppers.[73]

In this chapter, Committee reports on Rome Declaration on World Food Security, Committee on World Food Security, A World Free of Hunger, Declaration from Social movements, NGOs and CSOs – Parallel Forum to the World Food Summit on Food Security, G8 countries Pledge Food Security are discussed.

---

[73] Anuradha Mittal, Democracy Now, the United States

Rome Declaration on World Food Security

13 - 17 November 1996, Rome, Italy

The Heads of State and Government gathered at the World Food Summit at the invitation of the Food and Agriculture Organization of the United Nations to reaffirm the right of everyone to have access to safe and nutritious food. They pledged for to be consistent with the right to adequate food and the fundamental right of everyone, to be free from hunger. They pledged for common and national commitment to achieving food security for all and to an ongoing effort to eradicate hunger in all countries, with an immediate view to reducing the number of undernourished people to half their present level no later than 2015.

They considered it intolerable that more than 800 million people throughout the world, and particularly in developing countries, do not have enough food to meet their basic nutritional needs. This situation is unacceptable. Food supplies have increased substantially, but constraints on access to food and continuing inadequacy of household and national incomes to purchase food, instability of supply and demand, as well as natural and man-made disasters, prevent basic food needs from being fulfilled. The problems of hunger and food insecurity have global dimensions and are likely to persist, and even increase dramatically in some regions, unless urgent, determined and concerted action is taken, given the anticipated increase in the world's population and the stress on natural resources.

They reaffirmed that a peaceful, stable and enabling political, social and economic environment is the essential foundation, which will enable States to give adequate priority to food security and poverty eradication. Democracy, promotion and protection of human rights and fundamental freedoms, including the right to development, and the full and equal participation of men and women are essential for achieving sustainable food security for all.

Poverty is a major cause of food insecurity and sustainable progress in poverty eradication is critical to improve access to food. Conflict, terrorism, corruption and environmental degradation also contribute significantly to food insecurity. Increased food production, including staple food, must be undertaken. This should happen within the framework of sustainable management of natural resources, elimination of unsustainable patterns of consumption and production, particularly in industrialized countries, and early stabilization of the world population. They acknowledged the fundamental contribution to food security by women, particularly in rural areas of developing countries, and the need to ensure equality between men and women. Revitalization of rural areas must also be a priority to enhance social stability and help redress the excessive rate of rural-urban migration confronting many countries.

They emphasized the urgency of taking action now to fulfill their responsibility to achieve food security for present and future generations. Attaining food security is a complex task for which the primary responsibility rests with individual governments. They have to develop an enabling environment and have policies that ensure peace, as well as social, political and economic stability and equity and gender equality. They express deep concern over the persistence of hunger, which, on such a scale, constitutes a threat both to national societies and, through a variety of ways, to the stability of the international community itself. Within the global framework, governments should also cooperate actively with one another and with UNO, financial institutions, intergovernmental and non-governmental organizations, and public and private sectors, on program directed toward the achievement of food security for all.

Food should not be used as an instrument for political and economic pressure. The members reaffirm the importance of international cooperation and solidarity as well as the necessity of refraining from unilateral measures not in accordance with the international law and the Charter of the United Nations and that endangers food security.

They recognize the need to adopt policies conducive to investment in human resource development, research and infrastructure for achieving food security. The members pledged that they must encourage generation of employment and incomes, and promote equitable access to productive and financial resources. They agree that trade is a key element in achieving food security.

They resolved that 'we agree to pursue food trade and overall trade policies that will encourage our producers and consumers to utilize available resources in an economically sound and sustainable manner. We recognize the importance for food security of sustainable agriculture, fisheries, forestry and rural development in low as well as high potential areas. We acknowledge the fundamental role of farmers, fishers, foresters, indigenous people and their communities, and all other people involved in the food sector, and of their organizations, supported by effective research and extension, in attaining food security.' Sustainable development policies will promote full participation and empowerment of people, especially women, an equitable distribution of income, access to health care and education, and opportunities for youth. Particular attention should be given to those who cannot produce or procure enough food for an adequate diet, including those affected by war, civil strife, natural disaster or climate related ecological changes. The members are conscious of the need for urgent action to combat pests, drought, and natural resource degradation including desertification, over-fishing and erosion of biological diversity.

Commitments

Convinced that the multifaceted character of food security necessitates concerted national action, and effective international efforts to supplement and reinforce national action, the following commitments were accepted:

The governments will ensure an enabling political, social, and economic environment designed to create the best conditions for the eradication of poverty and for durable peace, based on full and equal participation of women and men, which is most conducive to achieving sustainable food security for all;

The governments will implement policies aimed at eradicating poverty and inequality and improving physical and economic access by all, at all times, to sufficient, nutritionally adequate and safe food and its effective utilization;

The governments will pursue participatory and sustainable food, agriculture, fisheries, forestry and rural development policies and practices in high and low potential areas, which are essential to adequate and reliable food supplies at the household, regional, national, and global levels, and combat pests, drought and desertification, considering the multifunctional character of agriculture;

The governments will strive to ensure that food, agricultural trade and overall trade policies are conducive to fostering food security for all through a fair and market-oriented world trade system;

The governments will endeavor to prevent and be prepared for natural disasters and man-made emergencies and to meet transitory and emergency food requirements in ways that encourage recovery, rehabilitation, development and a capacity to satisfy future needs;

The governments will promote optimal allocation and use of public and private investments to foster human resources, sustainable food, agriculture, fisheries and forestry systems, and rural development, in high and low potential areas; and

The governments will implement, monitor, and follow-up this Plan of Action at all levels in cooperation with the international community.

Plan of Action

1. The Rome Declaration on World Food Security and the World Food Summit Plan of Action laid the foundations for diverse paths to a common objective - food security, at the individual, household, national, regional and global levels. Food security exists when all people, at all times, have physical and economic access to sufficient, safe and nutritious food to meet their dietary needs and food preferences for an active and healthy life. In this regard, concerted action at all levels is required. Each nation must adopt a strategy consistent with its resources and capacities to achieve its individual goals and, at the same time, cooperate regionally and internationally in order to organize collective solutions to global issues of food security. In a world of increasingly inter-linked institutions, societies and economies, coordinated efforts and shared responsibilities are essential.

2. Poverty eradication is essential to improve access to food. The vast majority of those who are under-nourished either cannot produce or cannot afford to buy enough food. They have inadequate access to

means of production such as land, water, inputs, improved seeds and plants, appropriate technologies and farm credit. In addition, wars, civil strife, natural disasters, climate related ecological changes and environmental degradation have adversely affected millions of people. Although food assistance may be provided to ease their plight, it is not a long- term solution to the underlying causes of food insecurity. It is important to maintain an adequate capacity in the international community to provide food aid, whenever it is required, in response to emergencies. Equitable access to stable food supplies should be ensured.

3. A peaceful and stable environment in every country is a fundamental condition for the attainment of sustainable food security. Governments are responsible for creating an enabling environment for private and group initiatives to devote their skills, efforts and resources, and in particular investment, towards the common goal of food for all. This should be undertaken with the cooperation and participation of all members of society. Farmers, fishers and foresters and other food producers and providers, have critical roles in achieving food security, and their full involvement and engagement are crucial for success.

4. Poverty, hunger and malnutrition are some of the principal causes of accelerated migration from rural to urban areas in developing countries. The largest population shift of all times is now under way. Unless these problems are addressed in an appropriate and timely fashion, the political, economic and social stability of many countries and regions may well be seriously affected, perhaps even compromising world peace. It is necessary to target those people and areas suffering most from hunger and malnutrition and identify causes and take remedial action to improve the situation. A more complete, user-friendly source of information at all levels would enable this.

5. Availability of enough food for all can be attained. The 5.8 billion people in the world today (1996) have, on average, 15 percent more food per person than the global population of 4 billion people had 20 years ago. Yet, further large increases in world food production, through the sustainable management of natural resources, are required to feed a growing population, and achieve improved diets. Increased production, including traditional crops and their products, in efficient combination with food imports, reserves, and international trade can strengthen food security and address regional disparities. Food aid is one of the many instruments, which can help to promote food security. Long term investment in research and in cataloguing and conserving genetic resources, particularly at the national level, is essential. The link between sufficient food supplies and household food security must be ensured.

6. Harmful seasonal and inter-annual instability of food supplies can be reduced. Progress should include targeting on minimizing the vulnerability to, and impact of, climate fluctuations and pests and diseases. Timely transfers of supplies to deficit areas and the conservation and sustainable use of bio-diversity, early warning systems of climate, transfer and utilization of appropriate agricultural, fishery and forestry technologies, production, and reliable trade, storage and financial mechanisms can usher prosperity in agriculture. Natural and man-made disasters can often be anticipated or even prevented, and response must be timely and effective to assist recovery.

7. Unless national governments and the international community address the multifaceted causes underlying food insecurity, the number of hungry and malnourished people will remain very high in developing countries, particularly in Africa, south of the Sahara; and sustainable food security will not be achieved. This situation is unacceptable. This Plan of

Action envisages an ongoing effort to eradicate hunger in all countries, with an immediate view to reducing the number of undernourished people to half their present level no later than 2015, and a mid-term review to ascertain whether it is possible to achieve this target by 2010.

8. The resources required for investment will be generated mostly from domestic private and public sources. The international community has a key role to play in supporting the adoption of appropriate national policies and, where necessary and appropriate, in providing technical and financial assistance to assist developing countries and transitional countries in fostering food security.

9. The multi-dimensional nature of the follow-up to the World Food Summit includes actions at the national, intergovernmental and inter-agency levels. The international community, and the UN system, including FAO, as well as other agencies and bodies have important contributions to the implementation of the World Food Summit Plan of Action. The FAO Committee on World Food Security will have responsibility to monitor the implementation of the Plan of Action.

10. Reaching sustainable world food security is part and parcel of achieving the social, economic, environmental and human development objectives agreed upon in recent international conferences. The World Food Summit Plan of Action builds on consensus reached in these summits and is based on the conviction that although the world is faced with major food insecurity, solutions to these problems exist. If all parties at local, national, regional and international levels make determined and sustained efforts, then the overall goal of food for all, at all times, will be achieved.

11. The Plan of Action of the World Food Summit is in conformity with the purposes and principles of the UN Charter and international law and strives to consolidate the results of other UN conferences since 1990 on subjects having a bearing on food security.

12. The implementation of the recommendations contained in this Plan of Action is the sovereign right and responsibility of each State through national laws and the formulation of strategies, policies, programs, and development priorities. It should be in conformity with all human rights and fundamental freedoms, including the right to development, and the significance of and the full respect for various religious and ethical values, cultural backgrounds and philosophical convictions of individuals. They and their communities should contribute to the full enjoyment by all of their human rights in order to achieve the objective of food security for all.[74]

Committee on World Food Security

The Food and Agriculture Organization of United Nations Organization constituted a committee to study the number of under-nourished people in the world. The Committee on World Food Security (CFS) studied the prevalence and depth of undernourishment, classification of countries on the basis of food deprivation, economic performance and the health and nutrition performances.[75]

Responding to recommendations expressed by the Committee on World Food Security (CFS) at its 25th session, the document presents latest estimates of the number of undernourished persons and related

---

[74]World Food Summit, Rome Declaration on World Food Security), 13 – 17 November 1996, Rome Italy

[75] Assessment of the World Food Security Situation, Committee on World Food Security, Twenty- sixth Session, Rome, 18-21 September 2000

information about the food, health and nutrition situation worldwide. This is followed by a brief review of the current situation as regards access to food and food availability at global and national level. Finally progress in developing a set of core indicators and indices that can be used to monitor trends for both outcome and vulnerability factors are summarized.

In this context, overall economic performance as measured by GDP per caput is used to capture developments on the access side. As regards food availability, the current supply and demand situation for the main food commodities is to be assessed. Moreover, changes in selected market-based food security indicators; information on the prevalence of food emergencies, changes in food aid flows and current situation with regard to cereal import bill of developing countries are to be summarized.

Latest estimates of undernourishment indicate that 792 million people in the developing world and 34 million in the developed world remain undernourished in 1996-98. The total of 826 million undernourished people in the world represents no change from last year's estimate and at the regional level. This suggests that the trend in the decline in undernourishment observed in the first half of the nineties at an average of 8 million reductions each year, were interrupted in 1998. The probable explanation for this is severe economic and climatic conditions that affected large areas in the developing world (financial crisis, *el Nino*) in that year. According to these latest projections, the number of undernourished in the developing world could fall to around 580 million by 2015. However, the Summit target of no more than 400 million persons undernourished would only be reached towards 2030.

New projections reflect mainly the continuation of long-term declines in the prevalence of undernourishment in Asia that began in 1969-71 in East Asia and in 1979-81 in South Asia. India and

China, two most populous countries in the world are slowing down of population growth and strong growth of GDP would bring about significant increases in food availability per person between 1995-97 and 2015. The weighted average of the proportion of the undernourished for these two countries combined is projected to decline from 17 percent in 1995-97 to 7 percent in 2015.

In sub-Saharan Africa, prospects are not so favorable. Most of the world's poorest countries, where prevalence of undernourishment is high and opportunities for economic squeezed growthare found in this region, particularly in the central, southern and eastern parts of the continent. While prevalence of undernourishment is projected to decline from 33 percent in 1995-97 to 22 percent in 2015, the high rate of population growth means that the actual number of undernourished persons could increase slightly between now and 2015. Some very poor countries in East Asia, the Caribbean and the Near East exhibit similar characteristics and also have poor prospects for halving the number of undernourished by 2015.

It has to be taken into account that the minimum energy requirement represents only the amount needed to sustain life and undertake light physical activity. Therefore, the measure yields a conservative estimate of the dietary energy deficit of the undernourished. According to the calculations, average deficits of the undernourished lie within the range of 130 to 490 kcal per person per day, with figures varying considerably across countries of different regions and sub-regions.

For a first evaluation of the results obtained, the **151 countries** observed have been grouped according to the following classification:

(a) Low depth of undernourishment: average dietary energy deficit per person < 200 kcal/day was found in 68 countries.
(b) Moderate depth of undernourishment: average dietary energy deficit per person between 200 and 300 kcal/day was found in 60 countries.
(c) High depth of undernourishment: average dietary energy deficit per person > 300 kcal /day was found in 23 countries.

In order to give a more equal weight to both the prevalence and the depth of undernourishment in monitoring progress toward the Summit goals, a method for classifying countries according to the degree of food deprivation has been developed. To do this, three prevalence classes have been established, low (percentage of the undernourished < 5 percent), moderate (percentage of the undernourished between 5 and 20 percent) and high (percentage of the undernourished >20 percent). Then, in a second step, these have been combined with the three classes of depth of undernourishment mentioned above, and a matrix has been developed showing the number of countries for each of the nine possible combinations of prevalence and depth of undernourishment.

Country-by-country information about health and nutrition status presents:

(a) Three indicators of nutritional status i.e. percentage of children under five years old who were wasted, stunted or underweight at the time of the most recent survey, and
(b) Three indicators of health status i.e. life expectancy at birth, mortality rate for children under five and percentage of the population with access to adequate sanitation.

The occurrence of high levels of all these indicators together obviously indicates severe health and nutritional problems, and conversely, when all indicators are low, the situation is much more benign.

Among the approximately 80 countries that have been examined, nine achieved excellent scores for all indicators, while 16 scored very badly on all six of them. These 16 countries also suffered from moderately high or very high prevalence of undernourishment.

In general, it is expected that nutritional status of children would be associated with food intake, health status and sanitary conditions of the population as a whole. Although this association is quite common, there are some instances where high percentages of children are underweight even where prevalence of undernourishment is low or access to sanitary facilities is very high. This confirms that nutritional status is determined by a combination of many different factors. Improved understanding of the interplay among these factors requires more systematic data collection and more sophisticated analysis. Developing these tools represents a high priority challenge for all food deficit countries.

GNP per capita, although highly imperfect, does provide some indication of the extent to which a country's population will be able to afford the food needed to meet minimum dietary energy requirements for a normal and healthy life. Forecasts of GDP per person for 1999 and 2000 (using market exchange rates) indicate positive economic growth throughout world.

These show that in 2000 highest growth rates can be expected for sub-Saharan Africa, where due to their expanding mining industry. Mozambique, Botswana and Angola will be the best performing countries.

Strong growth rates are expected for North Africa and the Middle East. But it would be slow.

As the Brazilian economy recovered from its financial crisis in 1998 and 1999, regional GDP growth of Latin America and the Caribbean region increases from nil in 1999 to 3.4 percent in 2000. While slightly recovering from the severe financial crisis in 1998, with an average annual GDP growth of 2.7 percent in 2000,

Asia is still far from the growth patterns observed in the early 1990s. Slow progress in economic growth is expected for countries in transition, among which Moldova, Slovakia, Lithuania, Romania, Russia, Czech Republic, Belarus, Croatia and Kazakhstan are belonging to the group of the 20 slowest-growing countries.

Regular monitoring and assessment of global market conditions for basic foods is an integral part of FAO's activities related to providing early warning information on economic variables that have considerable impact on the status of food security at the national, regional and global level. An overview of the current outlook for food staples (cereals, roots and tubers) and other basic foods would guide the FAO to provide early warning information on changing status of food security of vulnerable groups. This needs commodity market analysis at the country level to the assess food security status of vulnerable groups.

Global production of food staples in 2000 is forecast to rise by about 1 percent from the previous year to 2,059 million tons.

World **cereal** output in 2000 is forecast to rise by about 1.3 percent from last year to 1896 million tons (including rice in milled equivalent), about 1 percent above the estimate for 1999. The expected increase is due to an anticipated expansion in coarse grains while wheat output could remain virtually unchanged from the previous season and rice production may decline below the record output in 1999.

Low international prices and changes in national policies are reported as the main causes for the reduction in rice output in 2000. Based on current forecasts, total cereal utilization in 2000/01 would exceed production and cause global cereal stocks to be drawn down for the second consecutive year. Consequently, the overall supply and demand balance for the coming season begins to look somewhat tighter than in the past two seasons and this could eventually result in higher prices. To avoid any further deterioration of the cereal supply and demand balance, a more significant increase in cereal production would be necessary in 2001.

World production of **roots and tubers** in 2000 is forecast at 652 million tons (in fresh roots equivalent) of which 72 percent is produced in developing countries, mainly in the LIFDCs (59 percent).

Potatoes, cassava and sweet potatoes account respectively for 45, 26 and 20 percent of the global production, the remainder being other roots and tubers such as taro, yautia and cocoyams. Only a small proportion of roots and tubers production is traded internationally mainly because most production occurs in developing countries for on-farm use, while the high degree of perishability and bulkiness makes the transportation costs very high. International trade is largely limited to processed cassava (chips and pellets) for feed and for potatoes.

Global production of **oils and fats** has continuously increased over the 1990s, reaching an estimated 114 million tons in the 1999/2000 seasons. All regions, except the group of CIS countries, participated in this increase.

The world's leading producing region is Asia, which in 1999/2000 was estimated to account for almost 40 percent of global production, followed by North and Central America (23 percent), Europe and South America (respectively 15 percent and 13 percent). At 50 million tons, Asia is also the world's leading consumer of oils and fats, followed by North and Central America and Europe. In recent years, consumption growth has been fastest in Asia and North/Central America. With regard to trade, in the last decade, Asia has consolidated its leading position in both the global export and import market for oils and fats. The region's imports have increased by almost 50 percent since the mid-1990s, reaching 23.5 million tons in 1999/2000. The world's second largest importing region is Europe (about 12 million tons), while the other two major exporting regions are North and South America (respectively, 11 and 10 million tons).

The growth in global **meat** production would be constrained to 2 percent in 2000, as low meat prices in 1999 dampen red meat output prospects in major countries. Exports by the United States in the context of lower supplies and higher domestic prices are set to increase only slightly. Likewise, EC exports will be compromised by a reduction in the WTO export ceiling for all meat exports and the prohibition on rolling over unused subsidies as of July 2000.

Global **milk** output is expected to rise by 2 percent during 2000, with production increasing in most countries. Positive growth is forecast for most regions of the world, in particular Oceania, South America and South Asia. Nevertheless, the likely expansion in production of milk among the major exporting countries may not be sufficient to meet the anticipated faster rise in world import demand in 2000. If this were to happen, supplies of some dairy products to the world market, especially skimmed milk powder, could be in short supply. As a result, average prices for 2000 are expected to be higher than the previous year.

The Committee prescribes seven indicators for the food security assessments. These are as follows:

1. Global stocks in relation to the likely level of market demand.

In general, the FAO Secretariat considers that a 17-18 percent ratio of end-of-season cereal stocks to trend utilization for the coming marketing year is the minimum necessary to safeguard world food security. This consists of a 12 percent working stock and a 5-6 percent reserve stock element. World cereal stocks by the close of the seasons ending in 2000 are put at 331 million tons, down 15 million tons, or slightly more than 4 percent below the previous year. All of the anticipated reduction is in stocks of wheat and coarse grains, as rice inventories are expected to increase for the second consecutive year.

Overall, the ratio of global cereal carryovers to trend utilization in 2000/01 is put at 17.4 percent, which is within the 17-18 percent minimum safeguard range. Based on the latest production outlook for 2000, world cereal stocks would have to be reduced further in order to meet the expected global utilization in 2000/01. Therefore, by the end of countries' marketing seasons in 2001, the level of global cereal stocks is forecast to be around 321 million tons, some 10 million tons, or 3 percent, below the already reduced opening level. Stocks of nearly all-major cereals are forecast to be smaller and this possible draw down of cereal stocks could lower the stocks-to-use ratio to 16.6 percent, which is slightly below the minimum safeguard level

2. Ability of the five major grain exporting countries to meet the import demand for wheat and coarse grains.

It is the ratio of the sum of their production, imports and opening stocks to the sum of their domestic utilization plus exports. This ratio for 1999/2000 is estimated at 1.17, down slightly from the previous year but higher than the long-term average of 1.14. Based on the preliminary supply and demand indications for 2000/01, this ratio could decline to 1.16 percent. On the supply side, the total grain production in major exporting countries is forecast to increase in 2000 but their combined opening stocks are lower than in the previous year. On the demand side, both domestic utilization and exports are likely to show an increase over the previous year.

3. Ratio of the volume of closing cereal stocks held by the major exporters of wheat, coarse grain and rice to the total disappearance of these cereals (domestic consumption plus exports).

Based on the latest estimates for 1999/2000, these ratios, except for rice, reflect a slight decline from the previous season. The main factor driving the ratios down in 1999/2000 is lower ending wheat and barley stocks in the EC, following last year's decline in their production. Looking further ahead into 2000/01, a likely increase in coarse grain production in Canada, the EC and the United States could result in a small recovery in the ratio for coarse grains. By contrast, smaller wheat production, especially in Canada and United States, could pull down the overall wheat ratio below the previous year. The ratio for rice is also expected to fall below the previous year's level, as production in China is likely to be smaller.

4. Changes in cereal production among the major cereal importing countries of China, India and the CIS against the trend and the preceding year.

For 1999, this indicator points to a significant improvement over the previous year, rising by 1.32

percent as compared to over 4 percent decline in 1998. For wheat, all the countries included in this category registered an increase in their output. Also for rice, the overall performance was a positive one as China's production was nearly the same as in the previous year while India harvested even bigger crops compared to 1998.

Recovery of coarse grains was confined to CIS but it failed in China and India. In 2000, the overall change is expected to be negative by (-) 1.38 percent from the previous year, although cereal output would rise in India and the CIS. The reason is entirely China, where cereal production would drop in output of about 12 million tonnes in 2000. It should be noted that, except for the CIS, cereal imports by China (mainland) and India have remained relatively small. China would be a net-cereal exporting country and India would import less cereal in future in response to bumper domestic crops.

5. Changes in aggregate cereal production of the Low Income Food Deficit Countries (L I F D C s).

For 1999, total cereal production in this group of countries fell only marginally compared to the previous year. The decline may prove more significant in 2000, with total output falling by about 1.22 percent compared to 1999.

6. **Changes in aggregate cereal production of the L I F D C s, excluding China and India.**

However, because production in China and India could heavily influence the overall effectiveness of this indicator, the sixth indicator measures the changes in aggregate cereal production of the LIFDCs, excluding China and India. In fact, for 1999, total cereal output for this group of countries are up slightly while, for 2000, it is forecast to show a 1.32

percent expansion; this compares to 1.22 percent decline when China and India were included.

7. Comparison of export prices for the major cereals.

Except for rice, international cereal prices continued to trend downward in 1998/99. Further drops in prices were registered for nearly all types of cereals during the 1999/2000 seasons. The main factor behind weak prices in recent years has been the large volume of export supplies, especially among the traditional cereal exporting countries, in view of only a modest growth in commercial trade of cereals (i.e. net of food aid).

Overall, the seven indicators point to a generally positive situation for the cereal importing countries in aggregate terms during the past marketing year. For 1999/2000, cereal supply proved adequate and prices were generally weak. Nevertheless, the outlook for 2000/01 suggests a somewhat tighter situation, with the general supply and demand picture pointing to a further reduction in stocks by the end of seasons in 2001. Currently, more than 100 million people in 26 countries in all regions of the world are drought affected. Although not all of these countries have declared formal food emergencies, the effects of widespread drought on the food security situation of both consumers and producers in affected countries, combined with the relatively low level of global cereal stocks, suggest that the coming year may be more difficult.

Food and agricultural emergencies, caused by civil conflict and natural or man-made disasters, far too often result in food insecurity in one part of the world or another. In 1999, natural disasters have been an important factor contributing to a decline in cereal production in developing countries. As of November 1999, the number of affected persons worldwide was

52 million people. As of end May 2000 thirty-six developing countries faced serious food shortages, primarily due to drought, but also due to civil strife and floods, particularly in Africa. In addition several countries in transition also faced considerable difficulties in ensuring that all segments of their populations were adequately fed. Locations of particular concern include:

(a) **In Africa** (16 countries), Angola, Burundi, Democratic Republic of Congo, Republic of Congo, Eritrea, Ethiopia, Kenya, Liberia, Madagascar, Mozambique, Rwanda, Sierra Leone, Somalia, Sudan, Tanzania and Uganda.
(b) **In Asia** (11 countries), Afghanistan, Armenia, Azerbaijan, East Timor, Georgia, Iraq, Jordan, Korea DPR, Mongolia, Syria, Tajikistan.
(c) **In Latin America** (7 countries), Cuba, El Salvador, Guatemala, Haiti, Honduras, Nicaragua, Venezuela.
(d) **In Europe** (2 countries), Russian Federation, Federal Republic of Yugoslavia.

Factors that reflect the performance of the general economy and the food economy enable the analyst to assess current conditions with respect to food availability and food access. Reasonably good estimates of food availability, expressed as **dietary energy supply per person**, can be obtained from the national food balance sheets that FAO maintains.

Good indicators of food access at national level are harder to come by. For example, in general **GNP per capita** is strongly associated with the proportion undernourished. Due to differences in distributional patterns from one country to another, this association is not a perfect fit. But when combined with an indicator of poverty and its impact on food consumption, such as the **percent of income spent on food**, GNP data can be relevant. Although widely-recognized as an important determinant of food security status for many poor people, indicators that can are/be used to monitor stability of supplies, prices and incomes are not readily available. Use of **an index of production variability** has been recommended as a proxy for stability of supplies and of farm income.

These relationships are also the ones that can be immediately affected by specific food, income, nutrition practice, health, and sanitation interventions. Outcome indicators are the focus of targets of specific summits and conferences. The intermediate outcomes are represented by percent of population undernourished such as food consumption, life expectancy at birth and under-five mortality rate that speak of health status, which affects the biological utilization of food. Finally, information is provided on proportion of children under five that are underweight, stunted or wasted – all good indicators of the ultimate outcome of nutritional status.

The relevance of income, price and health indicators for food access was frequently cited as important causes of vulnerability. The countries are: Benin, Cameroon, Chad, Guatemala, Liberia, Mauritania, Namibia, Nicaragua, Somalia, Tonga, Turkey and Vietnam.

From the perspective of intervention, the causes of most of the nutritional problems affecting population groups in developing countries are generally well known. The problems are more in conducting appropriate information collection to reveal the incidence of a problem with particular groups, organized by household characteristics and location, and determining the priority areas on which available resources should be focused to deal with problems that are of particular importance for specific groups or locations within the country.

Food and Agriculture Organization

FAO's top governing body has cleared the way for setting up a stronger and more effective system of global food security governance.

The conference of FAO's 192 members, which meets every two years, agreed to strengthen the Committee on World Food Security so it can become the foremost inclusive international platform for discussion, coordination and policy convergence in order to eliminate world hunger. The world summit on food security agreed that the Committee on Food Security should be a central component of the global partnership for agriculture, food security and nutrition. The approval by the FAO conference paves the way for the Committee on Food Security reform to become operational. The Committee on Food Security will be more inclusive to include, in addition to all member states of FAO and the United Nations, representatives of international organizations, NGOs, the private sector and civil society.

A high-level international network of experts would support the committee. Countries are encouraged to strengthen the committee's political clout by ensuring their representation at the highest possible level.

Budget: In a separate decision, the conference agreed to increase FAO's regular budget for the 2010-2011 biennium by 7.6 percent to US $1,000.5 million. The budget provides for implementation of a new results-based program of work as well as the immediate plan of action for FAO renewal.[76]

A World Free of Hunger

The Committee on World Food Security held its Thirty-second Session from 30 October to 4

---

[76]FAO Budget, FAO. Org , November 24, 2009

November 2006 at FAO Headquarters in Rome. The Session was attended by delegates from 116 out of 132 Members (Appendix 1) of the Committee, by observers from 6 other Member Nations of FAO, the Holy See, the Sovereign Order of Malta, by representatives from five United Nations Agencies and Programs; and observers from three intergovernmental and 41 international non-governmental organizations.[77]

The participants noted with regret that, ten years after the World Food Summit (WFS), no progress had been made towards the WFS target even though progress has been made towards the Millennium Development Goals (MDG) target. One in six of the developing world's population is chronically hungry. Efforts to reach the WFS target must be stepped up and new approaches will be needed. The lessons learned are:

(a) Political will is essential for hunger reduction;
(b) Agriculture-led growth is critical;
(c) Peace, stability and good governance are essential;
(d) Safety net programs for meeting immediate hunger needs are crucial; and
(e) Development assistance should be better targeted to the needy

The participants in the Multi-Stakeholder Dialogue recommended the following actions:

(a) Focus on hunger hotspots;
(b) Follow a twin-track approach that combines the promotion of broad-based, sustainable agricultural growth and rural development,

[77]Report of the 32nd Session of the Committee on World Food Security, Rome, 30 October – 4 November 2006 Appendix E - Progress and Prospects for Achieving the world food summit – plan of action

with targeted programs to ensure that hungry people who have neither the capacity to produce their own food nor the means to buy it can have access to adequate supplies;

(c) Empower smallholders, especially fisher-folk and women farmers;
(d) Promote pro-poor policies and strategies;
(e) Coordinate and enhance allocation of domestic and international resources to agriculture and rural development;
(f) Resolve conflicts;
(g) Strengthen institutions for promotion of food security;
(h) Protect human rights;
(i) Fight corruption; and
(j) Implement the Monterrey Declaration

On the following points, there were significant differences of opinions:

(a) Enhance productivity of smallholders through transfer of appropriate technology;
(b) Create an environment for private investment; and
(c) Make trade work for the poor

The Multi-stakeholder dialogue also urged all parties to pay special attention to the following and act upon as appropriate:

(a) Promote and support national alliances against hunger and facilitate international networking;
(b) Strengthen the capacity building of small producers;
(c) Promote food sovereignty;
(d) Place farmers at the center of national and international policies and strategies;
(e) Implement the rights of the Indigenous Peoples;
(f) Apply the Voluntary Guidelines on the Right to Food in the context of National Food Security;

(g) Link relief to rehabilitation and development;
(h) Enhance the role of women and their access to productive resources;
(i) Take care of marginal and neglected areas ;
(j) Target vulnerable groups;
(k) Involving NGO/CSO and private sector in monitoring WFS Plan of Action at the national levels;
(l) Reflect the contribution of NGO/CSO and the private sector in the implementation of national food security plans; and
(m) Involve youth in the formulation of the policies and interventions affecting their lives.

Action by FAO is essential in supporting national policies related to these points and in the defense of the role of small farmers and fisher-folk for food security.

Panel on Aid and Investment

The participants expressed great concern about the reduction of global investment in agriculture.
It was stressed that there is the need to:

(a) Boost both aid and investment in agriculture as an essential step to reducing hunger and food insecurity in the world;
(b) Give a central role to the voices of the poor;
(c) Support a more holistic approach to the issue of hunger reduction, viewing hunger in a wider context of the world's struggle against poverty;
(d) Provide strong support for greater coherence, coordination and harmonization of efforts at international level to make aid more effective, including the creation of interagency task forces at country level;
(e) Build new partnership arrangements and strengthen existing ones between governments, the private sector, civil society

organizations and local producer organizations; and

(f) Enhance stakeholder policy dialogue in order to promote good governance (a key to fighting food insecurity), bring about effective pro-poor reforms and create an enabling pro-poor policy environment.

Regarding investment, a number of participants stressed the need for:

(a)Targeting the poor and most vulnerable rural populations who form the bulk of the world's agricultural producers;
(b)Creating and strengthening of agricultural cooperatives and farmers organizations as essential in promoting food sovereignty as a key principle in achieving hunger reduction;
(c)Building capacities in rural areas to absorb investments and to empower smallholder groups/organizations to define their own agenda, to exchange knowledge amongst themselves and to press for their rights and interests in the political arena;
(d)Addressing the food chain, especially in post production activities and linkages to markets and rural infrastructure;
(e)Encouraging the local private sector to invest in rural areas; and
(f)Promoting investments in rural infrastructure and services: Key areas for investment mentioned included: physical rural infrastructure; local markets and market linkages; rural micro-finance services; basic low-cost technologies that are adaptable to the needs of the poor, especially women farmers.

There was also general agreement about the need to:

(a)Intensify efforts to understand poor people's livelihoods (including indigenous people and other minorities), their constraints, needs and priorities, and to make development interventions more people-centered and demand-driven; and

(b)Plan aid initiatives carefully, in order to avoid distorting local markets, and promote country and community level ownership of programs and projects.

Some disappointment was expressed in relation to technical assistance being inadequately responsive to local skills and potentials. Farmers Field Schools were cited as a positive example (to be up-scaled) of how to promote self-reliance, instill ownership and enhance the capacity of poor farmers to make sustainable use of aid and investments. Questions were raised that merit further examination, including a) effective participation of fishers in fisheries policies, and b) the impacts of trade liberalization, bio-fuels and GMOs on poor farmers' livelihoods.

There was convergence on strong support to FAO - both politically and financially – to maintain its important role in:

(a) Identifying best practices and proposing partnerships for the reduction of hunger and food insecurity;
(b) Developing capacities of governments to implement agricultural investments and aid programs;
(c) Facilitating donor coordination and taking the lead in disaster mitigation as well as in meeting key MDG goals on reducing hunger; and
(d) Providing valuable information to poor farmers - drawn on the Organization's knowledge and experience – through initiatives such as Farmer's Field Schools and participatory community projects.

Panel on Agrarian Reform and Rural Development

The participants noted that, twenty-seven years after the World Conference on Agrarian Reform and Rural Development (WCARRD, 1979), Agrarian Reform and sound land policies for rural development are still essential conditions for social cohesion, conflict reduction, food security, poverty eradication, and environmental rehabilitation. They agreed that some of the key current challenges lie in implementation, the need to mobilize resources and political will.

The lessons learned are:

(a) Family farms and rural communities are key actors for sustainable rural development;
(b) Rural producers - including women, pastoralists, Indigenous Peoples, tenants and the landless - need legal certainty about their rights, institutional strengthening and social empowerment;
(c) Reforms promoting equity, rule of law and good governance in land administration are essential;
(d) Equitable land rights for rural women need to be strengthened and legally secure; and
(e) The rights of specific groups, such as Indigenous Peoples, deserve special attention and equitable treatment.

The participants in the panel and many speakers stressed the need to:

(a) Promote dialogue at all levels, instead of confrontation, with a greater awareness of the different and complementary roles of States, Civil Society, and the private sector;
(b) Consider the diversity of situations, and the necessity to design context specific solutions in part through disaggregated information on gender and vulnerable groups;

(c) Learn from experiences, through knowledge sharing, research and dissemination of good practices;
(d) Address water scarcity and the linkages between access to water and access to land;
(e) Empower smallholders, particularly women farmers, fisher-folk, pastoralists and Indigenous Peoples;
(f) Promote diversified approaches, including legal support to common property regimes and not only individual titling;
(g) Consider that agrarian reform and land rights are defined through national legislations, and that country ownership of land policies is important; and
(h) Consider and address the fact that land policy choices are politically sensitive and that changes may require strong political willingness from governments.

A number of participants in the panel and speakers also recommended to FAO and its partners to consider the following actions:

(a) Strengthen the supportive role of FAO in the follow-up of ICARRD, notably through: (i) expert advice and dissemination of good practices and lessons learned; (ii) the establishment of a lasting platform and reporting mechanisms;
(b) Encourage and support Rome-based organizations working together either through existing or new mechanisms;
(c) Create a special fund to mobilize resources for rural development; and
(d) Work at country level for the follow-up actions, in addition to international level.

Trade and Globalization Panel

Panelists stated that improving productivity levels in small-scale agriculture is critical in achieving poverty reduction and enhancing food security through agriculture-led growth. They differed widely in their views on the influence of greater openness to trade on the scope for such improvements:

Downward trends in real agricultural prices are driven to a greater extent by changes in the structure of demand and by the emergence of lower cost suppliers. These trends will occur irrespective of changes in agricultural domestic and trade policies, as well as a WTO agreement;

The impact of further liberalization is unclear in the short to medium term. There is no simple relationship between greater openness to trade and poverty or food security levels. Trade is necessary but not sufficient for agricultural growth and poverty reduction;

The concentration of marketing chains is a continuing trend. Views differed on the extent to which changes in trade rules contribute to further concentration and on the extent to which local chains are negatively impacted by greater exposure to international competition;

There will be winners and losers from further openness to trade – the losers were generally identified as being small farmers, particularly women, while winners were identified as those with capital to invest. Poor producers risk losing market share through their inability to access markets on favorable terms and to meet increasingly stringent standards; and Current levels of protection vary widely by country, with poorer countries offering less protection to agriculture. Historical evidence suggests that, as countries develop, protection to agriculture relative to manufacturing increases. Countries are concerned to maintain the policy space to provide appropriate support to agriculture as their economies develop.

In this context, issues such as increasing protection as a means of supporting productivity growth, the relative benefits of food sovereignty, and the mechanisms by which agriculture can adjust to changing circumstances.

Against such issues, several roles for International Organizations such as FAO were identified:

(a) Objective information and analysis of globalization trends;
(b) Assessing the potential impact of trade agreements;
(c) Assisting governments to develop policies appropriate for the stage of development of their agriculture sectors;
(d) Assisting governments in promoting changes to the trade environment to make it consistent with their agriculture sector development objectives;
(e) Contributing to appropriate investments in public goods both to enhance productivity levels and rural investment opportunities – these include infrastructure, water control, meeting standards, creating improved investment environments through improved institutions;
(f) Programs to assist the emergence of farmer organizations to help increase returns to producers; and
(g) Programs to enhance local processing opportunities

Recommendations: The Committee called for urgent action to tackle the root causes of food insecurity in the most food insecure countries over the short and long term and made the following recommendations:

For Governments:

( ) Build capacity and institutions for better planning, coordination, implementation and monitoring of food security programs, including the collection of disaggregated data by gender and age;

(a) Improve early warning and disaster preparedness mechanisms integrated into national development plans;

(b) Strengthen veterinary services and raise bio-security standards to enable efficient prevention and rapid response to trans-boundary diseases;

(c) Incorporate compensation mechanisms for smallholders and other vulnerable groups that experience losses from mandatory culling and control programs;

(d) Empower women and promote their access to productive resources;

(e) For African Governments, take concrete measures in order to ensure the implementation of the Maputo Declaration to allocate 10% of the national budget to the agricultural sector;

(f) Create an enabling environment for investments in agriculture and rural development;

(g) Promote good governance; and

(h) Implement the Voluntary Guidelines to Support the Progressive Realization of the Right to Adequate Food in the Context of National Food Security.

For FAO

(a) Continue to develop and implement food security analysis and assessment tools such as the FAO Integrated Food Security & Humanitarian Phase Classification (IPC);

(b) Assist governments in elaborating and implementing food security strategies and programs;
(c) Strengthen the newly established FAO/OIE Crisis Management Centre to fight Avian Influenza and other major animal health or food health related emergencies;
(d) Refine the framework and methodology for assessing the impact on food security of trans-boundary diseases;
(e) Conduct specific detailed surveys and multi-disciplinary analysis to understand the linkages between food security and trans-boundary diseases, in particular Avian Influenza, in relation to different food insecure groups;
(f) Continue to work with at-risk and affected countries to enhance strategies for HPAI control through inclusion of livelihoods and food security concerns; and
(g) Explore the implications of bio-fuels for food security as a special issue for the 33rd Session of the CFS.

For all concerned parties

(a) Improve partnership of multiple stakeholders and interagency collaboration in the fight against hunger;
(b) Promote, support and follow regional food security initiatives such as the Latin America and Caribbean without Hunger 2025;
(c) Ensure cooperation and coordination on emergency response and long term policies in regard to trans-boundary diseases;
(d) Enhance sustainable agriculture and rural development, especially in Africa within the New Partnership for Africa's Development (NEPAD) and Comprehensive Africa Agriculture Development Programme (CAADP) framework;
(e) Make trade work for the poor;

(f) Enhance Official Development Assistance (ODA) and investment flows to the agriculture and rural sector;
(g) Promote women as equal and full partners;
(h) Promote South-South cooperation as a partnership tool for food security programs;
(i) Integrate food security in the fight against HIV/AIDS; and
(j) Strengthen countries' capacity in water management for agriculture, respecting relevant international obligations.

High Level Task Force on Global Food Security
August 2011

An international movement on food and nutrition security for all has evolved and — since 2008 — has grown in ways that involves multiple stakeholders. It catalyses concerted and focused action by governments, international and regional organizations, civil society, research institutions, the private sector, communities and individuals. It has been described as "**The Global Partnership for Agriculture, Food Security and Nutrition**".

The United Nations system's High Level Task Force (HLTF) on Global Food Security contributes to the movement through supporting a comprehensive approach to food and nutrition security. This focuses particularly on sustainable access to food by the people who are most at risk of poverty and hunger. The HLTF's Updated Comprehensive Framework for Action (UCFA) is the UN system-wide coordinated approach for supporting country action that leads to sustainable and resilient rural livelihoods and food and nutrition security for all.

Specific population groups are particularly at risk of being impoverished and becoming malnourished as a result of high and volatile food prices. Those who practice agriculture (growing crops, rearing livestock, producing fish and maintaining forests), especially smallholder farmers and rural entrepreneurs (the majority of whom are women) are less able to cope with such shocks. This is particularly so if they are exposed to climate-related weather events, are unable to access sufficient land and water, do not improve agricultural productivity, are subject to inappropriate government policies, or experience political crises (sometimes exacerbated by armed conflicts). Very poor households in urban or rural areas — especially those who are marginalized such as indigenous, nomadic or migrant communities — are also at particular risk. Women carry much of the burden — they have less access to productive resources, opportunities and services and may face legal and social barriers to their being able to adapt to and benefit from higher demand for and prices of food. They also provide for and nourish their households, and care for those who are dependent on others.

Pregnant and lactating women, very young children, people with disabilities, persons affected by chronic diseases (such as HIV/AIDS), and the elderly, face increased risks of hunger and under nutrition when exposed to food insecurity.

The emerging challenge of agricultural systems is to ensure the production and availability of sufficient nutritious foods to meet rising demands — in ways that are environmentally, socially and economically sustainable. This means ensuring functional links between policies and actions for food, land, water and energy security; environmental sustainability; adaptation to and mitigation of climate change; and relevant ecosystems services. Policy choices should be based on evidence, lead to better integration of institutional processes, and follow inclusive consultation among concerned stakeholders. Actions should at all times contribute to the realization of the right to food and be pursued along two tracks. The first is to respond to the immediate needs of the most vulnerable people through effective safety nets. The second is to build longer-term livelihood and food production resilience by eliminating the root causes of hunger, poverty and malnutrition while strengthening social protection. This twin-track approach requires a combination of political commitment; enlightened administration; focus on results; sustained increases in both public and private investments; robust partnerships between multiple stakeholders (including civil society, farmers' organizations, businesses and governments), and strengthened accountability.

The movement for food and nutrition security is advancing at a time when concerns about the functioning of agriculture, food and nutrition systems are increasingly being voiced indifferent political settings. Leaders of nations and relevant intergovernmental bodies are highlighting challenges posed by food and nutrition insecurity, food price volatility, dysfunctional food markets and trading systems and lack of farmer-accessible risk management mechanisms. They have recognized an urgent need for better functioning social protection and safety nets. They seek evidence-based solutions to current problems and those which lie ahead.

They call for coherent policies, aligned strategies and coordinated actions: this means transformed behaviors in ways that reflect common principles and institutional synergies. This will advance the international agenda on food and nutrition security.

This summary version of the UCFA — "Food and Nutrition Security: Comprehensive Framework for Action" — presents its ten key principles for action. These are the result of collective debate and discussion at global, regional and national levels. Efforts to achieve sustainable food and nutrition security should continue being inspired and guided by the principles:

(a) twin-tracks to food and nutrition security;
(b) the need for a comprehensive approach;
(c) smallholders, particularly women, at the centre of actions;
(d) increased focus on resilience of household livelihoods;
(e) more and better investments in food and nutrition security;
(f) importance of open and well-functioning markets and trade;
(g) the value of multi-stakeholder and multi-sectoral partnerships;
(h) sustained political commitment and good governance;
(i) strategies led by countries with regional support; and
(j) Accountability for results. [78]

The HLTF is committed to maintaining food and nutrition security at the top of its collective agenda. Its members will work in synergy to help governments, farmers' organizations, businesses and civil society to deliver results and measure their impacts — especially on the lives of the most vulnerable people. This UCFA summary is expected to enrich the movement for food and nutrition security; support comprehensive, country-led and people-focused action; contribute to results that are both visible and tangible; and help communities build sustainable and resilient livelihoods.

We anticipate that this will lead to reduced hunger and better nutrition management for all.

---

[78] High Level Task Force (HLTF) on Global Food Security - Coordination Team, IFAD, Via Paolo di Dono, 44, 00142 Rome, August 2011

Declaration by Social Movements by NGOs/CSOs

Parallel Forum to the World Food Summit on Food Security Rome, November 13-17, 2009

We, 642 persons coming from 93 countries and representing 450 organisations of peasant and family farmers, small scale fisher folk, pastoralists, indigenous peoples, youth, women, the urban people, agricultural workers, local and international NGOs, and other social actors, gathered in Rome[79] from the 13 -17 of November, 2009 united in our determination to work for and demand food sovereignty in a moment in which the growing numbers of the hungry has surpassed the one billion mark. Food sovereignty is the real solution to the tragedy of hunger in our world. Food sovereignty entails transforming the current food system to ensure that those who produce food have equitable access to, and control over, land water, seeds, fisheries and agricultural biodiversity. All people have a right and responsibility to participate in deciding how food is produced and distributed. Governments must respect, protect and fulfill the right to food as the right to adequate, available, accessible, culturally acceptable and nutritious food. Governments have obligations to provide emergency aid. But this must not undermine food sovereignty and human rights. Emergency aid should be procured as locally as possible and must not be used to pressure countries into accepting Genetically Modified Organisms (GMO).

Food must never be used as a political weapon.

We call attention to the violations of rights of people, urban and rural, living in areas under armed conflict or occupation and in emergency situations. The

---

[79]People's food Sovereignty 13-17 November 2009, Civil Society Organization (CSO) Forum parallel to World Summit on Food Security 2009

international community must urgently address violations of human rights like those related to forced displacement, confiscation and alien exploitation of property, land, and other productive resources, demographic manipulation and population transfers. We declare as follows:

We declare our support for the renewed Committee on World Food Security.

We take particular note of the commitment of those Heads of State present at the FAO Summit have shown to this important body in their Declaration.

We emphasize the fundamental importance of the renewed CFS as the foremost inclusive international policy body for food and agriculture within the UN system, and as an essential body where the knowledge and perspectives of those whose daily labour have fed humanity for generations are not only heard, but also acted upon. We assert the centrality of the Right to Food as a principle to guide all elements of the Committee on World Food Security's work.

We express concern that the CFS is not receiving the funding appropriate to the ambition of its work program. We urge FAO member states to back their political commitment with financial resources. We also note that much work remains to be done within the CFS to ensure that there is coherence between the different organs of the global food and agricultural institutional architecture. In this regard, we are extremely concerned by the proposed World Bank Global Agriculture and Food Security program whose governance mechanism appears undemocratic, un-transparent, and destined to lead to a replication of past mistakes. As long as institutions such as the WTO continue to privilege commercial interests over the globally marginalized and malnourished, hunger will continue to stalk the world.

Civil society has played a fundamentally important role in the CFS reform process, opening up a critical space, which we intend to fully occupy in a responsible and effective manner. In so doing we will ensure that the voices of the excluded continue to be heard at the heart of food and agricultural policy-making and governance, at all levels. However, whilst we value the work that has been done, and hold high expectations regarding the CFS's future achievements, we will vigilantly monitor its work to ensure that member states follow through on their commitment to create an effective mechanism that is strong in its powers of coordination at all levels; able to hold its members to account; and start now to realize its commitment to develop a Global Strategic Framework for food security and nutrition.

Ecological Food Provision

We reaffirm that our ecological food provision actually feeds the large majority of people all over the world in both rural and urban areas (more than 75 percent). Our practices focus on food for people not profit for corporations. It is healthy, diverse, localized and cools the planet.

We commit to strengthen and promote our ecological model of food provision in the framework of food sovereignty that feeds all populations including those in marginal zones like small islands and costal areas. Our practices, because they priorities feeding people locally, minimize waste and losses of food and do not create the damage caused by industrial production systems. Peasant agriculture is resilient and can adapt to and mitigate climate change.

We insist, however, that food and agriculture be kept out of carbon market. We will defend and develop our agricultural, fisheries and animal biodiversity in the face of the aggressive commoditization of nature, food and knowledge that is being facilitated by the 'new Green Revolutions'. We call for a global moratorium on GMO. Governments must protect and properly regulate domestic food markets. Our practices require supply management policies in order to secure availability of food and to guarantee decent wages and fair prices. We are ready to discuss new legal frameworks to support our practices.

We call for a reframing of research, using participatory methods that will support our ecological model of food provision. We are the innovators building on our knowledge and skills.

We rehabilitate local seeds systems and livestock breeds and fish/aquatic species for a changing climate. We commit to promote the findings of IAASTD (International Assessment of Agricultural Knowledge, Science and Technology for Development). We call for accountability by researchers. We reject corporations' control of research and will not engage in forums that are dominated by them. We will promote our innovations through our media and outreach programs for capacity building, education and information dissemination.

We will strengthen our interconnecting rural – urban food webs. We will build alliances within a Complex Alimentations – linking small-scale food providers, processors, scientists, institutions, and consumers – to replace the reductionist approach of the Codex Alimentations. We commit to shorten distances between food provider and consumer. We will strengthen urban food movements and advance urban and semi-urban agriculture. We will reclaim the language of food emphasizing nutrition and diversity in diets that exclude meat provided from industrial systems.

Control over food producing resources

Land grabbing by transnational capital must stop. Landlessness and land grabbing have intensified in the wake of the global food crisis, deforestation, sequestering of water bodies, privatization of the sea inland waters and coastal zones. Land and water confiscation and isolation practiced by occupying forces must be stopped. Countries and companies are colluding in alarming land grabbing practices. In less than a year, over 40 million hectares of fertile land in Africa, Asia, Latin America and Eastern Europe have been usurped through these deals, displacing local food production for export interests.

Instead of promoting large-scale industrial agricultural investments, we urge our governments and the FAO to implement structural changes implied in the Declaration of the International Conference on Agrarian Reform and Rural Development (ICARRD) and in the UN Declaration on the Rights of Indigenous Peoples. The International Planning Committee for Food Sovereignty (IPC) must play a critical role in ensuring the effective participation of social movements and civil society organizations.

We demand comprehensive agrarian reforms, which uphold the individual and collective/community rights of access to and control over territories. All States must implement effective public policies, which guarantee community (those derive their livelihood) control over all natural resources. Strong accountability mechanisms to redress violations of these rights need to be in place. Gender equity and the youth interests must be at the heart of genuine agrarian and aquatic reforms. Reforms should guarantee women and youth full equality of opportunities and rights to land and natural wealth, and redress historical and ongoing discrimination.

Access to water is a human right. Water must remain in the "commons" and not be subject to market mechanisms of use and governance. Aquatic reforms should give legal recognition, protection and enforcement of the collective rights of small-scale fishing communities to access and use fishing grounds and maritime resources.

Closure of pastoralists' routes and expropriation of lands, natural wealth and territories from local communities through economic concessions, big plantations, industrial agriculture and aquaculture, tourism and infrastructure projects and any other means must come to an end. Gathered food is also an important source to feed many of our communities and therefore deserves specific protection.

The rights to territory for indigenous peoples encompass nature as a living being essential to the identity and culture of particular communities or peoples. As guaranteed by Articles 41 and 42 of the UN Declaration on Indigenous Peoples Rights, we call FAO to adopt a policy for Indigenous Peoples, to recognize Indigenous Peoples' Territorial Rights, and to ensure their participation in resource decisions.

We urge FAO and IFAD to create a Working Group with Indigenous Peoples in the CFS.

We reject intellectual property rights over living resources including seeds, plants and animals. De facto biological monopolies -where the seed or breed is rendered sterile - must be banned.

We will keep the seeds in our hands. We will keep freely exchanging and saving our seeds and breeds. We value our traditional knowledge as fishers, livestock keepers, Indigenous Peoples and peasants and we will further develop it to be able to feed our communities in a sustainable way. Our songs and tales express our Cosmo-vision and are important to maintain our spiritual relationship with our lands.

Civil Society Commitments

We commit ourselves to increase our level of organization, build broad and strong alliances and promote joint actions, articulations, exchanges, and solidarity to speak with a strong voice for defending our food sovereignty. We are convinced that only the power of organized peoples and mobilization can achieve the needed changes, thus our principal task is to inform, raise awareness, debate, organize and mobilize people.

Women participants in the forum, noting the systematic oppression of women through the processes of globalization and corporatization of agriculture, fisheries and livestock, intensified by patriarchy, commit ourselves to achieving equality in representation and decision making bodies. We demand gender justice, peace and respect for the rights of women, including common property rights. Our rights over seeds, productive resources, our knowledge and our contributions to enhancing resilience must be respected, valued and protected. Women agricultural workers and their communities must be assured safe working conditions and fair wages. Youth participants of the forum reaffirm that young people are key to the development and implementation of ecologically and socially sustainable agriculture policies. All decision-making bodies must ensure the effective participation of young people. We insist on agricultural, fisheries and livestock education (formal and informal) from an early age, and the FAO and IFAD should provide adequate funds for capacity building training at all levels to address the needs of young people and rural women. Our commitment to food sovereignty includes a demand that the Committee on Food Security be transformed into the "Committee for Food

Sovereignty" and a call for a moratorium on agro-fuels.

We engage ourselves to collectively accept our responsibilities to mobilize from the local to the international levels in our struggles for food sovereignty. We claim the control and the autonomy of our processes of organization and alliances and we will further enhance our mutual accountability by valuing the wealth of our diversity and in the respect for our autonomies. We recognize the essential role of the IPC in the facilitation of alliance building. We demand Food Sovereignty now!

G8 Countries Pledge Food Security

The G8 countries in L'Aquila summit (2009) committed to addressing food security and sustainable agricultural development through a US $ 22 billion dedicated fund, but little clarity has been gained over how much new funding is actually being committed, and how the funds will be channeled to make a difference to the one billion hungry today, and the food and nutrition needs of the coming decades. As the G8 meets for the 2010 summit, Crop Life International calls on leaders to follow their commitment to food security by:

(a) Issuing a clear plan of action for implementation of the L'Aquila Food Security Initiative.
(b) Doing this in a way that is globally coordinated, yet locally adapted.
(c) Ensuring that action addresses the multiple issues that underpin food security, including the need to foster innovation.

The CEO and President of Crop Life International said that agriculture has to produce more food while preserving threatened natural resources, and mitigating and adapting to climate change. That is a huge undertaking – not just for farmers, but for legislators who must balance these concerns in a way that feeds our growing population. The plant science industry recognizes the valuable contribution that science and technology can make to achieve food security. Food security is achievable. However, the contribution of science and technology needs to be complemented by addressing six key issue areas that underpin food security. These are:

Agricultural productivity: We must increase productivity on existing lands. If plant science cannot help crop protection products, global crop losses would rise to 40-80 percent. Beyond existing yield benefits, biotech crops have the potential to further raise globally yields by up to 25 percent.

Fostering innovation: Increasing agricultural productivity sustainably requires continue innovation for new, improved technologies and knowledge. It also requires science-based regulation to make sure innovative technologies reach the market in a timely manner.

Sustainable resource management: Biodiversity and natural resources are under unprecedented pressure. To help ensure that agriculture helps preserve natural resources, policies must inform and award incentives to farmers for adoption of more sustainable farming practices.

Global and local trade: Efficient food production requires open, fair and well-functioning global markets.

Infrastructure: Infrastructure improvements are needed to improve crop production and quality, reduce post-harvest losses and secure farmers' access to inputs and markets.

Rural poverty: 75 percent of the poor in developing countries live in rural areas. With rising urbanization, there is a risk that policies will neglect the needs of rural and agricultural communities. This must be avoided.

While food security remains achievable, making it a reality requires genuine political will and investment in coordinated, targeted policies. The G8 has the opportunity to set an example through the L'Aquila Initiative and to make a difference to the food insecure of today, and those of the coming decades. The plant science industry calls on the G8 to take this opportunity and to ensure that their commitment translates into real change.[80]

Conclusion:

All the committee reports are excellent in their approaches to solve the problem of food insecurity. These reports should act as the guidelines for each country. There are variations in climate, soil type, crops grown, cultural practices and market demand among the countries and within each country. Economy of the state and consumers' behaviour control market demands and prices. Agricultural commodities, condiments, milk, poultry birds, prawn or fish could improve food security to all. Import and export of food items change food security of consumers and economy of the country.

All the committee reports need to be studied with particular reference to the country for which planning would be taken up. A group of committees of farm specialists, agricultural economists' and farmer organizations might be formed to find out the possibilities of ensuring 'food security' to each family in the country and submit a report to the government.

---

[80]Brussels, June 25, 2010, PR Newswire

Each country should take up land reform and allow the landless people to own at least a plot of land. This would allow the landless people to live with prestige, satisfaction and income to the family.

Agricultural land must not be transferred to industrialists and realtors by government law because it reduces farm land and reduces total agricultural yield in the country.

Food security must be awarded to the entire population. Each government must make plans to award food security to all for at least for 50 years phase-wise.

Water occupies the dynamics of successful agriculture; this resource must be utilized economically. Irrigation dams, ponds, wells and irrigation canal need repair each year. Water must be available for agriculture and animal husbandry and rural people throughout the year. **Availability of drinking water is a must for all people in the country.**

Efficient agricultural marketing is productive; it allows free movement of grains or other vegetables, poultry birds, eggs, fish, pulses, potato and onion to distant markets safely and quickly. Agricultural marketing such as retailing, wholesaling, storage, processing and distribution creates employment in private sectors.

If there would be a village market in each village for two hours once in a week on a particular day, a group of seven villages can make a chain of markets in a week. This would create employment opportunities for unemployed youths, widows and others. They would act as retailers or itinerant traders and earn an income daily even without investment. A career in trade or business would keep them engaged throughout the year.

Chapter VI

FOOD SECURITY FOR ALL

Hunger: One of the few cravings that cannot be appeased with another solution.

--- Irwin Van Grove

Food safety now requires attention to all aspects of the production of agricultural, horticultural, fishery, dairy, and poultry products from primary producers till marketing of all commodities to the final consumers. The problem is aggravated because more than 1 billion people are financially so weak that they do not have the purchasing capability to buy their requirements for consumption. They are hungry; food is available in the market but they cannot buy foodstuff. They need food; they need to live; and they have appealed their governments, national, international and world organizations for a solution of this 'Great Challenge'.

Hunger has created conflict zones, theft, beggary, displacement, insecurity, migration, sale of own sons and daughters, sex rackets, and has created

Terrorists, Maoists and Naxalites in most of the developing countries. Can the donors' organizations do undertake some positive steps in solving these burning crises?

In this chapter the activities of the United Nations, FAO, IFFRI, European Commission, CGAIR, the Pittsburgh Summit, activities of Australia, China, Canada, Japan, the US, the UK, the U N and IFAD have been discussed for a meaningful analysis.

The United Nations Action Plan

On Food Price Volatility and Agriculture

The French G20 presidency invited G20 Agriculture Ministers to meet in Paris on 23 June 2011. Ministers agreed an action plan on food price volatility and agriculture which focuses on stabilizing prices and increasing overall food supplies through sustainable investments in the production of nutritious foods. Their investments will make a comprehensive contribution to overall availability of food in the face of increasing demand, to improving people's food and nutrition security, and to reducing hunger. They agreed to remove food export restrictions or extraordinary taxes on food purchased for non-commercial humanitarian purposes by the World Food Programme: they also agreed not to impose them in the future. This was the first ever meeting of G20 Agriculture Ministers: it builds on a number of regional ministerial processes including the sequence of meetings sponsored by the Comprehensive Africa Agriculture Development Programme and last years' agriculture ministers' meeting under the APEC framework in Japan.

As they discussed global challenges Ministers highlighted the vital role of Agriculture in today's world. It deals with the production, processing and distribution of crops, livestock, fish and forest products. In many nations it determines the rate at which poverty is reduced and the potential for prosperity. It enables people in rural spaces to generate income. It enables farmers – especially smallholders – to be positive agents of change as they get better organized to participate in value production and benefit sharing. It can determine the quality of land, water, air and the sustainability of natural environments. It has a major influence on the price of energy and nutrients available in markets - and the nutritional status of children, women and men. It can determine whether people are healthy or at risk of disease. Agricultural policy choices influence rural economies, the availability and use of water and land, environmental quality, the rate of climate change, as well as people's nutrition and health status. In most countries, agricultural operations are relevant to the whole of government and many strands of society: Ministers of Agriculture have a place in a wide range of policy processes.

At least two billion people depend directly on agriculture for their livelihoods in the world.

Most of them are smallholder farming families, small-scale breeders and entrepreneurs, labourers working along food value chains, and nomadic groups. Farmer organizations, well-managed cooperatives, contract farming, franchise arrangements and agribusiness associations have a key role in ensuring that poor rural populations benefit from increased investments in agriculture and efforts to increase food production and supply so as to meet demands for nutritious food from increasing – and ever more demanding – populations. Farmers' organizations are best able to play these roles if they have strong capabilities for management, coordination and negotiation. Ministers indicated their increasing efforts to involve associations of small-scale farmers, food producers and processors in the development and implementation of agricultural policies at the same time as they work with those who own and farm larger landholdings on environmentally sustainable intensification of agricultural production.

During the discussions Ministers were explicit about their need to balance national interests with contributions to global benefits – including food price stabilization, hunger reduction and environmental sustainability. They were joined by a number of guests including representatives of the African Union and the CEO of the New Partnership for Africa's Development (NEPAD), the EU's Agricultural commissioner as well as the Heads of major international Organizations. The declaration had been negotiated through meetings lasting several days over a period of six months: some elements were resolved on June 23rd - in the early morning. After discussions had been concluded that day, the Ministers agreed their declaration. It sets out a range of principles for sustainable investments in increased food production; priorities for agricultural research that contributes to a broad range of critical outcomes; mechanisms for more comprehensive data collection, accumulation and analysis for better agricultural market information – and for responding effectively to that information; safety nets serve as a back-up for individuals, communities and nations that just cannot access and/or afford the food they need; better access to humanitarian food supplies, and freeing them from export bans or extraordinary taxes both now and in future; and desirable steps to accelerate agreements on more open trade in agricultural products. They agreed to establish an Agricultural Market Information System (AMIS) which will be housed in the Food and Agriculture Organization (FAO). Later this year G20 Finance Ministers are expected to examine options for regulating of food commodity markets so they permit price discovery and any necessary hedging.

The Ministers agreed that sustainable intensification of agriculture calls for increased financial investment in smallholders and enabling them to better connect with food value chains: this means farmers' organizations and agribusinesses (both big and small) working with governments in people-private-public partnerships that operate according to agreed principles: these include encouraging environmental sustainability, improving smallholder livelihoods, and contributing to better nutritional outcomes. It also means ensuring that farmers have access to market-based risk management systems (such as insurance against crop losses due to extreme weather or disease). Ministers were told about partnerships being developed in several African nations (for example - through investment in strategic corridors in Mozambique and Tanzania; and through a new African Agricultural Growth & Investment Task Force jointly sponsored by NEPAD, the African Union and the World Economic Forum). Ministers also noted country-led public-private partnerships catalyzed in Mexico and Indonesia, as well as Tanzania and Vietnam, by the Forum's New Vision for Agriculture initiative.

Some Ministers stressed the importance of grounding policies on food security within the framework of the Right to Food. Several recognized that better supplies of food are necessary - but not sufficient - to ensure food security. In their declaration Ministers are explicit about the need for safety nets to improve access to food by countries, communities and households at times when they are unaffordable because food prices rise, supply lines break or purchasing capacity is greatly diminished. The text on exempting humanitarian food supplies from export bans represents an advance on what has been written in the declaration of the 2009 World Summit on Food Security. This proposal could be taken forward by all WTO members at their Ministerial meeting later this year. Ministers agreed to ensure that national food-based safety nets can work at times when food prices rise sharply and governments cannot access the food required for these safety nets at an affordable price. They asked WFP to devise and then test an emergency humanitarian food reserve system and asked to more predictable long-term financing for the organization so that it can undertake advance purchases and set up pre-positioning arrangements for humanitarian food supplies. WFP has developed a five point action plan to take forward the letter and spirit of this declaration.

Several Ministers pointed out that the best agricultural development strategies are those which empower women and are sensitive to people's nutritional needs – they should address the drivers of under-nutrition especially in pregnancy and early childhood. This "nutrition-sensitive" approach to agriculture will help the increasing number of countries that are prioritizing efforts to scale up nutritional outcomes well before the 2015 target year for the Millennium Development Goals. The commitment – in the Ministers' declaration - to nutrition-sensitive agriculture should encourage similar engagement in Nutrition by Ministers of Agriculture throughout the world and will contribute to the acceleration of nutritional improvement.

Ministers recognized the absolute importance of open and well-functioning trade in agricultural goods and called for rapid completion of the Doha Development Agenda: in private conversation some suggested that least developed countries would better benefit from their products having tariff-free and quota-free access to other markets. They were also reminded about the need to facilitate in-country and regional trade.

The Ministerial Declaration calls for stronger international and regional networks for combined attention to public health, animal health and plant health. They also encourage international organizations – especially the Food and Agriculture

Organization, the World Health Organization and the World Organization for Animal Health – to take a lead on this issue.

Ministers acknowledged that strong global governance is an indispensable element for achieving food and nutrition security, and called for greater policy coherence, recognizing the critical role played by International and Regional Organizations. There was repeated recognition of the important role being played now, and in the future, by the Committee on Food Security (CFS), and of the contributions made by the three Rome-based UN agencies (FAO, WFP and IFAD) and by the UN system's High Level Task Force on Food Security (HLTF). The HLTF brings together 22 different UN system bodies, International Financial Institutions, the OECD and the World Trade Organization. Members of the HLTF contributed to this G20 meeting through the production of at least seven reports: FAO and OECD coordinated a total of 10 International Organizations (IOs) that contributed to the document on Food Price Volatility that served as a basis for discussions among the Agriculture Ministers' deputies.

The IOs would like to support the implementation of this action plan – with its comprehensive approach to food and nutrition security. It is in line with the HLTF's strategy – the Updated Comprehensive Framework of Action. HLTF members can also contribute to links between the G20 and the wider membership of the UN – for example, in the context of the Committee on World Food Security, the UN General Assembly (GA) and the Economic and Social Council (ECOSOC). This is particularly relevant as the G20 work is at the interface between food, land, water, energy, environment, climate change, health and nutrition. Lastly, the HLTF is committed to ensuring the overall accountability of a coordinated and synergized UN system: this may be helpful in the light of the broad ranging requests made of the system by the G20.

So, in conclusion, we congratulate the French Presidency and members of the G20 on this important declaration, on the political commitment being made to food and nutrition security and for their collective efforts to reduce hunger, enhance social protection and safety nets, improve food and nutrition security, and make agriculture a positive force for shaping the world of the future. We look forward to working on these issues in 2011 and beyond - not only with the G20 (in this year's Development Working Group and other processes on the road to Cannes in November, and then in Mexico next year), but also with all the members of the United Nations as well as their regional and global political bodies (including the Committee on World Food Security).[81]

The United Nations

High Level Task Force' to combat Global Food Security Crisis

Mr. Ban Ki-moon, United Nations Secretary - General, chaired the UN system high-level task force for the global food security crisis conveyed on September 30th 2009. The meeting included FAO, IFAD, ILO, IMF, UNHCR, OECD, UNICEF, UNCTAD, DESA, DPKO, DPA, DPI, UNDP, UNEP, OCHA, OHCHR, OHRLLS, The World Bank, WFP, WHO, WTO and Special Advisor on MDGs. The Coordination team of the UN System High Level Task Force (HLTF) for the Global Food Security Crisis advocated for greater national and international

[81]The Special Representative of the UN Secretary-General prepared the following commentary for Food Security and Nutrition and Coordinator of the High Level Task Force (HLTF) on Food Security, www. UN Org, January 2009

investments in global food security.[82] The meeting accepted the following programs:

(1)Helping national authorities to tackle food insecurity:

(a) Scaling up support for national authorities
(b) Results achieved after one year
(c) Sustaining intensified action in 2009 and 2010 with concerted focus on long-term issues

(2) Coordination within High Level Task Force (HLTF)

(a) Program of work and HLTF coordination team
(b) Concerted support to national authorities
(c) Coordination within regional entities
(d) Coordination with civil society and business, coordination - especially at country level - is valued by donors
(e) Coordination of multilateral financing for food security

(3) Implementing the Comprehensive Framework for Action

(a) The right to food
(b) Trade in food
(c) Employment

(4)Country level experience such as

(a) Hunger is a political liability for national governments
(b) A comprehensive response is essential
(c) The response should be generated from within commitments
(d) Multi-stakeholder partnerships are a vital platform for resilience
(e) Additional investment is necessary
(f) Interconnections

---

[82]Information Note on the work of the UN system high-level task force for the Global food Security Crisis, 2, UN plaza, New York, September 30, 2009

Food and Agriculture Organization (FAO)

The Food and Agriculture Organization (FAO) is the main United Nations agency specializing in all aspects of food quality and safety, and in all the different stages of food production, harvest, post-harvest handling, storage, transport, processing and distribution.

Food safety along the food chain:

FAO[83] adheres to the food chain approach in managing food safety and quality as recognition of the responsibility of all actors in the food chain for the supply of food that is safe, healthy and nutritious.

FAO's Food Quality and Standards Service (AGNS) is committed to the enhancement of food safety and quality along the food chain at all levels, with the aim of preventing food-borne diseases, protecting consumers and promoting fair practices in the food trade.

Food safety can be compromised at any point in the food chain. Threats posed by contaminated water and foods are interrelated and cannot be separated. In the case of natural disasters, poor sanitation, including lack of safe water and a shortage of suitable conditions to prepare food prior to consumption, can all lead to outbreaks of food-borne disease.

In crisis situations people may already be at risk through malnutrition, exposure, shock and other traumas, thus it becomes even more essential that the food they consume is safe. In any situation, this is particularly important for foods intended for people who are immune-compromised or suffering from

[83]Food and Agriculture Organization (UN), Food Safety and Control,

some underlying illness, infants, pregnant women and the elderly, who are often the most vulnerable.

The provision of food in crisis situations is often carried out under crude conditions, and the people available to organize and implement feeding operations may not have the necessary experience to manage food safety effectively.

AGNS can assist those involved in preparedness response planning and the overseeing of food operations in crisis situations to ensure food safety and consumer protection, to minimize the incidence of food-borne diseases and to manage related issues effectively.

In October 2006 FAO inaugurated a new Crisis Management Center (CMC) to fight avian influenza outbreaks and other major animal and plant health or food safety-related emergencies. The CMC will draw on the specialist services of AGNS when dealing with food safety crises.

Similarly, in 2005, FAO established a Nuclear Emergencies Crisis Network of Technical Experts (ECN) with members drawn from 11 units across FAO, including AGNS. Technical experts will be called upon to provide guidance in the case of a nuclear event concerning food safety and the contamination of food with radioactive substances.

EMPRES Food Safety: Emergency Prevention System for Food Safety Strategic Plan

An estimated three million people around the world, in developed and developing countries die every year from food and water-borne disease, with millions more becoming sick.

Occurrence of such disease can easily escalate to a food safety emergency situation, which can adversely impact national economies and livelihoods through reduced availability of food for national consumption, closure of export markets, and/or the high cost of addressing the effects of the threat.

The Food and Agriculture Organization of the United Nations (FAO) has established an Emergency Prevention System for Food Safety (EMPRES Food Safety) to reduce the adverse impact of food safety emergencies on global food security and public health. At the request of its members, EMPRES Food Safety will complement and enhance FAO's ongoing work in food safety, as well as in animal health and plant health emergencies.

The FAO in collaboration with other concerned technical divisions and units including the Nutrition and Consumer Protection Division (AGN) would implement the EMPRES Food Safety for making full use of relevant available expertise along the food chain within FAO. These units have prepared this strategic plan for comparative advantages of having a mandate covering the entire food chain, its status as a neutral international forum and its linkages with national governments, regional bodies, other international agencies, universities, research centers and the donor community. The Plan will be regularly updated to reflect the ever-changing nature of food safety emergencies.

FAO's Food Quality and Standards Service (AGNS) is committed to the enhancement of food safety and quality along the food chain at international, regional and national levels, with the aim of protecting consumers and promoting the production and trade of safe, quality food. We achieve this by:

(a) Establishing and improving national regulatory frameworks for food control and quality assurance compatible with international requirements, in particular those of the Codex Alimentarius;

(b) Supplying technical advice and expertise for the development of integrated food control systems, thus building capacity in food safety and quality throughout the food chain;
(c) Providing independent scientific advice, risk assessments and related guidance concerning food safety to the Codex Alimentarius and Governments, including the assessment of food additives, chemical and microbiological contaminants, naturally occurring toxicants, and foods derived from modern biotechnology;
(d) Developing guidelines and tools on food safety risk assessment and its use in food safety risk management, and on capacity building in various aspects of food safety and quality;
(e) Assisting in emergency or crisis situations through the provision of food safety guidance

In short, the FAO is prepared to supply technical advice to achieve food security to all countries.

Millions more food-insecure

Urgent action and substantial investments needed

Soaring food prices have triggered worldwide concern about threats to global food security, shaking the unjustified complacency created by many years of low commodity prices. From 3 to 5 June 2008, representatives of 180 countries plus the European Union, including many Heads of State and Government, met in Rome to express their conviction "that the international community needs to take urgent and coordinated action to combat the negative impacts of soaring food prices on the world's most vulnerable countries and populations". At the G8 Summit in Japan in July 2008, the leaders of the world's most industrialized nations voiced their deep concern "that the steep rise in global food prices, coupled with availability problems in a number of developing countries, is threatening global food security".

Moving away from hunger reduction goals:

The concerns of the international community are well founded. For the first time since FAO started monitoring undernourishment trends, the number of chronically hungry people is higher in the most recent period relative to the base period. FAO estimates that, mainly as a result of high food prices, the number of chronically hungry people in the world rose by 75 million in 2007 to reach 923 million. The devastating effects of high food prices on the number of hungry people compound already worrisome long-term trends. Our analysis shows that in 2003–05, before the recent rise in food prices, there were 6 million more chronically hungry people in the world than in 1990–92, the progress towards the World Food Summit and Millennium Summit hunger reduction targets is measured.

Early gains in hunger reduction achieved in a number of developing regions by the mid-1990s have not been sustained. Hunger has increased, as the world has grown richer and produced more food than ever in the last decade. As this report has pointed out many times, this disappointing outcome reflects the lack of concerted action to combat hunger despite global commitments.

Soaring food prices have reversed some of the gains and successes in hunger reduction, making the mission of achieving the internationally agreed goals on hunger reduction more difficult. The task of reducing the number of hungry people by 500 million in the remaining seven years to 2015 will require an enormous and resolute global effort and concrete actions.

Poorest and most vulnerable worst hit:

Food price increases have exacerbated the situation for many countries already in need of emergency interventions and food assistance due to other factors such as severe weather and conflict. Countries already afflicted by emergencies have to deal with the added burden of high food prices on food security, while others become more vulnerable to food insecurity because of high prices. Developing countries, especially the poorest, face difficult choices between maintaining macroeconomic stability and putting in place policies and program to deal with the negative impact of high food and fuel prices on their people.

Riots and civil disturbances, which have taken place in many low- and middle-income developing countries, signal the desperation caused by soaring food and fuel prices for millions of poor and also middleclass households. Analysis in this report shows that high food prices have a particularly devastating effect on the poorest in both urban and rural areas, the landless and female-headed households. Unless urgent measures are taken, high food prices may have detrimental long-term effects on human development as households, in their effort to deal with rising food bills, either reduce the quantity and quality of food consumed, cut expenditure on health and education or sell productive assets. Children, pregnant women and lactating mothers are at highest risk. Past experience with high food prices fully justifies such fears.

A strategic response: the twin-track approach

The food crisis brought about by soaring food prices in many developing countries needs an urgent and concrete response. At the same time, it should be recognized that high food prices are the result of a delicate balance between food supply and demand. These two facts show that, more than ever before, the twin-track approach to hunger reduction advocated by FAO and its development partners is key to addressing not only the threats to food security caused by high food prices but also the opportunities that arise. In the immediate term, carefully targeted safety nets and social protection programs are urgently required in order to ensure that everyone is able to access the food they need for a healthy life. In parallel, the focus should be on helping producers, especially small scale farmers, to boost food production, mainly by facilitating 'The State of Food Insecurity' in the World 2008 their access to seeds, fertilizers, animal feed and other inputs.

This should improve food supplies and lower prices in local markets. In the medium-to-long term, the focus should be on strengthening the agriculture sectors of developing countries to enable them to respond to growth in demand. Expanding food production in poor countries through enhanced productivity must constitute the cornerstone of policies, strategies and programs seeking to attain a sustainable solution for food security.

High food prices and the incentives they provide can be harnessed to re-launch agriculture in the developing world. This is essential not only to face the current crisis, but also to respond to the increasing demand for food, feed and bio-fuel production and to prevent the recurrence of such crises in the future. Re-launching agriculture in developing countries is also critical for the achievement of meaningful results in poverty and hunger reduction and to reverse the current worrisome trends.

This will entail empowering large numbers of small-scale farmers worldwide to expand agricultural output. Agricultural growth as an engine for poverty reduction means addressing the structural constraints facing agriculture, particularly for the millions of smallholder producers in agriculture-based economies. In other words, the state needs expanded public investment in rural infrastructure and essential services – in roads, irrigation facilities, water harvesting, and storage, slaughterhouses, fishing ports and credit, as well as electricity, schools and health services – in order to create favourable conditions for private investment in rural areas. At the same time, increased resources must be devoted to more sustainable technologies that support more-intensive agriculture and that assist farmers to increase the resilience of their food production systems and to cope with climate change.

A coherent and coordinated strategy is vital:

Many developing countries have taken unilateral action in efforts to contain the negative effects of high food prices, including the imposition of price controls and export restrictions. Such responses may not be sustainable and would actually contribute to further rises in world price levels and instability. To face threats and exploit opportunities posed by high food prices effectively and efficiently, strategies must be based on a comprehensive and coordinated multilateral response.

Urgent, broad-based and large-scale investments are needed in order to address in a sustainable manner the growing food-insecurity problems affecting the poor and hungry. No single country or institution will be able to resolve this crisis on its own. Governments of developing and developed countries, donors, United Nations agencies, international institutions, civil society and the private sector all have important roles to play in the global fight against hunger.

It is vital that the international community share a common vision of how best to assist governments in eradicating chronic hunger and that all parties work together to translate this vision into reality on the scale required. The situation cannot wait any longer.

The resolve of world leaders at the June 2008 Summit on World Food Security in Rome and the fact that the G8 Summit placed concerns surrounding high food and fuel prices at the top of its agenda demonstrates a growing political will to address hunger. Moreover, substantial commitments have been made for increased financial support to developing countries to address the food security threats caused by high food prices. Nevertheless, unless this political will and donor pledges are turned into urgent and real actions, millions more will fall into deep poverty and chronic hunger. The need for concerted action to combat hunger and malnutrition has never been stronger. I am hopeful that the global community will rise to the challenge.[84]

G 8 Summit must focus on food security

As the G8 leaders meet in the United States this week, agriculture and food security must be at the forefront of the discussions, and ways to prevent price volatility, including halting grain-based bio-fuels production, establishing grain reserves for emergency use, eliminating food export bans and increasing the transparency of food and agricultural market information, should be addressed.

Most importantly, the G8 leaders should fulfill their commitments on global food security.

In 2009, G8 leaders made considerable financial commitments to global agriculture and food security, pledging to mobilize $22 billion over three years through a coordinated, comprehensive strategy focused on sustainable agriculture development. But

---

[84]Jacques Diouf, FAO Director-General

as of May 2011, it was estimated that only 22 percent of these commitments had been disbursed.

In addition to the G8 leaders, the heads of states from Ethiopia, Ghana, Benin and Tanzania will take part in the summit discussions. The direct participation by these African leaders underscores the seriousness of the food security situation on the continent, where more than 220 million people are undernourished.

Millions suffer from micronutrient deficiencies, a total of 100 million women and children are iron deficient, and 33 million children have Vitamin A deficiencies.

The 2011 Global Hunger Index, a combined measure of the proportion of undernourishment, child malnutrition, and child mortality, shows that Sub-Saharan Africa is home to all the countries with "extremely alarming" scores and many of the countries with "alarming" scores.

In addition, it is projected that smallholder farmers, particularly those living in the highland areas and semi-arid savannahs in Sub-Saharan Africa, face increasing natural resource scarcity risks, including land degradation, which can cost as much as 10 percent of national GDP. Many parts of the region are extremely vulnerable to both man-made and natural shocks. Last year, more than 13 million people were affected by the drought in the Horn of Africa. This year more than 15 million people across seven countries in the Sahel region are already suffering from severe food insecurity or at risk.It is crucial that developed countries take action to fight starvation in Africa. The cost of hunger is high, and the damage is irreversible.

For over three decades now, the International Food Policy Research Institute has been engaged in promoting the transformation of smallholder agriculture across Africa through evidence-based research and support to country-driven development initiatives. Priority areas include: building capacity for agricultural and food policy analysis and supporting country-led development strategies; improving nutrition along value chains to increase poor people's access to nutritious foods and increasing the availability, access, and intake of nutrient-rich, bio-fortified staple foods for the poor; resilience-enhancing schemes such as productive social safety nets, weather insurance index, and other risk management tools that help reduce vulnerability and enhance resilience to shocks and contribute to overall long-term growth and prosperity.

Technological innovations such as biotechnology, nanotechnology, and bio-fortification are crucial to increasing agricultural productivity, building resilience to weather-related shocks, enhancing the nutritional value of food crops, and ensuring food safety. Biotechnology has great potential to improve crop yield, nutrition and resilience to weather shocks, which will be even more frequent in the future due to climate change.

As the world's population increases, there is enormous pressure on the planet's ecosystems. The most reasonable solution to feeding the ever-growing population is sustainably producing more food on the existing land. Scaled-up investments in science and technology and support for improved country capacities are essential to accelerate progress and achieve development objectives. While the governments of developing countries have taken important steps to boost food security-related investments, support from the G8 countries remains critical.[85]

---

[85]Shenggen Fan(2012), "G 8 Summit must focus on food security", China Daily, Page 9, May 18, 2012

FAO Projections for the United Kingdom

The projections made at the FAO food security conference are as follows:

1. At the World Food Security Conference in Rome, it was announced that there was a need to increase food production by 50 percent by 2030 and double it by 2050. These figures are based on assumptions about population growth and patterns of consumption. It is important to bear in mind that they are projections rather than targets. They are a useful way of focusing attention on food production. However, they should also be used to draw attention to population growth, diet, and waste at all stage of the food chain, and the need for policy responses in these areas.

2. More work is needed on future patterns of consumption. Doubling production by 2050 may focus the minds of policymakers, but, by itself, it is too broad a projection on which to base a response. We recommend that the Foresight Project on Global Food and Farming Futures, which is due to report in October 2010, provide a clear and accessible breakdown of this projection, encompassing where and at what rate the population increases are likely to take place, and how demand is likely to change. It should indicate the implications of these factors for world production of different food commodities. The UK should determine how it will monitor global food production and demand trends in order further to refine the projections in the future.

Sustainability

3. Producing sufficient food is only part of the challenge the world faces, the implications of the way in which it is produced are equally important. The only acceptable form of food production is that which meets the needs of the present without compromising

the ability of future generations to meet their needs. Applying this principle to food production requires a fundamental shift in thinking and an open-minded approach to embracing solutions from across the spectrum of production methods.

The head-in-the-sand approach

4. It is clear that maximizing food production does not depend on agriculture alone but also on infrastructure-transport systems, as well as food storage.

5. Doing nothing to contribute to the world's food supplies would be morally unacceptable: at a time when a fundamental shift in thinking is required, the UK should set an example, not bury its head in the sand. Land-rich countries such as Brazil have great potential to boost global food supplies, but neither their ability to realize this potential, nor a well-functioning global market, can be taken for granted. A healthy domestic agriculture is an essential component of a secure food system in the UK.

The self-sufficient approach

6. The Commission should investigate further what means would be at its disposal in the unlikely event of a breakdown of the single market. However, the fact that trading relationships are fragile is an argument in favour of spreading the risk by having relationships with multiple countries, working to build strong relationships, and having contingency plans, not an argument in favour of self-sufficiency.

7. The UK should not aim to be self-sufficient, even in indigenous foodstuffs. Total self-sufficiency would make the UK's food supplies less secure rather than more secure.

Food colonialism or Land-grabbing

8. We welcome the recent report by the UN Food and Agriculture Organization, the International Fund for Agricultural Development, and the International Institute for Environment and Development on the large-scale acquisition of farmland in sub- Saharan Africa by overseas investors. It is a first step towards exploring the implications of this global trend. We urge the bodies involved to continue their work on the phenomenon, with the aim of providing an accurate picture of the extent of the trend and of developing a set of international guidelines that include provisions for local producers, property rights, sustainable management and transparent rules.

We note the involvement of DFID in the initial study and urge it to continue to provide input to subsequent studies. DEFRA should report on the implications of the trend for UK food security.

The sustainable production approach

9. The UK should commission research to establish the reasons for the relatively low level of domestic fruit and vegetable production. This should include a study of the procurement practices of supermarkets, food manufacturers and the food service industry to establish how these practices impact on the problem. UK's new Council of Food Policy Advisers should consider how the barriers to increased domestic fruit and vegetable production could be removed.

10. The UK should produce its own estimate of the amount by which consumption of fruit and vegetables would rise if people in the UK followed the Government's five-a-day guidelines.

11. There is a big difference between aiming to be self-sufficient and aiming to increase production of certain commodities. The UK should aim to increase

its production of those fruit and vegetables that are suited to being grown here, particularly where there is evidence of an increase in demand. It should also explore the potential for an increase in cereal production. However, again, we emphasize that it is essential that this increase in production be carried out sustainably.

Meat and dairy production

12. The UK consumers buying meat and dairy products should be encouraged to consider the environmental, as well as the health, impacts of their choices. To enable consumers to make informed decisions, UK needs to do more work on what are the most sustainable methods of livestock production, and the balance to be struck between animal welfare, biodiversity, greenhouse gas emissions, and the need to conserve inputs such as water.

Fish

13. The marine environment is an important source of food. However, the current state of many fish stocks is a serious cause for concern. The Department of Health and the Food Standard Agency (UK) should consider the wisdom of continuing to advise consumers to eat at least two portions of fish a week at a time when the ability of the marine environment to meet this demand is questionable. The fishing industry and the Government have a duty to encourage consumers to try sustainable, less well known types of fish and shellfish. The UK and the devolved Administrations should produce a study evaluating the potential of sustainable aquaculture off the shores of the UK.

Environmental impact of increased population

14. The UK should produce a study setting out the volume of particular commodities that the UK would

be capable of producing under different scenarios and the impact that this production would have on the environment. This study into "The UK's Agricultural Potential" should include work on the most sustainable methods of both arable and livestock production.

Local and home production

15. We welcome the increasing enthusiasm among consumers for buying food that is local to a particular area of the UK, and also for growing their own food. In terms of overall production, these trends are a small contribution to a huge challenge, but they are a way of reconnecting people with food production and have an important part to play in encouraging the sort of changes in consumer behaviour that will be necessary for a sustainable system of food production. The role of local and home production, and of educating children about food, should be incorporated in UK vision and strategy for food. When it has been established that there is an unmet demand for allotments in a local authority area, the Government should require the local authority to publish, within three years, a plan setting out how it proposes to meet the demand.

The role of UK

16. UK's approach to the security of food supplies must take place in the context of the European Union. However, we believe that there is still scope for UK to develop its own food policy and that the clearer this policy and the stronger UK's leadership, the more chance the UK has of shaping the direction of any emerging EU policy on this issue.

17. It is beyond the scope of this inquiry to assess the impact of the new EU pesticides legislation on the security of food supplies. However, we note with concern that the Government's Chief Scientific

Adviser does not believe that it is an evidence-based policy. The UK should press for the EU to agree that the Council of Ministers or the European Parliament must not approve future changes of this nature until a full evidence-based evaluation of the proposals has been undertaken.

UK's progress so far

18. The vision and strategy for food, for which UK was assigned responsibility in the Cabinet Office's *Food Matters* report, must provide a long-term framework for the UK food and farming industries. It should commit the UK to increasing production of those commodities, which are best suited to being produced here, provided that this can be done in a sustainable way. UK must recognize that calling for more domestic food production is one thing, but it cannot order that this be done. It must; however, lay out clearly what role it has in helping the UK food and farming industries to achieve this objective. The vision and strategy cannot be expected to supply all the answers, but it must supply clear direction and indicate what further work is needed and the deadline for its completion. Cross-party consensus on the vision and strategy is essential.

Assessing the risks

19. We welcome the fact that UK is undertaking a comprehensive assessment of the risks to the security of the UK's food supplies. This work should be used as the basis for monitoring and managing risks, and should be regularly updated. Together with the vision and strategy for food, it should inform food policy decisions across all departments. It should also be used as a basis for contingency planning. The European Commission should undertake its own assessment of the risks to the security of food supplies in the EU.

The structure for delivering food policy

20. We believe that both the Food Strategy Task Force and the Cabinet Sub-Committee on Food could benefit from input from the food sector. They should set out how they intend to involve members of the sector in their deliberations.

21. The UK should use its review of its relationships with the food sector to consider how it can encourage the wider food sector to interact with the Council of Food Policy

Advisers

22. We extend a cautious welcome to the new groups working on food policy. The composition of the Food Strategy Task Force and the Cabinet Sub-Committee on Food means that they have the potential to improve co-ordination across Government. However, the Task Force and the Sub-Committee must be used as a way of facilitating action, rather than a substitute for it. To this end, as much information as possible about the groups' decisions and the work resulting from them should be published on the Internet. The Government should make use of modern, IT-based solutions as a way of engaging with consumers and the food and farming industries. The Council of Food Policy Advisers is already setting a good example. The Task Force should aim to publish more information about its work and the Sub-Committee should consider whether it can disclose any, even very basic, information—if not about its work, then at least about any work set in train as a result of its deliberations.

23. UK's vision for the UK food and farming industries is still being formulated. The UK has begun to recognize the importance of UK production, as well as trade in securing food supplies. It is essential that it develops and articulates this vision. The security of

the UK's food supplies is crucial because it will encourage the food and farming industries, and consumers, to respond in a coordinated way to the challenges posed by a growing global population, climate change, and increasingly scarce resources.

Targets for production

24. Targets are a crude and, in most cases, impractical way of increasing food production. We see no point in UK adopting production targets for particular commodities. Instead, UK should concentrate on helping to build capacity within the food and farming industries so that they are well placed to respond to market signals. However, if the global or national situation with regard to food were to worsen significantly, and the market did fail to deliver supplies of certain food stuffs, the possibility that the Government may need to consider production targets, and Government-held stocks of particular commodities, should not be ruled out altogether.

Common Agricultural Policy

25. We do not consider that the interests of food security would be served by a return to direct production subsides under the CAP, although, again, if the global situation with regard to food supplies were to worsen significantly, the possibility of some form of direct production subsidy should not be excluded altogether. The CAP is a way of rewarding farmers for the provision of environmental services. However, the focus of the post-2013 CAP should be on sustainable food production, rather than land management by itself. Europe has a responsibility to contribute to global food supplies and the EU must ensure that European countries are in a position to respond to increased demand. We are disappointed that the Lisbon Treaty did not address the out-of-date nature of European agricultural obligations and reflect

the increasing importance of sustainability. The principles of the new CAP should be reflected in future amendments of EU treaties.

Research and development

26. UK scientific research is crucial to the security of food supplies. Without adequately structured, funded and focused research, the challenge of producing more food and producing it sustainably will not be met. Concentrating on developing a strong research base in the UK could also have a beneficial impact on global food security. The Government should encourage UK research institutes and universities to build more links with research centers that are working on food and farming worldwide, particularly in developing countries.

Research budget

27. More money needs to be spent on public-sector food and farming research in the UK. The long-term nature of returns from research means that this money needs to be committed without delay. The UK urges the Government's Chief Scientific Adviser, and the BBSRC to continue to make the case for increased investment in food and farming research, using new structures such as the Food Research Sub-Group to convey their arguments in a coordinated and coherent way.

Focus of the research

28. The focus of public sector food and farming research should be on increasing production sustainably and on realizing benefits to the consumer and to the environment across the whole of the food chain. The UK should develop a long-term strategic research agenda, overseen by its Chief Scientific Adviser, rather than allowing its research priorities to be determined wholly or largely by policy teams.

Such an approach must reflect both the potential of UK agriculture, and the threats it faces from pests, diseases and climate change.

29. It is not within the scope of this report to offer a detailed assessment of the role of GM technology in securing food supplies up to 2050 and beyond. However, we believe that the potential of GM technology in the context of sustainable food production should be explored further. UK has a role to play not only in commissioning some of the research, but in gaining public trust through the provision of comprehensible information, based on evidence. It should make an effort to "negotiate a ceasefire" on the destruction of GM crop trials so that more facts can be established.

Transnational services and research

30. It is essential that, once research has been carried out, people working in the food and farming sectors can realize its benefits. The extent to which this was identified as a failing in the present system is a serious cause for concern. In conjunction with the BBSRC, the Department should set out what more it intends to do to address this failing. There is a case for the reinstatement of a public-sector provider of advice on best practice, similar to the old ADAS system, to co-ordinate and build on existing transnational services. It should act as an agricultural equivalent of Business Link.

Skills

31. We emphasize the urgency of addressing the potential gaps in food and farming skills. We are particularly concerned about the applied sciences. We believe that there is already sufficient evidence for the Department for Environment, Food and Rural Affairs to reintroduce a studentship scheme based on the scheme formerly run by MAFF, with the aim of

encouraging more young people to acquire the skills that will help the UK and the world to produce more food, more sustainably. We recommend that the Department of Environment, Food and Rural Affairs reintroduce such a scheme.

The food chain

32. The Department for Environment, Food and Rural Affairs should set out how it plans to address the perceived weaknesses in its understanding of the food supply chain and what measures it intends to take to ensure that dialogue with the food industry leads to action. As a first step, it should arrange for more of its officials to undertake work placements in different sectors of the food and farming industries so that they can experience the problems, challenges and possibilities at first hand.

33. Food must be affordable to the consumer, but its prices must also make it worthwhile to produce in the first place. An agricultural system must be profitable to be healthy. The Department should initiate work to establish whether the different agricultural sectors are currently sufficiently profitable to enable them to invest, and therefore improve productivity in the long term.

34. Strong relationships in the food chain are an important element of securing food supplies over the long term. The Department of Environment Food and Rural Affairs (DEFRA) should consider applying the principle of the Pig Meat Supply Chain Task Force to other sectors where necessary.

35. The Department should monitor the supply chain infrastructure in the short-term to ensure that potentially damaging trends are identified and addressed before they affect the UK's abilities to secure its food supplies in the long term.

In short, FAO suggested the following:

36. We are broadly satisfied that the Department for Environment, Food and Rural Affairs is beginning to move in the right direction. However, there is a great deal still to do. The scale and importance of the challenge is such that we recommend that the Department publish a supplement to its Departmental Annual Report, detailing what it is doing to ensure the long-term security of the UK's food supplies, both through trade and domestic production.

37. Securing food supplies is a vast subject and there are many aspects that we have not been able to cover in this report. We regard this as the first in a series of food-related inquiries to be undertaken by this Committee. It is likely that our subsequent work will focus on some of the solutions to the challenges we have outlined. We would welcome feedback and suggestions for future work. We propose to hold a public discussion to enable people to respond to the report and to the Government's reply, and to shape the direction of future inquiries on this subject.

The report was prepared with the following terms of reference. These are:

(a) How robust is the current UK food system? What are its main strengths and weaknesses?
(b) How well placed is the UK to make the most of its opportunities in responding to the challenge of increasing global food production by 50% by 2030 and doubling it by 2050, while ensuring that such production is sustainable?
(c) In particular, what are the challenges the UK faces in relation to the following aspects of the supply side of the food system?
(d) The way in which land is farmed and managed
(e) What trends are likely to emerge on the demand side of the food system in the UK, in terms of consumer taste and habits, and what

will be their main effect? What use could be made of local food networks?

(f) What role should UK play both in ensuring that the strengths of the UK food system are maintained and in addressing the weaknesses that have been identified? What leadership and assistance should UK provide to the food industry?

(g) How well does UK engage with other relevant departments across Government, and with European and international bodies, on food policy and the regulatory framework for the food supply chain? Is there a coherent cross-Government food strategy?

(h) What criteria should UK use to monitor how well the UK is doing in responding to the challenge of doubling global food production by 2050 while ensuring that such production is sustainable?

(i) The FAO also studied soil quality, water availability, the marine environment, the science base, the provision of training, and trade barriers to recommend further actions to the UK government.[86]

International Alliance against Hunger

We, the Heads of State and Government, or our representatives, assembled in Rome at the World Food Summit: *five years later* at the invitation of the Food and Agriculture Organization of the United Nations (FAO)[87]:

Recalling the World Food Summit (WFS) held in Rome in November 1996 at which Heads of State and Government, or their representatives, adopted the Rome Declaration on World Food Security and the WFS Plan of Action and pledged their political will and

[86]FAO Food Security Report

[87] World Food Summit: Five Years later

their common and national commitment to achieving food security for all and to an ongoing effort to eradicate hunger in all countries, with an immediate view to reducing the number of undernourished people to half their level no later than 2015;

Recognizing the urgent need to reinforce the efforts of all concerned partners as an international alliance against hunger, for the fulfillment of the objectives of the 1996 Summit;

Reaffirming the right of everyone to have access to safe and nutritious food;

Reiterating that food should not be used as an instrument for political and economic pressure and reaffirming the importance of international cooperation and solidarity as well as the necessity of refraining from unilateral measures not in accordance with the international law and the Charter of the United Nations and that endanger food security,

Reaffirming the commitments that we assumed with the Rome Declaration and Plan of Action, which taking into consideration the multifaceted character of food security, encompass national action and effective international efforts to supplement and reinforce national action,

Acknowledging the considerable efforts, which have been made in many countries to reduce poverty and improve food security, and recognizing the commitment of the international community to assisting this effort as expressed in the United Nations Millennium Declaration,

Noting that the average annual rate of reduction in the number of undernourished people in the world was eight million and that if this trend continues, the WFS target of reducing the number of the undernourished by half by 2015, reaffirmed by the Millennium Declaration, will not be attained;

Noting that hunger is both a cause and an effect of extreme poverty, and prevents the poor from taking advantage of development opportunities, that hunger eradication is a vital step in alleviating poverty and inequality, and that the international community has restated its commitment to the reduction of poverty. Observing further that 70 percent of the world's poor live in rural areas and depend almost entirely on agriculture and rural development for their livelihood; and noting the rapid increase in the numbers and proportion of urban people affected by poverty, hunger and malnutrition;

Conscious of the particular difficulties faced by all developing countries, in particular by the least developed countries (LDC), the low-income food-deficit countries (LIFDC), the small island developing states, and countries affected by violent conflicts, civil strife, land mines and unexploded ordnance, or exposed to desertification and natural disasters; noting further that global warming and climate change can have serious implications for food and livelihood security, especially in these countries;

Recognizing also the difficulties faced by the countries with economies in transition in addressing their food security needs in the process of conducting market-oriented reforms;

Concerned with the current estimates of the overall downward trend in the national budgets of developing countries and the decline in Official Development Assistance (ODA) and International Financial Institutions (IFIs) portfolios directly allocated for agriculture and rural development, as a contribution to food security,

Recognizing the important role of food assistance in situations of humanitarian crisis as well as an instrument for development, acting as an enabling pre-investment;

Reaffirming Commitment 4 of the WFS Plan of Action that trade is a key element in achieving world food security,

Reaffirming the fundamental importance of national production and distribution of food, sustainable agriculture and rural development, fisheries and forestry, in achieving food security,

Reiterating our deep concern at the debt burden on developing countries in particular the heavily indebted poor countries, and at its negative impact on resources for food security, in spite of progress in implementing the Heavily Indebted Poor Countries (HIPC) initiative;

Recognizing that international economic and financial crises have shown dramatically the vulnerability of developing countries;

Noting with concern the acute threat of the HIV/AIDS pandemic, and the incidence of malaria, tuberculosis and other diseases, in particular those caused by water contamination in developing countries, and their devastating impact on food security;

Reaffirming our commitment to the Monterrey Consensus, which referenced the need to develop effective partnerships between developed and developing countries, based on the recognition of national leadership and ownership of development plans that embody poverty reduction strategies, and recognizing the value of exploring innovative sources of finance provided that those sources do not unduly burden developing countries, as important steps towards achieving sustainable food security;

Recognizing the importance of the International Treaty on Plant Genetic Resources for Food and Agriculture in support of food security objectives; and if the population growth is higher than expected.

Noting the outcomes of the world conferences:

(a) Including the International Conference on Financing for Development,
(b) The United Nations General Assembly (UNGA) Special Sessions on HIV/AIDS in 2001,
(c) The UNGA Session on Children in 2002 and
(d) The 4th Ministerial Conference of the World Trade Organization (WTO) at Doha,
(e) And highlighting the forthcoming World Summit on Sustainable Development of 2002.

Political will

1. We renew our global commitments made in the Rome Declaration at the World Food Summit in 1996 in particular to halve the number of hungry in the world no later than 2015, as reaffirmed in the United Nations Millennium Declaration. We resolve to accelerate the implementation of the WFS Plan of Action.

2. We call on all parties (governments, international organizations, civil society organizations and the private sector) to reinforce their efforts so as to act, as an international alliance against hunger to achieve the WFS targets no later than 2015. With this aim, parties should promote coordinated action. Bearing in mind the contribution of all parties, countries should continue to report on progress to the Committee on World Food Security (CFS), within its mandate as a focal point for the implementation of the WFS Plan of Action.

3. We recognize that progress had not been adequate to reach the WFS target. Recognizing that responsibility for assuring national food security rests with national governments in cooperation with civil society and the private sector and with the support of the international community, we resolve to accelerate implementation of action to halve hunger by no later than 2015. This requires a rate of hunger reduction of more than 22 million per year on average.

4. We stress that poverty reduction and food security strategies should, *inter alia*, include measures to increase agricultural productivity, food production and distribution. We agree to promote equal access for men and women to food, water, land, credit and technology which will also help in generating income and creating employment opportunities for the poor, thus contributing to reduction of poverty and hunger.

5. We reaffirm the importance of strengthening the respect of all human rights and fundamental freedoms including the right to development, democracy, the rule of law, good governance, sound economic policies, the equality of rights for all without distinction as to sex, race, language, religion, the resolution of conflicts in accordance with the UN Charter and respect for international humanitarian law, and international cooperation so as to solve economic, social, cultural and humanitarian problems, which are essential for achieving food security.

6. We call upon the concerned development partners to exert all necessary efforts to achieve the international development goals of the Millennium Declaration, particularly, those related to halving poverty and hunger by 2015, to improve and strengthen the indicators necessary for measuring progress and to monitor progress within their mandate; and to renew and strengthen the commitment to national and international systems in place to assess food security. We reaffirm the role of

FAO, with World Health Organization (WHO) and UNICEF in monitoring progress towards the Millennium Development Goal on hunger and the importance of the Inter- Agency Working Group on FIVIMS (Food Insecurity and Vulnerability Information and Mapping Systems) in strengthening national and international monitoring of food security.

7. The vast majority of the hungry and those living in absolute poverty are in rural areas. We recognize that reaching the goal of halving the number of hungry requires that the most food insecure and impoverished countries promote the alleviation of rural poverty especially through sustained growth of agricultural production, particularly in sub-Saharan Africa.

8. We reconfirm that FAO has a major role to play in assisting countries to implement the provisions of the WFS Plan of Action within its mandate, keeping in mind that the WFS entrusted the Committee on World Food Security to monitor progress.

9. We believe that broad international partnerships are of utmost importance for the implementation of the WFS Plan of Action. We call on governments, the international organizations and financial institutions to utilize their resources effectively, to improve their performance and strengthen cooperation and to undertake joint efforts to combat hunger, and reinforce the key role of sustainable agriculture and rural development in food security.

10. We invite the FAO Council to establish at its One Hundred and Twenty-third Session an Intergovernmental Working Group, with the participation of stakeholders, in the context of the WFS follow-up, to elaborate, in a period of two years, a set of voluntary guidelines to support Member States' efforts to achieve the progressive realization of the right to adequate food in the context of

national food security; we ask the FAO, in close collaboration with relevant treaty bodies, agencies and programs of the UN System, to assist the Intergovernmental Working Group, which shall report on its work to the Committee on World Food Security.

11. We specifically urge governments to review their ongoing national food security policies with a view to filling gaps, identifying new initiatives, removing implementation obstacles and streamlining inter-ministerial and inter-departmental policy initiatives.

12. We reaffirm the Monterrey Consensus and we urge all members of the WTO to implement the outcome of the Doha Conference, especially the commitments regarding the reform of the international agricultural trading system, with particular reference to paragraphs 13 and 14, given that international agricultural trade has a role to play, consistent with Commitment 4 of the WFS Plan of Action, in promoting economic development, alleviating poverty and achieving the objectives of the World Food Summit, in particular in developing countries.

Challenges

13. We reaffirm the need to assure gender equality and to support empowerment of women. We recognize and value the continuing and vital role of women in agriculture, nutrition and food security and the need to integrate a gender perspective in all aspects of food security; and we recognize the need to adopt measures to ensure that the work of rural women is recognized and valued in order to enhance their economic security, and their access to and control over resources and credit schemes, services and benefits.

14. We emphasize the need for nutritionally adequate and safe food and highlight the need for attention to

nutritional issues as an integral part of addressing food security. The recent UNGA Special Session on Children addressed the need for investments in basic economic and social infrastructure and social services, as well as social protection for vulnerable and disadvantaged groups. Attention should be given to improving the quality of diet; access to potable water, health care, and education; and sanitation. We recognize the importance of interventions to tackle micronutrient deficiencies, which are cost-effective and locally acceptable.

15. We reaffirm our pledge to the fight against world-wide conditions that pose severe health threats, and especially the spread of HIV/AIDS, which can have a uniquely devastating impact on all sectors and levels of society and consequently on food security. This requires new approaches, technologies and crops for labour-deficient HIV / AIDS - affected farming households. In this regard, we welcome the establishment of the Global Fund to Fight AIDS, Tuberculosis and Malaria, which constitutes an important step forward for concerted action at country level, as well as for the mobilization of new and additional resources aimed at the prevention and treatment of these diseases.

16. We reaffirm the important role of Codex Alimentations, the International Plant Protection Convention (IPPC) and the Office International des Epizooties (OIE) to provide effective, science-based, internationally-accepted standards of food safety, plant and animal health, as well as to facilitate international food and agricultural trade in their role as the WTO Agreement on Sanitary and Phyto - sanitary Measures (SPS)-recognized standard-setting bodies.

17. We pledge to continue to support efforts to strengthen developing countries' capacity with

respect to the management of food safety and plant and animal health.

18. We should strengthen national and international action to prepare for contingencies and emergencies and to improve the effectiveness of emergency actions both through food and non-food based intervention. These actions must be integrated into sustainable development efforts with all stakeholders involved to achieve sustainable food security. We underscore the importance of developing the scope and coverage of social protection mechanisms, in particular of safety nets for vulnerable and food insecure households. We are committed to ensuring, through economic development, the use of early warning systems, and emergency assistance, that famine will never again be seen.

19. We recognize the merit of school feeding as a social development program. It should be based on local or regional purchase where possible, and managed in a way to respect local consumption habits. In this regard, we encourage the development of the World Food Program's (WFP's) school feeding programs, among others, when implemented in accordance with national priorities and educational programs.

20. We resolve to contribute to the outcome of the World Summit on Sustainable Development, recognizing the important role of the three Rome-based organizations, FAO, WFP and the International Fund for Agricultural Development (IFAD), and to strengthen coordination and cooperation among national and international organizations, in order to make efficient use of resources, particularly in the areas of technical and financial cooperation, sustainable management of natural resources, fighting trans-boundary animal and plant diseases and securing food safety.

21. We stress the need to further promote sustainable forest and fisheries management, including sustainable use and conservation of aquatic living resources, in view of the contribution of those sectors to food security and poverty eradication.

22. We stress the importance of supporting alternative development activities that enable people engaged in illicit crop cultivation to reach sustainable food security and live in dignity.

23. Recognizing the extent of poverty in the mountain zones, we emphasize the vital role of mountain zones and they're potential for sustainable agriculture and rural development in order to achieve food security. We stress the need to build partnerships between developing and developed countries in this regard.

24. We pledge to work in the spirit of cooperation and solidarity to strengthen FAO activities, within its mandate, that enable the developing countries and countries with economies in transition to meet food safety issues, to make better use of the benefits of research and technologies and to respond effectively to the challenges and opportunities of globalization, in particular with respect to agriculture and food security. We also pledge to assist those countries, particularly their food producers, to make informed choices about, and to have access to, the necessary scientific and technical knowledge related to these new technologies targeted at poverty and hunger reduction.

25. We call on the FAO, in conjunction with the CGIAR and other international research institutes, to advance agricultural research and research into new technologies, including biotechnology. The introduction of tried and tested new technologies including biotechnology should be accomplished in a safe manner and adapted to local conditions to help improve agricultural productivity in developing

countries. We are committed to study, share and facilitate the responsible use of biotechnology in addressing development needs.

26. We recognize that the developing countries and countries in economic transition are facing difficulties in responding to the challenges and opportunities of globalization, in particular with respect to agriculture and food security, and we therefore agree in a spirit of cooperation and solidarity to consolidate FAO activities, in support of these countries to enable them to cope with the challenges and reap the benefits of globalization.

Resources

27. We call on all Member States, intergovernmental and non-governmental organizations, the private sector and all other partners in development to consider voluntary contributions to the FAO Trust Fund for Food Security and Food Safety and other voluntary instruments. The Trust Fund should serve as a catalyst for accelerating food production and improving food access in LDCs, LIFDCs and Small Island Developing States, and for the prevention, control and eradication of trans-boundary pests and plant and animal diseases, and the preparation of investment projects, and South-South cooperation, in the aforementioned areas.

28. We stress the inherent linkage between rapid progress towards the targets of the World Food Summit Plan of Action, as reaffirmed by the United Nations Millennium Declaration, and the size, direction and efficient use of investment in food security, agriculture, rural development, food production, processing and distribution. As we agreed in the Monterrey Consensus, mobilizing domestic and international resources to reach those objectives is contingent on several factors, *inter alia*:

(a) An enabling environment for savings and investment in rural areas within the framework of a sound national macro-economic system,
(b) A broad-based national poverty reduction strategy aiming at improving access to food including through increasing food production and distribution,
(c) Promoting opportunities for internal and external private investment,
(d) Trade,
(e) Adequate attention in the national budget towards social-economic development,
(f) Complementing national efforts with ODA in critical areas of social infrastructure and human development and
(g) Transparent and effective management of public resources.

29. We urge developed countries that have not done so to make concrete efforts towards the target of 0.7 percent of Gross National Product (GNP) as ODA to developing countries, and 0.15 percent to 0.20 percent of GNP of developed countries to least developed countries, as reconfirmed at the Third United Nations Conference on Least Developed Countries, and we encourage developing countries to build on progress achieved in ensuring that ODA is used effectively to help achieve development goals and targets. We acknowledge the efforts of all donors, commend those donors whose ODA contributions exceed, reach or are increasing towards the targets, and underline the importance of undertaking to examine the means and timeframes for achieving the targets and goals.

30. We welcome the adoption of the New Partnership for Africa's Development (NEPAD), and the inclusion of agriculture and food security as a component of this initiative. We invite the international community to respond to this initiative by financing programs or

projects, in the most appropriate manner that reflects NEPAD principles and commitments.

31. We will encourage the international community to continue to provide technical and financial assistance to the countries with economies in transition with a view to fostering their food security;

32. With a view to reversing the overall decline of agriculture and rural development in the national budgets of developing countries, in ODA and in total lending in international financial institutions, we call for an adequate share for those sectors of bilateral and multilateral ODA, lending by IFIs and budgetary allocations of developing countries, within the framework of the Monterrey Consensus.

33. We reaffirm that the enhanced Heavily Indebted Poor Countries (HIPC) Initiative provides an opportunity to strengthen the economic prospects and poverty reduction efforts of its beneficiary countries, thereby increasing food security. Speedy, effective and full implementation of the enhanced Initiative, which should be fully financed through additional resources, is critical. Heavily indebted poor countries should take the policy measures necessary to become eligible for the initiative.

34. We also reaffirm the Monterrey consensus to encourage exploring innovative mechanisms to address debt problems of developing countries, including middle-income countries and countries with economies in transition.

35. We call on all countries that have not yet done so, to consider signing and ratifying the International Treaty on Plant Genetic Resources for Food and Agriculture in order that it shall enter into force as soon as possible.

The International Food Policy Research Institute (IFPRI)

IFPRI seeks sustainable solutions for ending hunger and poverty. IFPRI is one of 15 centers supported by the Consultative Group on International Agricultural Research (CGIAR), an alliance of 64 governments, private foundations, and international and regional organizations.

IFPRI's Vision: The vision is based on the human rights to adequate food and freedom from hunger, and the recognition of the dignity inherent in all human beings. It is a vision of a world where every person has secure access to sufficient and safe food to sustain a healthy and productive life and where food-related policy decisions are made transparently, including the participation of consumers and producers.

IFPRI's Mission

(a)To provide policy solutions that reduces poverty and end hunger and malnutrition

(b)To achieve sustainable food security and reduce poverty in developing countries through scientific research and research-related activities in the fields of agriculture, livestock, forestry, fisheries, policy, and natural resources management.

Two key premises underlie IFPRI's mission:

(a) Sound and appropriate local, national, and international public policies are essential to achieving sustainable food security and nutritional improvement.
(b) Research and the dissemination of its results are critical inputs into the process of raising the quality of food policy debate and formulating sound and appropriate policies.

IFPRI's mission focuses on:

(a) Identifying and analyzing alternative international, national, and local policies in support of improved food security and nutrition, emphasizing low-income countries and poor people and the sound management of the natural resource base that supports agriculture;

(b) Contributing to capacity strengthening of people and institutions in developing countries that conduct research on food, agriculture, and nutrition policies; and

(c) Actively engaging in policy communications, making research results available to all those in a position to apply or use them, and carrying out dialogues with those users to link research and policy action.

(d)IFPRI places priority on activities that benefit the greatest number of poor people in greatest need in the developing world. In carrying out its activities, IFPRI seeks to focus on vulnerable groups, as influenced by class, religion, ethnicity, agro-ecological location, and gender.

(e)IFPRI is committed to providing global food policy knowledge as an international public good; that is, it provides knowledge relevant to decision makers both inside and outside the countries in which it undertakes research. New knowledge on how to improve the food security of low-income people in developing countries is expected to result in large social benefits, but in most instances the private sector is unlikely to carry out research to generate such knowledge. IFPRI views both public organizations and the private sector in food systems as objects of study and as partners.

(f)Given the large body of national and international food policy research, IFPRI's added-value derives from its own cutting-edge research linked with academic excellence in other institutions, such as other CGIAR centers, universities, and other research institutes in the South and the North, and from its application of this knowledge to national and international food policy problems.

Guiding Principles

IFPRI's research is guided by a mission of generating knowledge to reduce poverty, hunger, and malnutrition. IFPRI's strategy describes the Institute's programs and its research and capacity strengthening goals. In pursuit of these goals, IFPRI research staff should adhere to the following guiding principles:

Integrity and Transparency

IFPRI generates knowledge and makes it available to all key stakeholders, without supporting any political regime or ideology.

The processes by which IFPRI's research topics are identified and its priorities are set are transparent.

IFPRI's research approaches, methodologies, and results are state-of-the-art and are subject to peer review;

IFPRI publishes its peer-reviewed research results and makes them available to all stakeholders.

IFPRI recognizes that in some instances, initial research findings must be made available (with appropriate qualifications) to policymakers before a full, formal peer-review process is complete. Such research, including IFPRI discussion papers, is marked as "research in progress."

IFPRI does not shy away from making its voice heard regarding peer-reviewed research findings even if they conflict with conventional wisdom or certain stakeholder interests.

Because some of IFPRI's work is undertaken in complex political environments, the Institute is mindful that controversial policy research findings produced with research partners should not put those partners at risk.

IFPRI's policy advice is guided by research and not by individual opinions (about a country, government, etc.). IFPRI researchers must engage stakeholders with care, bearing in mind that as researchers, their primary role is to inform the debate and not advocate for a cause.

In order to maintain its integrity and transparency, IFPRI discourages its research staff from working as de facto consultants for individual policymakers.

Partners and Donors

IFPRI research aims to serve the poor, food insecure, and malnourished. Because these clients often do not have a strong voice, IFPRI researchers seek to take their interests into account when conducting and communicating research and capacity strengthening initiatives.

IFPRI's research is conceived and conducted in consultation with stakeholders in an open manner. Exceptions to stakeholder consultation may include exploratory research or literature reviews.

In principle, IFPRI aims to be financially independent. This entails that research programs be funded by multiple donors to avoid dependence on a single donor, though IFPRI recognizes this may not always be possible.

The host institutions of IFPRI country- or regional-based programs are selected on the basis of the institutions' strength in the area of policy research within the country, and on the basis of maximizing their impact on poverty reduction by generating public goods and knowledge and by strengthening national capacity. Host institutions with strong affiliations to particular political interest groups are avoided.

Research partners are chosen on the basis of their professional competence or potential for competence; research program advisory committees should consist of a broad range of members, including nongovernmental organizations such as universities, farmer and consumer organizations, and private-sector groups.

IFPRI undertakes policy research wherever the expected results will have global or regional impact (international public goods). Among other considerations, country-specific studies are selected where a significant poverty-reduction impact can be expected and where the knowledge generated can have a broader impact beyond the country studied.

Guiding Principles:

(a) Research should directly or indirectly serve the poor—IFPRI's ultimate clients.
(b) Research should be conceived and conducted in consultation with stakeholders in an open manner (exceptions noted above).
(c) Research funding should not be linked to pre-conceived research results.
(d) Research should be conducted in accordance with the principles of sound scholarship.
(e) Research should be freely disseminated, without censorship beyond normal quality controls.

(f) Context-specific research should create international public goods by having effects beyond the research site.[88]

The European Commission:
Food Facility Interim Report

On 12 March 2010, the European Commission adopted the Food Facility Interim Report. This Document reports on the measures taken by the Commission in 2009 to implement the Food Facility. It shows that, financially, implementation is ahead of schedule with more commitments and payments made than anticipated. Moreover, the overall plan for the Food facility, as approved by Council and Parliament in March 2009, has been respected with less than 5% change in financial planning. The report also indicates monitoring arrangements made to assess the effects of the Food Facility projects.

The UN Food and Agriculture Organization declared that it would work till:

All people, at all times have physical and economic access to sufficient, safe and nutritious food to meet their dietary needs and food preferences for an active and healthy life through an epoch-making declaration known as "Rome Declaration on World Food Security".

But in the developing world, nearly ONE billion people are unable to meet their dietary needs. Another 5-10 percent people are at risk of 'acute' food insecurity in times of crisis. Despite improvements, the millennium development goal on hunger is likely to be missed by a wide margin in Sub-Saharan Africa, where persistent food insecurity is compounded by widespread political instability, conflict and the HIV/AIDS pandemic.

---

[88] IFPRI Report

Lack of food – the defining feature of poverty

Food insecurity is directly linked to poverty, which means that it is a priority for the European Union consensus on development. So the European Union decided that support must be given at the right time because even a transitory crisis can trigger chronic food problems, as assets are quickly depleted and livelihoods undermined.

EU food security policy

(a) Puts food availability, access to food, responses to food shortages and nutritional problems at the center of poverty-reduction strategies

(b) Acknowledges the causes of food insecurity – environmental degradation, poor productive systems, badly functioning markets, limited human capacity and inequality

(c) Recognizes the social factors affecting access to food – gender, age and ethnicity

(d) Supports broad based food-security strategies at the national and regional level in preference to handing out food aid directly

(e) Is based on the premise that the long-term objectives of meeting millennium development goals and eradicating food insecurity will only be met through nationally owned poverty-reduction strategies

Food insecurity in crisis situations

Food insecurity is particularly hard to tackle in complex, ongoing crises and in the fragile transition to stability. During a crisis, fragile states may lack the capacity or institutional frameworks to implement long-term food security solutions – a situation that may be compounded by poor governance, conflicts, man-made disasters, HIV/AIDS and other diseases.

The EU – a mainstay of support for food security

Because food aid is primarily a humanitarian tool, it is managed by ECHO and administered through:

(a) European Development Fund (EDF)
(b) Development Cooperation Instrument (DCI)
(c) European Neighborhood and Partnership Instrument (ENPI)
(d) The Food security thematic programs address food security at global, continental and regional level in countries where the other, geography-based, instruments cannot be used.
(e) EU actions tackle the structural causes of food insecurity on three levels
(f) National level – inadequate food and water availability
(g) Household level – poverty resulting in insufficient access to food
(h) Individual level – food use and nutritional adequacy

In assessing and implementing support for food security the EU attaches importance to:

(a) Consistency with EU development policy and the Commission's country and regional support strategies
(b) Close coordination with other EU financial instruments, ECHO, EU member countries and major donors. This ensures external coherence and complementarities. Food security programs support changes to policies and institutions to achieve sustained economic growth and reduce poverty.
(c) Building on nationally owned policies and strategies for poverty reduction and social cohesion
(d) Reinforcing national capacity and supporting local partnerships

(e) Measure that have an impact – direct or indirect – on incomes for the poor and most vulnerable
(f) Disaster preparedness and crisis prevention
(g) The link between relief, rehabilitation and development in protracted and post-crisis situations
(h) Code of Conduct for Food Aid
(i) Efficiency in reducing poverty and food insecurity in a specific environment where possible, relief materials will be purchased in the country or region.
(j) Sustainability of food security programs – insofar as possible.
(k) Collaboration with FAO
(l) European Union and FAO cooperation is based on the 2004 EC – FAO Partnership.

The focus is on: [89]

(a) Increasing the ability of countries and regions to design and implement food insecurity information systems
(b) Increasing awareness in government and local circles of the links between food insecurity and poverty
(c) Using food insecurity information systems to help design and implement food security strategies
(d) Support through the FAO targets crosscutting activities particularly relevant to food security and poverty reduction in fields where FAO has a comparative advantage – such as support to the agricultural sector after a natural disaster.

[89]Food Facility Interim Report, The European Commission, March 12, 2010

The Consultative Group on International Agricultural Research (CGIAR)

Consultative Group on International Agricultural Research (CGIAR) is at the forefront of research in food security and natural resources management, genetic resources and international policy. EU resources are allocated to a CGIAR programmes closely related to food security in the fields of genetic resources and international policies related to water management and the new initiative of the International Assessment of Agricultural Knowledge, Science and Technology for Development.

Instruments

Financial aid can be provided either as budgetary support through (national procedures apply) projects (Commission procedures apply) or food aid – and at national level (agreement with the country's government) or international level (cooperation with international organisations).

Budgetary support

Budgetary support is provided as financial assistance through the government budget and aims to:

(a) Support policy and institutional reforms related to food security
(b) Facilitate import of food by the private sector
(c) Promote employment and income generation to improve access to food
(d) Help provide safety nets
(e) Budgetary aid is provided under well-defined conditions:
(f) To low-income and least developed countries
(g) To countries with a strong macroeconomic framework demonstrating fiscal sustainability
(h) To countries with good governance, including sound public-finance management and

effective public and private sectors where policies and programs exist to promote food security and reduce poverty

Project support

(a) Support to country/ regional strategies and programs
(b) Project support is provided in countries with a weak institutional framework where the policy environment does not allow budgetary aid. Support will:
(c) Ensure financial support is routed to "food insecure" groups
(d) Ensure that development assistance is managed properly and promote capacity building where the public sector is weak and realistic avenues for improvement are lacking
(e) Make it possible to test pilot approaches to tackling food insecurity
(f) Make it possible to address key bottlenecks in food availability and access to food
(g) Ensure that aid recipients participate actively in project design and implementation.

Food security projects are supported for a limited time - during a transition from relief to long-term development or when food insecurity is structural. Projects focus on improving access to food through support to production systems, other income-generating activities and social safety nets. Regional strategies on food security should be promoted and - when justified - supported.

Food aid should be:

(a) Considered a tool for humanitarian assistance. In grant form, it should be provided only in acute, protracted crises to meet well-identified and internationally recognized needs.

(b) Restricted to situations where it is the best tool to solve an immediate problem.

(c) Delivered in response to a food-related emergency (man-made and natural disasters, calamity or similar circumstances creating severe food insecurity that local government is unable to handle).

(d) Targeted to the most vulnerable groups, while respecting their nutritional requirements and habits. Preference will be given to local and regional purchases.

(e) Based on reliable, objective, credible and transparent assessments of needs.

(f) Fully de-linked, cash only, and donors should buy locally and regionally in order to stimulate agricultural production, sustain local markets and enhance the livelihood of producers.

(g) Demand-driven and provided in compliance with broader food security strategies.

EU food aid is targeted by means of a continuous process of analysis, needs assessment, information and consultation between ECHO and the main UN and NGO partners. Other Directorates General may be involved, particularly DG Development and DG RELEX. The EU is committed to work actively towards making food aid more effective and minimizing any negative impacts. Soaring food prices have brought poverty, hunger and malnutrition to millions throughout the developing world in the last few years. In 2007 the number of undernourished people in the world rose to 923 million according to FAO estimates – most of them in South Asia and Sub-Saharan Africa. After dramatic price rises in late 2007, prices eased in the second half of 2008. But, despite record production figures, prices are still very high in some developing countries, affecting access to food for low-income population groups.

The EU responses: The commission has responded quickly

(a) Additional €140m in humanitarian aid authorized in 2008

(b) Additional €50m made available from food security thematic program

(c) Additional €200m in emergency funding from the 10th EDF proposal to set up a special €1 billion food facility – now in operation

Food facility: The € ONE billion food facility (see EU regulation 1337 / 2008) will enable the EU to respond rapidly to problems caused by soaring food prices in developing countries. Operating over a 3-year period from 2009-2011, the fund will bridge the gap between emergency aid and medium to long-term development aid.

Its chief objectives are to:

(a) Encourage food producers to increase supply

(b) Deal directly with the effects of volatile food prices on local populations

(c) Increase food production capacity and improve the way agriculture is managed in the longer term.

In concrete terms, it will support:

(a) Measures to improve access to agricultural inputs and services including fertilizers and seeds – with special attention to local facilities and availability

(b) Safety-net measures to maintain or increase agricultural production capacity and help meet the basic food needs of the most vulnerable populations, including children

(c) Other small-scale production-boosting measures based on countries' individual needs – micro credit, investment, equipment, infrastructure and storage – and vocational training and support for agricultural professionals. [90]

The Pittsburgh Summit:
Partnering On Food Security

At the Summit in L'Aquila, Italy in July, Leaders from thirty-six countries and international organizations committed to five principles for a food security initiative:

(a) Stronger coordination among donors
(b) Support of comprehensive strategies
(c) Investment through country-owned plans
(d) Leveraging effective multilateral institutions
(e) Sustained commitments.

As part of that sustained commitment, fourteen countries and the European Commission committed at least $20 billion over three years to agriculture development, in addition to their assistance for emergency food aid and nutrition programs. These countries included: Australia, Canada, Denmark, France, Germany, Italy, Japan, The Netherlands, Republic of Korea, Russia, Spain, Sweden, the United Kingdom, and the United States.

Since the L'Aquila Summit, we have seen further progress to launch this important partnership:

New Partners: Additional countries, such as Belgium, Finland, Ireland, Norway, and Switzerland have pledged their support for the initiative and its approach, helping to bring total pledges towards agriculture development to $22 billion over the next three years. In addition, other countries have pledged to provide technical assistance as part of this initiative. Some of these countries include Argentina, Brazil, Indonesia, and Mexico.

---

[90]Food Facility Interim Report, The European Commission, March 12, 2010

G-20 Call for World Bank Food Security Trust Fund:

In addition, the United States has been working with donor partners and the World Bank since L'Aquila to develop a multi-donor trust fund that supports the initiative, building on the success of the World Bank's Food Crisis Response Fund (GFRP) to finance medium- and long-term investments that boost agricultural productivity and market access in low-income countries.

Development of Implementation Plan: On September 14th and 15th, senior technical experts from over forty developing and developed countries, regional and international organizations came together to begin implementing the L'Aquila commitments. This event generated agreement on actions that we collectively need to take to help developing countries put together, resource, and implement country-led food security strategies. Secretary Clinton and U.N. Secretary General Ban Ki-moon will take the implementation of our commitments a step further on September 26th when they host a forum for the leaders of countries and international, public, and private organizations to affirm our shared approach to achieving food security and outline the key steps that we will take to realize our commitments.

Engaging the Private Sector and Philanthropy:

One of the key elements of the U.S. approach to this initiative is to use development assistance to explore synergies with private philanthropy and private sector actors. As an example, we have been working with several foundations and businesses deeply involved in food security to see how best to coordinate our efforts:

Gates Foundation: The Bill & Melinda Gates Foundation, which has to date committed $1.4 billion as part of a new effort to boost agricultural development focused on smallholder farmers in the developing world and another half billion dollars for nutrition-related investments largely for children and their mothers around the globe, has strongly endorsed the new food security initiative, and agreed to work closely with the G-20 and its partners to better align their activities and explore areas of collaboration and partnership to maximize impact on the ground.

Rockefeller Foundation: The Rockefeller Foundation will bring over sixty years of experience in food security and agricultural development to bear, working with us to explore how we can take to scale successful programs on agricultural inputs and market development, and will share with us its research and field testing on critical issues including, for example, building climate change resilience into agricultural development programs and facilitating greater private sector investments in agricultural development.

Hewlett Foundation: We are collaborating with The William and Flora Hewlett Foundation to develop the most effective ways to integrate smallholder farmers into commercial agricultural value chains, especially along Africa's regional infrastructure corridors. We will work with the Hewlett Foundation and others to increase market efficiencies and reduce barriers along these regional development corridors, through improved infrastructure and policies along these corridors.

Rabo bank Foundation: This Foundation from the Netherlands, which supports cooperative micro finance institutions, producers organizations and local savings- and credit cooperatives in twenty-five countries, has endorsed the new food security initiative, and agreed to work closely with the G-20 and its partners to help us find ways to use small scale donations, technical assistance, fair trade-financing, micro finance lending, guarantees, and other tools to improve access to capital for small scale farmers and cooperatives.

World Economic Forum: The World Economic Forum is collaborating with partners in the L'Aquila initiative as part of a broader effort to facilitate public-private collaboration to improve food security and sustainable agriculture. Forum partners develop and catalyze scalable business models that contribute to sustainable food production. We will work with the Forum to harness business expertise, in partnership with other sectors, to generate sustainable, market-based solutions to hunger and poverty.

Initiative for Global Development: We are working with the Initiative for Global Development (IGD), whose members comprise business leaders from the United States and Africa, to help build market linkages that serve small producers by identifying both barriers to agricultural development and new opportunities for investment. IGD provides a forum for regular consultation with its members, which can facilitate private-sector participation in this global food security initiative. Over the next several months, we expect to work with donor and target countries, foundations and private sector actors to further development the implementation plan for this initiative.

China Helps African Countries

The People's Republic of China (PRC)[91] is home to 22 percent of the world's population, but has only 7 percent of its total arable land. Following the Chinese people's recovery from the humanitarian disaster of

---

[91]LoroHorta, "Food Security in Africa: China's New Rice Bowl", Jamestown Foundation, May 27, 2009

the "Great Famine," which according to one authoritative account contributed to the death of 36 million Chinese between 1958 and 1961 (South China Morning Post, July 6, 2008), the Beijing government has made it a priority to ensure self-sufficiency in the supply of basic products for the Chinese diet (e.g. rice and grain). In the past three decade, the country's breakneck economic growth has led to the rise of a new wealthy class in Chinese society made up of hundreds of thousands of Chinese people whose dietary demands have changed and who consumes more food. Starting in the 1990s, in order to accommodate this growing demand, China began encouraging its citizens to establish agricultural-businesses overseas. Initially, most of this investment went to nearby countries such as Laos, Burma and Cambodia. Yet, scarcity of land and sprawling overpopulation in these countries have led to political backlashes that prompted the central government to turn its attention to Africa at the beginning of this decade to fill its people's rice bowl.

To put this growing demand into perspective, the Chinese were consuming 25 kilograms (kg) of meat a year in 1985. Two decades later, its consumption reached 52 kg, and it is expected to climb as high as 70 kg by 2020. The consumption of more agriculturally intensive products such as soybeans, potatoes and cereals has increased between 16 and 30 percent in the past decade[92]. Rice consumption is declining as a more wealthy urban population develops a taste for a Western-style diet. The consumption of seafood has increased significantly in the past decade, with shortages of certain products now common. The increase in China's food consumption also comes at a time when arable land in the country is sharply shrinking as a result of over

---

[92]Hongbo Liu and Claus Diblitz, "Determinants of meat consumption in China" Working Paper 40, December 2007, Asian Agribusiness Research Centre, Stuart University

planting and land loss due to environmental damage caused by rapid industrialization. According to Yang Xiong[93] at the ministry of agriculture, China lost 8.9 million hectares of farmland between 1995 and 2007.

The Scramble for African Land

African nations, with their vast and sparsely populated fertile lands, offer China a solution to its rising food demand. Most Chinese investment in African agriculture is concentrated in southern Africa: Mozambique, Tanzania, and Malawi and, increasingly, Angola. The first major Chinese investment in Africa's agricultural sector was in 1995 when Zhongkan Farm, a private company, invested $220,000 in a farm project in Zambia (Xinhua News Agency, March 21, 2006). By 2007 China had some 63 agricultural investment projects in southern Africa ranging from small-scale farms to large cattle-raising grounds.[94]

In the past two years the central government has taken the lead and encouraged Chinese state-owned enterprises to invest in Africa's farms. In August 2008, the Governor of China Development Bank Chen Yuan told a gathering of African finance ministers in Mauritania:

China Development Bank is anxious to work in the area of agriculture. Given the current scenario of a great shortage of food and food price hikes I believe African countries should put agricultural development as their top priority. (Source: Reuters, August 1, 2008).

---

[93]Interview with Yang Xiong, Ministry of Agriculture of the People's Republic of China, Beijing, September 12, 2008.
[94] This figure was given during a seminar attended by the author on Trade and Investment between China and the Portuguese Speaking Countries, hosted by the Chinese Ministry of Commerce Central School in Changing, Beijing between September 7-10, 2008

Mozambique, Tanzania and Angola

In early 2008 the Chinese government pledged to invest $800 million to modernize Mozambique's agricultural sector. The plan includes increasing the rice production of the former Portuguese colony from its current 100,000 tons to 500,000 tons per year in the next five years. With this objective in mind, Beijing is bankrolling the establishment of an Advance Crop Research Institute and several other small agricultural schools throughout the country. Over 100 Chinese agricultural specialists are currently stationed in Mozambique, including teams from the Hunan Hybrid Rice Institute, China's top institution in the field of hybrid rice research.[95]

Other major Chinese projects include the construction of numerous irrigation and canal networks, including a massive canal connecting land-locked Malawi by way of Lake Malawi—the second largest in the continent—to rivers and dams in Mozambique. In the past two years, the search for new land has led Beijing to aggressively seek large land leases in Mozambique, especially in its most fertile areas, such as the Zambezi valley in the north and the Limpopo valley in the south. The Zambezi valley is the richest agricultural region of Mozambique with an area of 230,000 kilometers spread between Tete and Zambezi a provinces.[96]

Chinese investment in the Zambezi valley started in mid-2006 when China's state-owned bank Eximbank (Import Export Bank) granted $2.3 billion in soft loans to the Mozambican government to build the

---

[95]Statement by Tomas Mandiate, Minister of Agriculture and Fisheries of Mozambique on March 30, 2006

[96]Loro Horta, "China's relations with Mozambique: A Mixed Blessing," April 1, 2008 Online Africa Policy Forum Center for Strategic and International Studies (CSIS) Washington D. C.

Mpanda Nkua mega dam on the Zambezi stretch of Tete province. Since then China has been requesting large land leases to establish Chinese-run mega farms and pasture areas for cattle rising. A memorandum of understanding (MoU) was reportedly signed in June 2007, under which an initial 3,000 Chinese settlers were to move to Zambezia and Tete provinces to run farms along the valley.[97]

The Chinese Ambassador to Tanzania, Liu Xinsheng, announced in April 2008 that China may invest upward of $400 million to modernize the local agricultural sector while in Beijing the Chinese Ministry of Agriculture has pledged to assist Africa in creating a "green revolution," a process of rapid increase in agricultural production that results from the introduction of advanced biotechnology, modern irrigation and better managerial skills. According to a ministry of commerce official, China currently has 1,134 agricultural experts serving in Africa and has given $600 million in assistance to the sector since 2002. This assistance ranges from major irrigation projects to donations of agricultural equipment to extending generous credit lines. Another former Portuguese colony, Angola, is fast becoming a major destination for Chinese agri-business. [98]

Angola is already China's biggest trading partner in Africa and its single largest oil supplier accounting for 15 percent of the PRC's total oil imports. The country, with its vast land—1,246,700 square kilometers—and a population of just 16 million, offers China great opportunities, particularly in beef production, but also

---

[97] NoticiasLusofunas "Empres schinesasanunciam investimentos no Vale do Zambeze" Chinese companies announce investment in the Zambezi Valley); June 3, 2006 Lusophone News,

[98]Jornal de Angola "Banco Chines propoencreditopara agricultura" Marco 13 2009 (Chinese bank proposes agriculture credit line).

in some luxury items now in ever greater demand in China such as coffee, spices, tropical fruits, sugar and cotton. China's agricultural investments, which were primarily concentrated on Southern Africa, are now slowly spreading to other parts of the continent such as Guinea Bissau in West Africa where China recently established several hybrid rice experimentation farms. In early 2007 Chinese businessmen pledged to invest $60 million in the country's cashew nut industry, which is one of the biggest such industries on the continent.

While China may be primarily motivated by its need to meet its rising food demand, the modernization of the African agricultural sector is also likely to benefit the people of that continent. In 2007 the Ugandan government thanked China for its support in developing the country's agricultural industry. After serious food shortages last year that degenerated into violent riots, the Senegalese government was eager to attract Chinese investment.

Africans desperately need to modernize their agriculture both to insure their food security and to earn hard currency by exporting it. China needs to deal with its growing food demand and Africa seems to offer the solution.[99] This version was revealed by Professor Li Anshan, one of China's top African specialists at Beijing University.

In short, China is indeed able to help launch a "green revolution" in Africa; millions of Africans will have a chance at a better future. At the same time, however, if China's ambitious plans are not carried out with proper considerations for the environment and its impact on Africa's agricultural land, the continent may one day find itself in a similar predicament to the one confronting China today.

---

[99] Interview with Professor Li Anshan, Department of History University of Beijing, September 14, 2008, Beijing

For instance, various NGOs in Mozambique and foreign experts have begun to express concern over the environmental impact of the Mpanda Nkua mega dam on the ecosystem of the Zambezi valley. Daniel Ribeiro[100], a biologist and the head of Justica Ambiental, a local NGO, argued that, "No serious environmental impact study was conducted, the people whose land will be flood were not consulted or properly compensated. No doubts that we need electricity and to modernize our agriculture. But at what cost?"

While considerable attention has been paid to Chinese interest in African oil and other mineral resources, it is perhaps in the agricultural and food processing sector where China may have a more significant impact on the continent's future. Yet, whether Beijing's grand plans for Africa will really materialize and help the continent alleviate its chronic food shortages, or will it become another of the many empty promises made to Africa remains to be seen.

Australia helps African Countries in food security

Australia will help improve food security in eastern and southern Africa through a new $20 million program to substantially boost agricultural production and improve market opportunities for farmers. The program will operate in five countries, Ethiopia, Kenya, Malawi, Mozambique and Tanzania, with the benefits expected to spill over into other countries in eastern and southern Africa.

Food availability and access are major concerns in this region. More than half the population of 400 million people lives in extreme poverty and about 70 per cent depends on agriculture. Maize is the staple food crop in the region, with legumes providing a

[100]Interview with Daniel Ribeiro, Beijing May 15, 2008

valuable source of dietary protein. Demand for maize and legumes are likely to increase considerably over coming years. However, poor weather conditions and weaknesses in crop management and varieties are holding back production of these important food crops.

The Australian Centre for International Agricultural Research (ACIAR) will work with the Association for Strengthening Agricultural Research in Eastern and Central Africa (ASARECA), the International Maize and Wheat Improvement Center (CIMMYT) and national agricultural research institutes in each of the five partner countries to help boost food security in eastern and southern Africa. Australia's assistance will support research, testing and development of farming techniques specific to drought-affected regions. It will also help develop drought and disease tolerant maize and legume varieties and educate farmers about new crop varieties and technologies. The program aims to lift crop productivity by 30 per cent and reduce year-to-year produce variation by 30 per cent on approximately half a million farms within 10 years.

A number of agricultural research centers, including the International Center for Research in the Semi-Arid Tropics (ICRISAT), and partners including the Queens land Department of Employment, Economic Development and Innovation, Murdoch University and the Agricultural Research Council (ARC) of South Africa will also provide support. Short-term training opportunities and postgraduate fellowships will also be offered to help build the capacity of African scientists involved in the program.[101]

---

[101]Australian Government / Aus AID, Ministry of Foreign Affairs- Media Release, April 14, 2010

Soaring food prices intensifying African crisis

A volatile global food supply is deepening the humanitarian catastrophe in the Horn of Africa, the World Bank warns in a new report. Shortages and near-historic prices for staples such as corn, wheat and sugar have magnified the impact of the drought now ravaging the Horn of Africa, the Food Price Watch report said. There exists emergency in the Horn of Africa because of prolonged droughts, conflicts and internal displacement such as Somalia, food prices that are near the record high levels seen in 2008 also contributed to the situation.

More than 12 million people are in urgent need of humanitarian assistance in the Horn of Africa, the report said. In some areas of Somalia, more than 40 per cent of children under five are suffering from acute malnutrition. The report also warned that production of bio-fuels — specifically America's production of corn ethanol — was contributing to rising food prices. In global terms, food prices last month (JUL) were on average 33 per cent higher than a year ago, the report warned. Corn, or maize, has risen by 84 per cent; sugar 62 per cent and wheat 55 per cent. Shortages and near-historic prices for staples have magnified the impact of the drought.

But the price rises were particularly severe in Africa. Corn prices doubled in Kampala, Mogadishu and Kigali over the last year. Sorghum prices have increased more than fourfold, 240 per cent, over last year in parts of Somalia. It blamed the soaring prices on poor local harvests as well as shrinking global food stocks. The report said corn stocks were at their lowest levels since the 1970s creating a situation in which even small shortfalls in yields can have amplified effects on prices. U.S. production of corn ethanol — which the report said rose by eight per cent in the first three months of this year — was also eating into supplies.

Another factor that adds to the potential upward pressure on the price of maize is the diversion into the production of bio-fuels. Aid organizations have also connected rising food prices to the use of food crops for energy. Some prices had fallen back slightly since last February, but the bank warned the volatility still left the most vulnerable populations, in the Horn of Africa, dangerously exposed. Shortages and high prices for staples have magnified the impact of drought in African countries.

Persistently high food prices and low food stocks indicate that we're still in the danger zone. --Robert Zoellick[102]

IFAD

The International Fund for Agricultural Development (IFAD) works with poor rural people to enable them to grow and sell more food, increase their incomes and determine the direction of their own lives. Since 1978, IFAD has invested over US $11 billion in grants and low-interest loans to developing countries, empowering some 350 million people to break out of poverty.

IFAD[103] is an international financial institution and a specialized UN agency based in Rome – the UN's food and agricultural hub. It is a unique partnership of 165 members from the Organization of the Petroleum Exporting Countries (OPEC), other developing countries and the Organization for Economic Co-operation and Development (O E CD).

---

[102] Suzanne Goldenberg (2011), "Soaring food prices intensifying African crisis", Guardian Newspaper Limited, 2011

[103] Press release No.: IFAD, Rome, 18 February 2010 -

Developed countries and the World Bank on Food Security

With malnutrition causing the deaths of as many as 3 million mothers and young children every year, ministers, heads of development agencies, and civil society organizations, who attended the World Bank and IMF Spring Meetings, appealed to governments worldwide to invest more in halving the rate of malnutrition - one of the 2015 Millennium Development Goals (MDGs).

Meeting for a high-level nutrition roundtable in Washington-co-hosted by Canada, Japan, the United States, through the U.S. Agency for International Development (USAID), and the World Bank-ministers and other senior representatives heard how better nutrition called the "forgotten MDG" for its historical neglect by aid donors would not only sharply reduce hunger and malnutrition but also would significantly improve the health of mothers and children worldwide since research shows that malnourished mothers cannot deliver healthy children, and undernourished children are more likely to die. Focusing nutrition interventions on this special window of opportunity from pre-pregnancy until 2 years of age is therefore crucial to achieving many of the MDGs, especially MDG-4 and MDG-5. Despite the potential high returns to nutrition investments, latest OECD figures show that overseas development aid for nutrition has been modest, with commitments of less than **$300 million a year.**

Rwanda, Guatemala, Bolivia, and Ethiopia, and UN World Food Programme attended the meeting, which announced two new significant initiatives and commitments to invest more in nutrition and its broader development gains.

Canada: We have been working hard with our global nutrition partners to build this momentum and will champion nutrition as part of the maternal and child health initiative at the G8 Summit in June 2010.

The meeting also endorsed a new multi-partner effort called **Scaling up Nutrition: a Framework for Action** to fight malnutrition using cost-effective and proven interventions to prioritize actions for pregnant women and children under the age of 24 months. The framework carries the endorsement of more than 80 multilateral, bilateral, academic, and civil society agencies and institutions that are active in the nutrition and development field. Held at World Bank headquarters, the nutrition meeting described the new framework as "historic" for the way in which the global nutrition community had rallied for the first time around a common agenda and solutions to the problems of malnutrition.

World Bank: Malnutrition is a leading cause of death of mothers and young children worldwide and even for those fortunate enough to survive it in early childhood, its harmful effects stay with them for the rest of their lives. Survivors are likely to start school later, more likely to drop out of school, and less able to learn because their brain functioning and learning capacities were compromised during early years. Malnourishment not only means children have to suffer but it also makes them less-productive adults. The World Bank needs to break the vicious cycle of poverty and malnutrition to give people opportunity and to achieve sustained economic growth. The new multi-partner Framework for Action represents a united call to action for this **'Forgotten Millennium Development Goals.**

United States of America: During the meeting, USAID announced, for the first time, the **Feed the Future** priority countries. USAID's Feed the Future strategy is a comprehensive initiative that targets the causes of hunger and aims to reduce poverty, hunger, and under nutrition at national scale. USAID is working with governments in Africa, Asia, and Latin America to develop comprehensive, multi-sectoral plans to invest in food security and nutrition, including programs to boost agricultural productivity, expand access to markets, reduce under nutrition, and improve resilience to food security shocks.

The Lancet says as many as 3 million mothers and young children die of malnutrition each year. For too long, nutrition has been separated from agricultural practices and food policy. They must strive to make fortified foods more available and step up proven ways to change women's and young infants' feeding and caring behavior where needed, through community-based programs. The approach that they are working out today marks a turning point in how agriculture and nutrition policy interact.

As announced at the meeting, **Feed the Future priority countries** include Ethiopia, Ghana, Kenya, Liberia, Mali, Malawi, Mozambique, Rwanda, Senegal, Tanzania, Uganda, and Zambia in Africa; Bangladesh, Cambodia, Nepal, and Tajikistan in Asia; and Guatemala, Haiti, Honduras, and Nicaragua in Latin America. With 2010 marking the five-year countdown to achieving the 2015 MDGs and evidence that food prices are increasing again in developing countries. Food and nutrition security is the prerequisite for a decent and productive life and the achievement of all Millennium Development Goals. It is a collective responsibility to ensure food and nutrition security for all through synergy across the full range of sectors. The Scaling Up Nutrition or SUN-Framework has the potential to mobilize all behind a smart new approach for vastly better development outcomes.

Japan: Japan has created the **Japan Trust Fund** for scaling up nutrition investments to build operational capacities for nutrition interventions in high-malnutrition-burden countries. This would support the International Development Association. It aims to establish a common platform for the international community to boost necessary resources for enhanced service delivery in most high-burden countries. By addressing the multiple facets of under nutrition of the youngest children of today, countries and communities will be stronger and more resilient in the face of future shocks such as the food, fuel, and financial crises. Now is the time to coordinate action and harmonize funding at the global and national levels.

The United Kingdom: Department for International Development (DFID) also announced during the meeting that the South Asia Food and Nutrition Security Initiative (SAFANS) would support work in Afghanistan, Bangladesh, India, Nepal, and Pakistan. The joint DFID/World Bank initiative aims to improve food security and nutritional outcomes across the South Asia region, which will be accomplished through improving the evidence base, increasing awareness, and building capacity. Throughout the meeting, members of country delegations from many sectors-including finance, health, planning, agriculture, and social protection - as well as civil society organizations and bilateral partners, highlighted progress in and challenges to scaling up proven, effective approaches to address the scourge of under nutrition. Many civil society groups around the world are thrilled that there is now international consensus about the most effective strategy to tackle under nutrition. That provides a solid, politically attractive basis for action.[104]

Let's Grow Together and agree that nutrition investments need to target the window of minus 9 months and 2 years of age for the highest impacts on child mortality, maternal health, optimal physical and

---

[104]Government of Canada, Gov Monitor Public Sector News and Information, April 27, 2010, Appeal for Faster Coordinated Action in Battling Malnutrition: April 27, 2010

intellectual development of children, and future economic productivity and growth. This approach needs to work in tandem with better results in reproductive health, social protection, gender, early childhood development, and agriculture and food security and overall poverty-fighting programs. Participants stressed that good nutrition is a basic human right for all children.

Conclusion:

The world organizations and donor countries have accepted the challenges for assuring food security to all the food insecure families around the world. The procedures to achieve success in food security are:

(a)Regulating of food commodity markets

(b) Arrangement for humanitarian food supplies;

(c)Women's participation and empowerment

(d)Increasing people's nutritional needs,

(e)Tariff free and quota free access to other markets;

(f)Strong international and national network to public health, animal health and plant health;

(g)Strong global governance for achieving food and nutrition security;

(h)Making agriculture a positive force for shaping the world of the future;

(i)Use of biotechnology, nanotechnology and bio-fortification are crucial for increasing agricultural productivity and ensuring food security;

(j)Food security is possible by political will, meeting the challenges, utilizing resources and guiding principles;

(k)Academic excellence;

(l)Collaboration with FAO;

(m)CGIAR is ready for budgetary support, project support and food aid support;

(n)Stronger coordination among donors;

(o)Support of comprehensive strategies;

(p)Investment through country-owned plans;

(q)Leveraging effective multilateral institutions, and Sustained commitments.

Chapter VII

WORLD PEACE IS POSSIBLE

Poverty and deprivation are seen as underlying causes of endemic conflict and civil violence.
The Brunt land Commission (1987)

We are living in this planet where more than one billion people are hungry; we are faced with serious risks of peace and security; there is fear of atomic wars; we are confronted with new diseases and health risks never before; there is rise of Terrorists, Maoists and Naxalites in all low-income countries; the gap between the rich and poor is increasing at a very fast rate; there is religious rivalry among the religions; the nature shows sharp variations in climate; even different countries have permitted legally same-sex marriage.

The scientific achievements have ensured us many facilities to lead immense pleasure and we have achieved every step for a peaceful life today that only few could have imagined half a century back. We have also controlled the nature, but all of us are expecting a fearful future. Why? Why everyone dreads that we are advancing for tensions and sorrows? Why a man hates another? Why a nation fights against another country? Why a rich country desires to cheat a poor country?

We need a better standard of living – a peaceful life – a life free of tensions and rivalry among people. Simply can we try for peace at home, in the town, in the state for peace? It is cheap and very easy to live in peace if each one at least thinks for a minute that 'we are all human beings and we want our world a paradise of peace'.

We should treat that we belong to same genre; same aspirations and all people are our brethren's.

We have to create 'peace' everywhere.

Peace is a heavenly endowment, the best policy for a healthy life and amiable society.

Most of the problems can be fulfilled if everyone is food secured. We are confident that food security would strengthen World Peace. But how can we ensure food to additional one billion people who are hungry?

A peaceful and stable environment in every country is a fundamental condition for the attainment of sustainable food security. We have incorporated the following topics such as "Food for Peace, The Marshall Plan, Conflict and Food Insecurity, World Food Shortage is a British Policy Success, Will the World Achieve Food Security?, Reports for a possible solution of the greatest danger that confronts more than three billion of people in more than 62 countries of the World. Food security might challenge the whole human civilization, if appropriate policy decisions are not devised long before the catastrophe. The following suggestions are mentioned to the world organizations and all governments for achieving 'food security', which could promote world peace forever.

Food for Peace

For more than 50 years, the Food for Peace program has brought hope and nourishment to the hungry corners of the world. Approximately 3 billion people in 150 countries have benefited directly from our food. The secret of Food for Peace's success lies in the unique combination of American compassion together with the unmatched efficiency of our nation's farmers. It is less a triumph of government than of working Americans, for in its essence, Food for Peace is the work of farmers, businessmen, grain elevator operators, truckers, bargemen, freight forwarders, port operations, private voluntary organizations, and government officials. Together they form an unbroken chain of humanity stretching from this country's fertile fields to hungry families half a world away. In the end, hope is what America has promised, and hope is what Food for Peace delivers around the world every day.

Upon reaching its destination, the food is used in a variety of ways, and always for the people most vulnerable to the effects of hunger: children under age 5, pregnant women, the elderly, and the poorest families in a community. During an emergency in which people face threat of imminent starvation, food - wheat, sorghum, corn and other commodities are distributed to save their lives. If the symptoms of extreme malnutrition have already appeared, a nutritionally fortified ration with blended, fortified, and processed food is provided. In less dire circumstances, food can be used to compensate people for work, such as building roads or repairing water and irrigation systems. In turn, these projects help protect communities from future hunger by providing them access to local markets for their produce, keeping them healthy, and improving their harvests.

Other methods of using food aid include:

(a) Working with farmers to identify better ways to sow and tend their fields or providing improved seed, thus improving their harvest by linking them with American know how
(b) Improving women's education about nutrition, resulting in healthier babies and children
(c) Encouraging the production of higher value commodities that could earn money in local markets
(d) Providing micronutrients, such as vitamin A, iodine, zinc, and iron, that hungry children often lack
(e) Feeding children at school to encourage attendance and improve academic performance
(f) Though there are many ways of providing food aid, Food for Peace's goal remains constant: to minimize hunger in the world so that people everywhere can enjoy active and productive lives and, ultimately, to ensure that one day no one needs food aid.[105]

The Marshall Plan

At the same time the UNRRA and private relief was being extended to Europe, the U.S. government was attempting to help repair war torn economies. In 1946 and '47, the U.S. approved nearly $20 billion in long-term, low interest loans. But the loans weren't enough. European economies still struggled to rise anywhere close to their former levels.

Former Army General George Marshall was now the U.S. Secretary of State, and he was also concerned with the expanding influence of the Soviet Union in Europe. Marshall decided decisive action was needed.

---

[105]Food for Peace, USAID

What he proposed in June 1947 was that the nations of Europe get together and devise a rational, multilateral approach to their common economic problems. Helping only one nation at a time was not working. He said that if Europe could come up with a coordinated plan, the U.S. would give Europe billions of dollars in aid, but only for a limited four year period. One month after Marshall's proposal, 16 European nations met in Paris to work out their plan. The nations included Austria, Belgium, Denmark, France, Great Britain, Greece, Iceland, Ireland, Italy, Luxembourg, the Netherlands, Norway, Portugal, Sweden, Switzerland and Turkey.

Germany was not included in the conference because it had no government, yet. Germany was being ruled by the conquering powers of Russia, the U.S., France and Great Britain. But everyone agreed that the economic health of Germany was the key to the revitalization of Europe. Spain was also not included because Fascist Gen. Francisco Franco ruled the country and the west had isolated him politically. Russia walked out of the meeting and prevented any of the eastern European countries behind the Iron Curtain from participating.

The group's first request from the U.S. was for food. As Allen W. Dulles (who later became director of the CIA) argued, "What do we contribute? In first line, it will be food, fuel and fertilizer, to keep body and soul together, so that there will be men and women in Europe with the strength and the will to work. And then they will be given some of the tools so that they can increase their own production of food, fuel, and fertilizer."

At first, the nations at the Paris conference came up with a plan that totaled $29 billion. Through some quiet diplomacy, the U.S. scaled that figure down to a $22 billion request over four years. The request included foodstuffs, fuel, cotton, agricultural and mining machinery, transportation equipment, iron and steel manufacturing equipment, and tobacco. Combining the food, fuel, cotton and tobacco products totaled over 75 percent of all requests for assistance.

Three-quarters of the proposed plan would go to buy products from American farmers. The proposal came at a good time because, in 1947, U.S. farmers had harvested the greatest wheat crop in history. Many agricultural commodities were in excess supply, and Europe didn't have the money to buy them. The European proposal was on the table, and Gen. Marshall had to sell the plan to the American public. He approached the task as if it were a campaign for the presidency. In December 1947, President Truman submitted a $17 billion plan before Congress – scaled down from the European proposal. [106]

Marshall crisscrossed the country speaking to the National Cotton Council, the National Farm Institute, House and Senate committees, chambers of commerce, women's clubs and the nation as a whole over radio. By the spring of 1948, both houses of Congress approved what had become known as the Marshall Plan by surprisingly wide margins. Food and fuel began pouring across the Atlantic soon after. Over the next four years, $11.8 billion in aid and another $1.56 billion in loans were extended to Europe. Once again, the American farmer was feeding the world.

George Marshall received the Nobel Peace Prize in 1953 although he claimed his only real contribution was in convincing the American people that a secure and stable Europe was good for America.

---

[106] Farming in the 1950s and 1960s, Weasels; Living History Farm, Nebraska

World Food Shortage is a British Policy Success

Marcia Merry Baker (2010) opines that food security must be awarded to all people, all countries now and in future but we have rethink and change certain policy issues of the government.[107]

At this time of spring planting in the Northern Hemisphere (and near-harvest in the Southern), a snapshot picture of world agriculture shows a fast-worsening loss of farm capacity, and increase in food scarcity. This is the result not of failed policies or "adverse nature," but is, in fact, a British policy success.

There are over 1.02 billion people going hungry. Farm capacity and production are declining. The 2010 prospective crop plantings and anticipated harvests are way below requirements, yet projects are underway that are known in advance to make the situation worse, e.g. 30 percent of the U.S. corn crop is going to bio-fuels; international neo-plantations, for export only, are spreading. Meantime, desperately needed water-supply projects and related infrastructure are blocked.

Why? It is because scarcity and national breakdown are the goals behind the last 50 years of globalization of agriculture. Today's crises are not failures from wrong-headedness. They mark the successful imposition of deliberate British neo-imperial policies against nation-states, policies that have wiped out the most basic condition for national survival: food self-sufficiency. The mechanisms in this subversion are familiar:

---

[107] Marcia Merry Baker (2010), "World food Shortage is a British Policy Success", The Schiller Institute – Food For Peace, Quoted from Executive Intelligence Review of April 16, 2010

(a) The World Trade Organization's "free trade" and "global sourcing" of food;
(b) Mega-commodity cartels;
(c) Hoaxes about global warming, the environment, and consequent demand for bio-fuels; and
(d) The extension of so-called intellectual property rights to private patent-control over food seeds and improvement of technologies by themselves

A Depopulation Agenda

Behind all this stand the London-centered financial interests, backing destruction of national economies, and depopulation. Break with these policies, destroy their control, and all can be fed. Continue these policies, and biological holocaust is ensured. There is no leeway at this point for niche appeals to "defeat hunger by 2050," or for scheming to produce food on the sidelines of the WTO world. The WTO itself, the thinking behind it, and all the practices associated with it, must end.

This is the import of Lyndon La Rouche drive for the four world powers—China, India, Russia, and the United States—to break with the failed world monetarist system, and implement a new credit system that will launch agro-industrial and infrastructure projects to rebuild national economies.

In direct opposition to this, a slew of policy statements has issued forth from London circles over the last 20 months, during the tumult of the financial blowout and food crisis. They are all demanding a continuation of the policies that created the world crisis. Typical is a review by ten British authors, including from the U.K. Office of Science, in Science magazine, **"Food Security: The Challenge of Feeding 9 Billion People"** (February 12, 2010). They conclude: Any optimism for "sustainably feeding

9 billion people" must be tempered by the enormous challenges of making food production sustainable while controlling greenhouse gas emission and conserving dwindling water supplies, as well as meeting the Millennium Development Goal of ending hunger..." blah, blah.

In fact, such "tempering" ensures that the world population cannot be fed; because it rules out the very infrastructure and technological advances that human survival depends upon. The focus on feeding **"9 billion people by 2050"** has become the sick theme phrase for demanding more globalization, and opposing moves to change the system now.

The following is a snapshot of the scope of the current crisis, and documentation of the British pedigree behind what constitutes a world famine policy.

A few crop updates, and associated patterns of agriculture degradation, give a picture of the food supply and farm capacity crisis generally.

The total world production of grains this current crop year of 2009-10, is projected to be 2.218 billion metric tons, which is below the 2007-08 output of 2.223 billion, and well below last year's 2.235 billion (2008-09). (USDA and World Agriculture Supply and Demand Estimates, March 2010.)

This year's output of rice, the staple for billions, is projected to be 440 million metric tons, down 7.2 million metric tons from last year.

The rough estimate is that for today's 6.8 billion populations, some 4 billion tons of annual grain output is the level required for adequate diets, in the form of direct cereals consumption, cultural preferences for animal protein, and for reserves.

Even worse than the underproduction of grains itself, more and more of the world's grain and oilseed crops are going into bio-fuels. In the United States, which alone accounts for 40 percent of world corn (maize) production, 34 percent of the entire 2009 corn crop went for fuel ethanol! This year is running at the same pace.

Less than 1 percent of the U.S. corn harvest went for fuel ethanol in the early 1980s. At that time, the shift to bio-fuels was not yet a "policy," but a subsidy to the processors—Cargill and ADM—for what was termed innovation in the "industrial, non-food uses" of corn, and a foot-in-the-door for the insane policy shift that was to come under the G. W. Bush Administration, when Federal mandates for fuel from food-biomass were decreed. Today, there are 12 billion gallons of blended bio-fuels (mostly corn ethanol) consumed yearly in the U.S., and President Obama's Bio-fuels Interagency Working Group is intent on upping this to 15 billion gal/yr by 2015, and 36 billion gal/yr by 2022 (including visions of 16 billion of that to come from cellulose ethanol), as mandated by the crazed 2007 renewable fuels law.

That's food out of people's mouths. By simple math, over 300 million people could have been fed for a year by the 2009 flow of 107 million tons of U.S. corn that went to ethanol. American corn farmers—who have gone along with the policy, in hopes of surviving a few more years—are quick to point out caveats. The corn in question is "field corn," i.e., livestock-grade, and would have to be intensively processed for meal for humans. And the corn ethanol by-product, dried distillers' grains (DDG), is fed to cattle, and as of 2008, has even become a new U.S. export commodity. But these points only underscore the deeper principle involved.

The imposition of the system of bio-fuels is undermining the capacity of the U.S. farm belt, and agriculture everywhere. In the traditional U.S. Corn

Belt now, instead of high-tech farmers, populous towns, industry, and regional food production (milk, orchards, diversified crops, meat animals), the pattern is monoculture, imported food, ghost towns, and decay throughout Iowa, Illinois, Nebraska, and the rest.

Besides grain crops, animal protein output is level or falling on a world scale. In the United States, the numbers of cattle, hogs, and chickens have fallen 3 percent below last year this time. Worldwide, milk production for 2009-10 is projected, at best, to remain at the levels of the year before, around 700 million tons, whereas, rapid growth is needed.

Dominating and enforcing these patterns is an interlock of commodity cartels of mega-companies in fertilizers, agro-chemicals, seeds, processing and distribution, integrated in policy with the WTO, World Bank, and IMF, and private, London-centered financial networks.

The dairy cartel is especially emblematic of the pattern of the globalization of what, instead, should be nation - and region-serving farming and food processing, since milk is a perishable product, and tastes for processed dairy foods vary locally (butter, cheese, yogurt, etc). Nevertheless, a few mega-firms, under the WTO system, now dominate dairy foods internationally. These companies are: Nestlé (Switzerland), Danone (France), Dean Foods (U.S.A.), Lactalis (France), Kraft Foods (U.S.A.), Unilever (U.K. and the Netherlands), Fonterra (New Zealand). Lactalis operates in 150 countries, with 16,500 workers outside France, at 44 worksites.

The British Commonwealth firm Fonterra is situated in Auckland and it accounts for 30 percent of the world's dairy exports. Recently it established an electronic auction, global Dairy Trade, for dairy commodities, including anhydrous milk fat.

Cargill, ADM, Bunge, Dreyfus, and others dominate the world grain trade today. The mega-processor JBS, based in Brazil, has arisen to top rank in world meats.

There is tight control over seeds and high-yield traits. The top ten world seed companies account for over 60 percent of all world sales, with the top three—Monsanto, DuPont, and Syngenta — accounting for half of all sales of proprietary (patented) seeds. Monsanto alone accounts for 60 percent of the corn and soybean seed market in the U.S., through direct sales, and trait-licensing agreements. Monsanto's patented biotech traits are in 90 percent of U.S. soybeans, and 80 percent of U.S. corn. U.S. farmers have seen a 64 percent rise in seed prices in the past three years, directly to this cartel.

Double Food Production

To reverse the food supply and agriculture collapse, the physical economic emergency measures are straightforward. Within a few years, production levels could be doubled, and then increased steadily for future generations. These are the possibilities under three broad headings.

1. Build Infrastructure

On every continent, there are large-scale infrastructures, especially water, but also transportation, power, and storage facilities—that must proceed, to create the environment for raised and constantly intensifying levels of farming.

Depletion and saline infection of fresh water is now beyond the danger point in almost every farming region, not due to "natural" doom, but from the lack of infrastructure building and maintenance over the last 60 years. In many cases, detailed plans were already worked out, but shelved during the shift-period of the 1970s, into what became the WTO-era of cheap-labor, below-cost outsourcing.

The kinds of geo-engineering for increasing water supply are indicated by Mexico's PHLINO (Hydraulic Project for the Northwest) proposal, ready to go since the 1960s. It would divert surplus run-off from the southwestern slopes of the Sierra Madre, to the water-short northwest, for a vast increase in farm output. Farther north, the NAWAPA (North American Water and Power Alliance) has long been proposed to divert southward part of the run-off from the Alaska and Mackenzie River run-off, through Canada, and into Great American Desert of the USA.

In Africa, there are long-standing projects on the drawing boards, including diverting part of the tributary flow from the Congo Basin, northward to the arid Chad Basin, and dry Sahel.

In Asia, only last month, the proposal was made to develop the Central Brahmaputra River Basin. Bangladesh Prime Minister Sheikh Hasina issued the call, especially to India and China, for flood control, agriculture, power, and other programs, to the mutual benefit of the five nations sharing the Basin.

The other source of enhancing the natural resource base by man-made intervention is that of nuclear-powered desalination. Coastal duplexes for water and power are in order as fast as possible in multiple sites, from North Africa and Southwestern Asia, to Australia, to the dry or water-short littorals in the Americas—California, the Florida peninsula, Chile, the Caribbean island nations, and many other locations.

But foremost of all infrastructures is nuclear power itself—necessary for transportation, energy inputs into advanced agriculture, and the advancement of science. Take just one obvious example of what plentiful power means: the reopening of the Arctic

Frontier for agriculture, for the eight countries of the Far North. Besides special agronomy for new arable lands during the "24-hour daytime" of summer, inexpensive, ample energy allows for soil less agriculture, whether night or day, in any challenging climate, anywhere.

The resurgence of nuclear energy for power generation in a large section of the world today—China, India, South Korea, and Russia—provides an opportunity for these countries to use natural gas for fertilizer production, and not divert it for power generation. Power, water, fertilizer, and seeds, guided by dedicated agronomists, lay the foundation for food production. On this issue, the train is now arriving at the station. We all must get aboard now.

Resuming space exploration is essential. Pursuing the R&D to produce food in space opens vast possibilities on Earth. Look ahead to hydroponics "family farms" in water-short northern China.

2. Restore Bio-science for Public Good

A vast potential exists for increasing yields in crop and livestock production through R&D in bioscience—not simply genetics, but investigation into basics of photosynthesis and photo morphogenesis. In recent decades, there have been bio-engineered genetic improvements in many crops, and gains in conventional hybridization; but the privatized controls, and reductionism in research that have come to dominate the entire field, must be replaced by science for the public good. There must be an anti-trust bust-up of the seed and agro-chemical control by the Big Agro-Pharmacy cartel, and restoration of research, education, and production facilities in separate and regional groups of nations, serving the public interest of all.

Today's cartels have no right—historically, morally, or economically—to hold power over the means to life. This was arrogated only over the last 40 years of GATT (General Agreement on Tariffs and Trade) and the WTO. A short recap of the history is useful.

The 1800s saw great advances in the understanding of micro-level plant genetics, bacteria, and related processes, by Louis Pasteur, Gregory Mendel (1822-84), and others. Even before that, there were key contributions by those of the Leibniz faction, including Carl Linnaeus, and in colonial Pennsylvania, James Logan (1674-1751) and others.

A marker of advance in the 20th Century was the work by Henry Wallace in Iowa, to master producing and selling mass-scale hybridized seeds and poultry; in 1926, he established his commercial operation, Hi-Bred Corn Co., in Des Moines. By 1940, fully 90% of all corn seed in the U.S. was hybridized. Wallace backed the principle of R&D, as a three-term Agriculture Secretary (following on his father's term in the same office), putting out a landmark edition of the USDA Yearbook in 1936, featuring chemist Dmitri Mendelyev, and dedicated to, "the creative development of new forms of life through plant and animal breeding." In the U.S., for example, corn yields per acre rose from an average 29 bushels per acre in 1900, to 165 today.

Wallace, while Vice President under Franklin Delano Roosevelt, also promoted agriculture development as foreign policy. He initiated what became the International Center for Wheat and Corn Research (CIMMYT) research in Mexico City, where the Green Revolution of new "miracle" corn and wheat seeds originated. By means of collaboration between the governments of Mexico and the new nation of India—always food short under British rule—India became grain self-sufficient as of 1974.

Thus, the advances in science, agriculture, and the public good, are directly associated with nation-states. All that changed with the 1970s shift to post-industrialism and globalization.

A series of U.S. law changes, court decisions, and non-enforcement of anti-trust law by the Justice Department overturned the standing principle in the United States, against using industrial patent law for food seeds and methods. This change allowed the wrongful takeover of genetically altered food seeds, bio-engineering methods, and the direction of research, by a financial network operating through agro-chemical and pharmaceutical multinational companies. They claimed patent rights, enforcement, and sweeping control. In brief:

In 1970, the Plant Variety Protection Act (PCPA) was enacted in the U.S., which specifically counteracted the 1930 Plant Patent Act (PPA), which, though it gave some protection to the breeders of new flower and ornamental types of plants, specifically prohibited the patenting of any food crop plants, in recognition that these patents could threaten the food supply. The 1970 PVPA, for the first time, gave protection for 25 years to developers of specific varieties of crop seeds.

In 1980, the U.S. Supreme Court made a landmark decision (Diamond vs. Chakraverty) that living organisms could be patented. The decision allowed the patenting of genetically engineered microbes, which opened the door to the patenting of any life form.

In 1985, the U.S. Patent Office ruled that plants could be protected under the powerful industrial patent.

In 1994, the PVPA of 1970 was amended in accordance with the GATT regulations, to make it illegal for U.S. farmers to resell or exchange seed of patent-protected crop, cotton, or any future varieties. The GATT agreement was further extended to force developing nations to to do likewise, and to pay stiff license fees for the use of seeds patented by corporations in fellow GATT member-nations. This was further extended under the WTO.

All along, the consolidation of companies concentrated control over staple crop seeds and biotechnology in the hands of a very few cartel firms. True, many of the seed varieties perform excellently (to resist insects, survive drought, and other desirable traits), when grown for where they were custom-bred. But that is not the point.

The patent-holders have relentlessly sued and ruined farmers for claims of infringement of license-to-use the seeds, including just the presence of seed genetic material in farm fields, or charges of holding over seeds from one year to the next. In North America, Monsanto has a record of hundreds of lawsuits. Cargill, Monsanto, and others have laid siege to national governments, in an attempt to coerce them to force their farmers into compliance. In India now, for example, a Monsanto-related firm is demanding licensing rights to their biotech okra, no matter what the opposition by the government or population.

As a cynical counterpoint to this, the same financial circles backing cartel control over food have also sponsored the "organic," chemical-free, and GMO-free foods movements, just to sow superstition and mis-blame among a confused public. All this must be rolled back.

3. Restore Nations: Kill the World Trade Organization (WTO)

Finally, the entire apparatus of globalism, beginning with the World Trade Organization, should be obliterated. This includes the range of globalist networks, from the IMF and so-called "independent" central banks (outside the control of national governments), such as the Federal Reserve Bank of the United States, right on through to the upstart entities, such as the UN Intergovernmental Panel on Climate Change (IPCC), attempting to thwart development in the national interest.

One central tenet of the WTO-era must be singled out for elimination: the decree that no nation has the right to seek food self-sufficiency, but instead, must operate on the definition of "food security" as "access to world markets." This assertion was, from its inception in the GATT Uruguay Round (1984-94), just a sophistical cover for an attack on national sovereignty. The founding rules of the WTO rationalized its claim that member-nations have no right to support their own farmers, because that would be "depriving their citizenry" of the superior right to access world markets for potentially cheaper and better food. Behind this and other sophistries stand the same Anglo-imperial money crowd positioned in the globalist banking and commodities cartels?

The record of destruction is awful. Look at the case of Mexico. As of the 1960s, Mexico was a net food exporter, with water-management projects planned, a program for nuclear power development, and a growing industrial base. All this was undermined, under the 1980s onslaught for free trade, then the 1992 NAFTA (North American Free Trade Alliance), and finally the 1995 WTO. Mexico was ordered to become corn and beans import-dependent, all the while, serving as a cheap-labor outsourcing zone for cartel exports of frozen foods and fresh produce for the U.S. market. Now, hunger stalks Mexico. Millions fled looking for work. And drug running and death are displacing the farming that remains. This is the successful result of the British free-trade agriculture program.

There are two principal areas that need immediate action:

(a) Restore national sovereignty over currencies, trade, debt, and the right to build and protect all aspects of national economy, especially farming and food supply. In tandem, exert the right of sovereignty against the anti-nation-state assault underway from supranational agencies peddling the global warming hoax.

(b) The continuing failure of the WTO Doha Round (begun in 2001) for yet more agriculture free trade is an indication of the repugnance felt for the concept. The WTO meets the definition of a true zombie—dead, but still walking. What remains is to kill it off once and for all.

What about the IPCC? A stream of evidence is pouring forth to document, for those still needing proof, that the entire assertion of global warming was a geopolitical hoax, to further globalization, and depopulation.

Fraudulent Slogan: **'Feed NINE Billion'**

In defense of globalization, London-centered financial operations are conducting an elaborate pseudo-support campaign in the name of feeding the hungry, which most commonly goes under a cynical banner of calling for food security for 9 billion people by 2050.

Besides crocodile tears—or even genuine sorrow from some of the unthinking advocates—the core demands are exactly the opposite of the three action categories outlined above. In other words, this hoax campaign opposes restoring nations and building agriculture. Namely:

Don't build large-scale water, nuclear power, or any kind of modern infrastructure. Instead, assert that resources are fixed; scarce water can only be shared, conserved, and used in "smart" farming. This is rationalized as the only way to have "sustainable" agriculture.

Accept the global warming hoax. Go for only "green and alternative" power, such as windmills and bio-fuels, to reduce greenhouse gases. Engage in extended debates about the merits and demerits of food-biomass vs. non-food bio-fuels (jatropha, future cellulosic); but whatever you do, don't go for nuclear power or electrified transportation, or modern infrastructure.

Finally, and most of all, don't expand population. Cut population down, under the ruse of downsizing to match dwindling natural resources.

Don't seek to have public-interest science for crop genetics or medicine, and certainly not basic research. Leave it to the cartels, to own, control, and decide. There are two ways of remaining compliant: Either oppose the bio-tech science itself, and fall in line with the cartel-backed movements for "pure," organic, chemical-free, free-range livestock, etc. Or call for the extension of GMO high-yield seed stocks to more farmers in poor lands, but all the while leaving the patent-rights and controls intact with the genetics cartel now dominating the food chain. This latter is the favored choice of many who are now calling for a "Second Green Revolution," but minus the nation-state system of the first!

Expand free trade to the limit. End all national barriers to the cartels. Allow food from poor countries, especially from public/private projects run by the cartels, duty-free entry anywhere in the "developed" world. Serve the globalist cartels now dominating the food chain to the hilt. The watchword can be, "fair" trade under a new Doha Round. Retain floating currencies. Bring on the financial crash.

The kick-off for these policies, as a **"feed the hungry"** mobilization, came from UN Secretary General Ban Ki-moon, and the UN Food and Agriculture Organization (FAO) in Spring 2008, in the midst of the worldwide food riots crisis, which began with the crack-up of the global monetary system beginning in the Summer of 2007. In April 2008, Ban established a High Level Task Force on the Global Food Security, headed by British foreign office careerist Sir John Holmes (later headed by another British diplomat, Dr. David Nabbaro). In June, FAO Director Jacques Diouf, at the Rome Food Summit, called for doubling world food production — but by 2050.

Ban and Diouf repeatedly struck the theme in follow-on meetings in New York in July 2008 and Madrid in January 2009. Diouf used the exact British imperial script in a letter of congratulations to Barack Obama, on winning the U.S. Presidential election in November 2008. Calling for a 2009 food summit, Diouf said, "The summit must find $30 billion per year to develop rural infrastructures and increase agricultural productivity in the developing world, particularly in low-income food-deficit countries, with a view to doubling production to ensure food security for a world population expected to reach 9 billion by 2050...." When the summit did occur in Rome, in November 2009, Diouf changed the goal to increasing food production by 70 percent by 2050. But it doesn't matter. The goal is a cover story slogan for keeping the free trade/famine policy intact.

Made in London

In tandem with the UN, reports and articles have come from Britain directly, over the 2008-09 period, issuing commands on how the present system must be retained. For example, on Nov. 2-3, 2009 in London, this command was featured at a conference held by Chatham House (the Royal Institute of

International Affairs), titled, "Food Security 2009—achieving Long-term Solutions." The panel topics illustrate the globalization focus: "What More Is Needed To Ensure ... the Proper Functioning of Global Food Markets?" and "How Can the Benefits of International Investment in Land Be Maximized and the Risks Controlled?" The overseas "land" issue refers to the neo-plantation movement for establishing huge for-export farm operations in desperate, food-short nations in Africa and Asia, to provide food supplies to the Persian Gulf states, Britain, and elsewhere.

To help shop these views into the United States, the Chicago Council on Global Affairs was enlisted to issue a report in 2009— funded by the Bill and Melinda Gates Foundation —formulating London's approved themes for incorporation into legislation. Senator Richard Lugar (R-Ind.) and Senator Robert Casey (D-Penn.) introduced a draft U.S. law entitled "Global Food Security Act of 2009" (S.B. 384). It now has 14 sponsors. The bill calls for more aid to agriculture around the world, but retains all the Made-in-London demands for free trade, private "intellectual property rights" for cartels, etc. The special humanitarian-sounding twist is to speak of providing help to the 200 million "smallholder" farmers of the world.

In the front ranks of this fake fight-hunger mobilization of globalize, are the Bill and Melinda Gates Foundation and their Associates. In 2006, this foundation, along with the Rockefeller Foundation, had already set up the Alliance for a Green Revolution in Africa (AGRA), to promote selected policies in the name of addressing hunger, but in free-trade terms. This was a message Gates gave at the January 2009 Davos Forum. In May 2009, Bill Gates met in New York City with Warren Buffett, George Soros, and others, to discuss significant world depopulation as a goal.

In the fall last year, Gates issued a book on agriculture success stories (Millions Fed: Proven Successes in Agriculture Development), from his depopulation vantage point of calling for a Second Green Revolution amidst the globalize world. Gates gave the keynote for the World Food Prize in Des Moines, Iowa in October, on the same perspective.

By this time, new appointments in the Obama Administration were made in accordance with the London-serving outlook and networks. An eight-year Gates Foundation personage, Dr. Rajiv Shah, was made Chief Science Advisor to the U.S. Department of Agriculture (USDA) in June 2009; and was made to head the State Department's U.S. Agency for International Development (USAID) in October 2009. Dr. Roger Beachey, directly associated with Monsanto, was made the Science Advisor to the USDA. Dr. Nina Fedoroff, Science and Technology Advisor to the U.S. Secretary of State and to the AID Administrator plays a key role in publicizing 'Rethinking Agriculture in a Warming Climate' and 'regulatory framework to give even more power to the private GM seed patent-holders' and 'Intellectual property rights'.

When Marcia Merry Baker challenged Fedoroff, on the point that patenting of food genetics — a hallmark of Globalization —was always against the American System, explicitly opposed by the FDR Administration's Agriculture Secretary Henry Wallace, and should be rolled back now, Fedoroff replied with a defense of the cartels.

She said sternly that no rollback of privatized patenting is going to happen. The train has left the station.

The exchange included the further point, by this author, that in the midst of today's economic breakdown, there is potential for turnaround to rebuild national economies through the right emergency measures. Specifically, look at the surge of commitment to nuclear power in Asia—in Russia, China, India, and others. This "going nuclear" marks a policy shift potential, in which we must unleash real scientific research, promote vast agriculture expansion, and end the wrongful free-trade practices of the last 40 years, including private patenting of food genetics. There must be science for the public sector.

Genocide

The definition of genocide is action to exterminate a group of people deliberately. That applies equally to those who devise and implement policies with the stroke of a pen, as well as those who carry out bloody slaughter with their own hands.

British imperialists have always preferred the former method, wishing to let others get their hands dirty, while they sit back and reap the advantage. This has emphatically been the case with food policy, which has increasingly been administered by faceless bureaucrats and cartels, not the British in their own name. By this method, mankind has already reached the point where it is producing less than is required for its survival, and that of the next generations. Indeed, we are on the edge of collapse into a New Dark Age—genocide worse than mankind has ever experienced before.

In our opinion, the British and the USA are trying to control all people, all nations for all time to come. Let this horror be stopped by the people themselves. Let the governments of low-income countries beware of these facts.

Similarly, China is interested to control Asian continent at present and desires that the whole world should come under the administration of China and follow the East and Maoism. Why these countries are worried to rule the world, where billions of people are hungry, illiterate and without shelter. They could donate a portion of their military expenses for these starving people and they have the power to make the World free of conflicts and permanent peace everywhere.

Do we need to double food production?

The world has to increase food production by 50 percent by 2030 and double it by 2050 to meet future demand. This seems to be the consensus among economists, scientists, politicians and representatives of the agricultural industry. But does the world really have to do so? Even if the global population crosses 9 billion by 2050, the world may not need to **double** its food production if food is not wasted and dietary habits change to healthier ways?

The need for a 100 percent rise in food production was based on a UN Food and Agriculture Organization report. But recent studies show the report implies that global food production during the 45 years from 2005 need to be raised by about **70 percent**. The 30 percent gap is huge. In fact, it is equivalent to the food produced by the whole of the American continent. So, what is the message? The world has to increase, by hook or crook, the output of agricultural and livestock (milk, meat and eggs) products by at least 70 percent.

It is a tough task, because urbanization across the world is eating into agricultural land, and once agricultural-surplus nations have been forced to become food-scarce countries today.

For example, Mexico, the land where corn originated has to import corn.

Isn't it surprising that China, where rice was first cultivated and which is still its largest producer, has to import its staple? Isn't it surprising that not China, where tea originated and which is still its largest producer and consumer, but Kenya is its largest exporter? Isn't it surprising that India, which introduced sugar to the world, has to import sugar today? And isn't it surprising that India and Pakistan, where cotton was first cultivated, has to import cotton today?

The answer to all the questions is "no", for that is the natural outcome of market economy and globalization policies. Global food production and distribution no longer depends on the simple laws of demand and supply. Instead, they depend on the intricate and complicated policies of the World Trade Organization (WTO) and the whims of multinational companies. Such policies and whims have given rise to supermarkets in vegetables and fruits in the developing world too.

If we can save food from being wasted (wasting food is a common phenomenon throughout world, but more intense in the West), and if we can change our unhealthy eating habits, the world may not even have to increase the food production by 70 percent to feed the projected population of more than 9 billion people by 2050. But that would be contrary to the demands of market economy.

Market economy is all about increasing production infinitely and making money. So, if millions of tons of food grains rot in Indian government warehouses, we should let them rot, instead of trying to distribute them among the poor and hungry people of the country. Why? Because distributing food for free goes against the laws of market economy.

Despite what Economics Nobel laureate Amartya Sen says, a democratically elected government is no guarantee against famine. Or else how starvation can be explained in a democratic country like India? Food is no longer dependent on the backbreaking labor of farmers? It is not dependent on the whims of nature or proper irrigation, either? It depends on market laws worked out by international organizations such as the WTO, International Monetary Fund, World Bank and multinational corporations.

It is their laws and schemes that have forced almost all or most of the African nations to become food-insufficient.

It is their plans that force most of the developing world to depend on supplies from the developed countries, which perforce subsidize their agricultural products.

The world today has more than 1 billion hungry people. And even it were to double its food production, as demanded by international organizations, by 2050, it would still have 290 million hungry people. Where wills this cycle of poverty and hunger end? The answer is no one knows, not as long as the Bretton - Woods institutes and multinational corporations are allowed to decide the fate of the world.[108]

Governance of Food Security

The Director General of the Food and Agriculture Organization of the United Nations, Rome has advised that governance of food security should aim at:

(a) Keep agriculture and food security at top of the international agenda for the eradication of hunger and malnutrition in the world;

---

[108]O. P. Rana, "Will the World Achieve Food Security" China Daily September 25, 2010

(b) Fully understand the factors that affect world food security, the associated risks and remedial actions;
(c) Ensure close links between technical expertise and policy-making;
(d) See that the international community adopts a coherent and systematic approach to food security:
(e) To respond rapidly to situations of food crisis and emergency in order to mitigate their negative effects;
(f) To stimulate investment in agriculture and rural development and mobilize the funding required ensuring the food security of local populations.
(g) To help bolster the governance of food security in a framework of coherence and synergy of policies, strategies and actions at all levels – national, regional and international.[109]

World Hunger 2012

The British Prime Minister, David Cameron, will have to strike a delicate balance as the convener of the global "hunger summit". If an Oxfam report is any indication, the outlook for the world is grim; the food shortage is said to be unparalleled with **an additional 43 million going hungry this year**. Part of the problem is drought. India may be on the edge of this phenomenon but the paradox here is perhaps unique ~ abundant grain, a substantial quantity rotting, the political class splitting hairs over food security, and a large segment of the populace contending with malnutrition. It is (Altogether suggestive of the) virtual collapse of governance.

---

[109]Report of the 36th Session of the Committee on World Food Security (CFS), Rome 18-23 November 2009

The food crisis is particularly acute in Yemen, West Africa and East Africa ~ the three regions of the Dark Continent suffering from poverty and the withering effects of drought. Almost a billion people are now hungry; indeed one in seven of the global population and the number of acutely malnourished children have risen for the first time this decade. The warning by the charity organizations, notably Oxfam and UNICEF, must serve as a curtain-raiser to the "hunger summit". It has been relayed sufficiently in advance before the world leaders ~ representing both the hungry and the affluent nations ~ gather at the high table to devise strategies. The international community will have to respond with urgent dispatch. It didn't last year despite warnings of a famine in Somalia. And that response must of necessity be tangible, transcending the rock concerts that were organized some years ago to raise funds for tackling poverty. There is a profound message in Sunday's lament of the Harry Potter actress, Bonnie Wright, after a visit to Senegal ~ "We need to help now, rather than wait until we're in such an extreme situation that we're already losing people by the second."

It can't be crueler on the pangs of hunger. The summit will be expected to unveil the "biggest-ever push" to combat malnutrition and starvation.

It will have to set a target to reduce the number of under-fives ~ currently the figure is 180 per million ~ who suffer from physical and mental stunting due to poor nutrition.

The global nutrition event has been packaged as a "positive move forward". It cannot lessen the pangs of world hunger without concerted action, however. The Oxfam message could be the determinant of success or failure:

We will have to address the shocking fact that while we produce enough food to feed everyone on the planet, about a billion will tonight go to bed hungry.

One crisis spawns another. And central to world hunger are dwindling natural resources and climate change ~ leading to murderous drought.[110]

World Peace is Possible

Food aid to the hungry is the best form of aid; it is an act of humanity. The fact is that when the Almighty God desires to give food to the hungry; He does it through the donors, as He has no hands to give alms to the poor.

The world has enough food for all human beings, but it is not possible because some people are greedier, who capture all properties of these unfortunate brethrens.

The rich people, rich nations, and rich organizations should not impose their policies in poor countries. It has created **negative results** in debtor countries and the number of hungry people is increasing in all debtor countries. Moreover, child mortality, maternity mortality and farmers' suicides are increasing. Improper policies have caused uprisings, wars and have caused the growth of Naxalltes, Maoists and terrorists.

These developed countries should award debt relief to all indebted countries without any pre-condition. The debtor countries should pay back the principal amount to the developed countries, the World Bank and the IMF. The interest portion of the debt should be waived out for greater interest of human civilization.

---

[110]Editorial, The Statesman, August 07, 2012

The causes of poverty must be solved; each individual should have a piece of land legally; each one should be engaged to earn an income; each individual should be permitted to live a life of a human being.

Food security is primarily necessary for hungry people. The government should see that these people are the beneficiaries of food aid. Subsidized food enters into black market and leads to corruption, dumping and wastage even in government warehouses, transit, fair price shops and midday meals centers. Subsidized rice and wheat cause excessive harm to the farmers and peasants as their produce are devoid of remunerative prices and no-buyers in the market.

Poverty is the root cause of hunger, lawlessness and suicides. This should be checked or halted by law and action. The causes of poverty should be identified and attempts must be taken to solve causes of poverty.

Hunger can change the governments; hunger can create world instability; hunger can challenge the state laws. Hence, the world organizations, governments or funding institutions should try to solve hunger, and should not encourage hunger. Unless all countries secure food security by themselves, the food deficit countries would witness growth of Terrorists, Maoists and Naxalites. These food deficit countries would also loss independence forever.

Suggestions and Policy options

(A)Donor countries and World Organizations:
The world organizations and developed countries are advancing huge credit to the developing countries for infrastructure development such as roads, dams, warehouses, cold storages, office buildings, irrigation projects, rural development and for strengthening

research organizations. The world organizations finance pro-poor projects for uplift of vulnerable people. But these funds are mostly mis-utilized and enter into personal accounts of politicians, government employees, contractors and dealers.

The World Trade Organization has been created to harass the low-income countries and control the whole world through food. The best of charity is 'donating food to the hungry' in all religions. The WTO is acting in the reverse direction. It causes food war.

The slogan for '9 billion of people by 2050' neither is a good hypothesis nor is the slogan 'produce more or we may perish' an appropriate call. The slogan should be 'we can produce more to award food security to all'.

The world organizations are frightening the innocent people without any cause. It is simply political. We do not know why food security would include balanced diet like fruits, milk, eggs, fish, meat, vitamins, and iodine. Food security should include two full meals a day. Why the developed countries emphasize on doctors prescribed meals? It is possible when 'poverty' can be found in dictionary only.

The world bodies should make international law that food materials would not be imported or exported by any country in future. This would make each country self-sufficient. In case of natural calamities a country can donate food materials to the victims through the Marshall Plan or free charitable donations.

Foreign funding has caused massive corruption, unemployment, immoral politics, and corrupt bureaucracy. A corrupt country needs more foreign funds; and corrupt politicians need power for generations.

Black money or illegal funds is utilized or invested in elections, land and buildings, foreign trips, shares, gold and other valuables. Black money is deposited in fake names, Swiss Banks or as hidden treasure. The politicians, government servants, contractors, business organizations and industrialists are capable of acquiring unsolicited funds earmarked for development of the state. This illegal money could be collected from the culprits, if corruption cases are finalized within a year. The culprits should be sentenced to rigorous punishment and confiscation of their property as punishment. The government has to check black money, corruption and mismanagement of public investment.

Food security is possible when all families have an income, such as monthly salary or income from business or family pension scheme or income from agriculture, horticultural plantations, bamboo cultivation, goat or sheep or swine rearing, dairying, fish farming or as agricultural labourers.

The United Nations must strengthen international laws, human rights, and peace forums to allow the poorest of the poor for a peaceful living. The United Nations Organization should solve the problems of: country boundaries, increasing pollution, religious conflicts, production of defense arms and armaments, and debt relief for developing nations. The world now faces grave dangers of climate change, growth of terrorists and corruption in high offices.

Let the world organizations invite the advices and services of philosophers, Nobel laureates, economists, thinkers and ex-presidents of countries for finding out the solutions of the challenges the people of world face today.

The United Nations, developed countries, world organizations, and charitable institutions should award assistance to the hungry people and the Least and Less Developed Countries for agricultural development.

The USA, the UK, Australia and Canada should consult with the food scarcity nations for providing food aid in natural calamities. The planners of developed countries should not impose policies that are detrimental to local situations. They should make plans as per requirement of the farmers. It should base on participatory approach.

The foreign delegates should not be biased with the politicians or bureaucrats of food scarcity nations. They must be aware that poor governance prevails in all developing countries.

The governments of food deficit countries should pay more attention to absolute poor people residing in forest areas, isolated areas covered by rivers or lakes and in rural areas. All absolute food-insecure families are landless, widow-headed and have no-income. They are alive to commit suicides in future. The governments should rescue them; prevent them to commit suicides by donating two quintals of paddy (Rice with husk) or wheat free of costs. When the hungry families have something; they would try to earn something to live. This benevolent act of the government would be treated as God-sent.

The subsidy amount awarded to companies of fertilizers, pesticides, diesel pumps, tractors, housing schemes and banks are deliberately mis-utilized and do not reach the farmers.

The donor countries should advise the peasants of developing countries to utilize own resources to increase food production. And they should not sanction mega projects, infrastructure projects and rural development projects. Simply they can donate all fertilizer and pesticides requirements free of cost.

Donor countries can create, energize, and stabilize WORLD PEACE, if they do not wish to control politics of low-income countries. Can't we eradicate poverty, hunger and war even in the twenty-first century?

(B) Food insecure countries

All the food deficit countries must emphasize on production of cereals, vegetables and pulses to provide two meals a day for total population of the country. These countries must be self-sufficient to protect their sovereignty and prestige. A food deficit country is treated as a hungry country. Moreover, the government should take up special care for development of dairy, horticulture, fishery, poultry and goat rearing to supply milk, fruits, fish, and meat as food packets for healthy diet for all people.

Food security should include vitamins, iron and iodine when they have sufficient disposable income.

All the farmers of a district should be assisted to grow at least 10 fruit trees to create an export market and to earn an additional income daily during fruiting season. For example, a district may be declared as kagzi lime district or lemon or banana or cocoanut or apple or pineapple district. All the farmers would be supplied with saplings/seedlings as per advice of horticulturists and accepted by the farmers of the district. It is because each market could collect at least one truckload of the fruit each day, which could be dispatched to a distant city for sale. Small lots of any commodity cannot have a wider market. There are some fruit varieties that grow all round the year.

Most of the developing countries give more emphasis on 'receiving more foreign funds as debt' to prove good governance to the voters. They run after debt for road construction, industrialization and fight against Naxalites, Maoists and Terrorists. But they prepare for unwanted war against neighbor countries.

It is because these developing countries have adopted pro-rich, pro-industrial and pro-urban approaches in planning. But their approaches should be pro-poor, pro-rural and pro-agricultural policies.

If developing countries borrow to invest in infrastructure and enjoy city life, they cannot achieve food security. The farm sector would suffer and all agricultural labourers would move to towns for better amenities.

In all developing countries, towns are expanding more than expected; agricultural land is being converted to industrial areas or buildings; there is rampant growth of English medium schools and private clinics; agricultural prices galloping; mobile phones, TVs and drinks are treated as most wanted commodities for all people. But insecurity of life increases continuously. There is growth of anti-socials, drug addicts, and lawlessness. The growth of Terrorists, Maoists and Naxalites has challenged the very existence of the elected governments. Cheap bank loans have caused purchase of motorcycles, cars and other automobiles. Forests are converted to industrial houses. Rivers are polluted. Tigers and elephants are poached. Budgets for education and healthcare are less than loan installments. The elected governments are more corrupt than the kings and emperors of yester years. Now the questions are:

Who would produce agricultural commodities? Who would assure food security?

Agriculture has become a loss-bearing profession. It has become a punishment for all peasants. So, farm youths prefer to join political parties as politics has become a business in India.

Agricultural labourers are scanty in all rural areas. The governments reduce prices of raw agricultural produce for procurement and sell through public distribution system at nominal prices. The subsidy earmarked for agriculture is mis-appropriated by industrialists, traders, and government functionaries. The governments import cooking oil, wheat, rice, Soya bin, and milk powder from foreign countries and supply to the consumers. The heavy burden of foreign debt on the developing countries is galloping.

Food security is possible in all developing countries when agriculture becomes a remunerative enterprise and profession. The price of agricultural produce should be linked to remuneration of government employees or gold prices. If value of Gold or salary of a clerical post increases four times at a time or over a period, procurement prices of wheat or rice should be increased four times during the same period.

The governments of developing countries should provide drinking water facility, school education facility, market yards in each village; peasants would remain in villages and grow crops to meet the consumption demand of the area. If rural markets are developed, agricultural production would grow and excess agricultural produce would move to distant markets.

Every person is alive with hope, faith and future. Let the poorest of the poor hope that there is a future for his family. Let the poor people have faith in the government. Let the governments implement the following programs for a safer world. These are:

(a) Life Insurance for all (up to a limit)
(b) Pension for all senior citizens
(c) A Bank Account for all adults
(d) A piece of land for each adult
(e) Free primary education and healthcare for all

Farmers should not be evacuated forcefully by the police force for the purpose of an industry or a project. State laws should prohibit conversion of agricultural land into industrial purposes. If farmers commit suicides as a routine event, the constitution of the country should be amended to give weight-age to save the life of peasants. The State Laws should dismiss an elected government, if it fails to save the farmers.

Each country must ensure food security to all people. A farmer must be saved from these drastic consequences.

(C) Suggestions for India

Land is the real asset. Therefore it is complicated. Each family in each country should have at least a piece of land. If a family does not own any land, the government must allot land for farming purposes that cannot be sold to others at any time.

Agricultural land should not be transferred or acquired for industries at any cost either by the government or by the industrial houses. Farmers should not be treated as beggars. They must be honored as '**Peace Workers**' as they devote their whole life in agriculture and supply food grains to the nation.

All farmers must be awarded 'Pensioners' benefits' after completion of 60 years in age by the state.

Cost of production of cereals (wheat, Rice) must include interest of land value, farmers' own labour charges, family laborer's wages, bullock labour charges, storage charges, and cost of fertilizers, pesticides, insecticides and transportation charges. It also includes irrigation charges, management costs, interest on own funds utilized for crop raising, risk and un-certainties, insurance etc.

The market price of rice and wheat must be compared against price of gold or share market prices or government employees' salary / wage as compared with a base year. If Members of Parliament increase their own pay and perks four times, the price of cereals must be increased to four times. The state laws should protect the farmers and peasants.

There should be total decontrol of agricultural commodities in the country. The Central Control Orders such as 'Movement Restriction Orders of 1964' and 'Restrictions on Rail Bookings Order, 1957' must be abandoned at once. All political parties in India must admit, say and practice that India is one.

But the government must procure rice/paddy and wheat to the extent of 1 million tones cereals for emergency purposes such as flood, cyclone, drought, and other natural calamities. Government should undertake import and export of cereals as and when necessary.

The **subsidy amount** earmarked for agriculture should be utilized for pension, insurance, healthcare or scholarships to farm boys for higher education. The absolute hungry families should be given two quintals of un-husked rice or wheat free of cost to save the family from starvation linked deaths provided the family is 'No-income family.

Charity is above market laws.

Hungry people reside in rural areas. They do not have any source of income; generally these families are female - headed or no-income families. These families must be cared for by the administration. The monthly financial assistance for food security could be awarded to only absolute hungry families without earning members.

A portion of the total subsidy amount must be utilized to procure cereals (Wheat and Rice) from the farmers in villages directly by the government and the procured quantities must be distributed among the hungry families **free of cost** in the same village or in a nearby village. Wheat and Paddy (rice + husk) should be distributed in raw form. As a result, marketing expenses on transport, storage, loss in transit, pilferage or storage loss would not happen. Each "No income' or hungry family would be given only 2 quintals of raw cereal per year in five bags with symbol / emblem of government.

All Fair Price Shops must be closed as these are the sources of black marketing, corruption and political hobnobs. Food security is never possible through present system of food administration. The government regulation to low procurement prices of cereals hinders agricultural growth. Rural youths are coming to cities for more income and there is shortage of agricultural workers in rural areas.

The government should watch open market prices; and create a wider market to dispose of cereals. The Ministry of Agricultural Marketing in each state or country should dispose of all stocks before procurement season to accommodate new stocks. The export or import duties must be waived out to allow quicker movement of grains. .

The government of India is supplying clean rice at the rate of 3 rupees (INR) per kilo of rice. The government supplies 35 kilo of rice and 10 kilo of wheat to the Below Poverty Line (BPL) families. This has resulted in massive corruption and wastage of food grains in public institutions. This has caused also dearth of agricultural labourers for agricultural operations. The landlords have made their land fallow.

Cheap rice or cheap wheat is regarded as an election – winning instrument in India. This populist measure has resulted in sharp fall of yield in cereals in the country in successive years. It has also made agriculture a loss-bearing enterprise; has caused wide spread of Naxalites, Maoists and Terrorists in about 40 percent of total geographical area in the country.

Cheap rice or wheat cannot ensure food security over a period of time. Higher price or favourable price of rice or wheat can induce the farmers to grow more cereals to meet the requirements of the country.

The present low procurement prices of paddy (rice with husk) or wheat should be increased to triple of the cost for maximization of production. Agriculture should be converted as a profit generating profession for food security. Hence, all countries should be debarred to allow subsidy to agriculture. Higher price for wheat and rice would increase agricultural production and assure food security to all.

The western countries are allowing high subsidy to compete the international market.

Agricultural research has been slowed down for the last two or three decades in all countries. The universities and the national agricultural institutes are more interested for self-publicity rather than new research findings.

There should be a "Fact Finding Commission for Agricultural Research' in each country and let them evaluate 'how much has been invested and what is the outcome'.

Money spent in research is also mis-utilized, as all researchers are neither loyal to the farmers nor to the state. Even high officials engaged in agricultural research and extension services are hard-core corrupt people.

India should have a full-time Cabinet Minister in agriculture. A full time Minister could do justice to the farmers in the country.

(a) Who would examine the working of 'Bharat Krushak Samaj'?
(b) Who would be responsible for farmer suicides in the country?
(c) Who would bear the storage loss of rice and wheat of FCI in Punjab and Haryana state?
(d) Who would be punished to convert human foods to cattle feeds in government organizations?

Mechanization of agriculture helps in maximization of yield. But the government must execute plans to employ more labourers in agriculture. The 'big farm' concept in thickly populated countries would cause unemployment and loss of peace. Similarly, the implementation of Mahatma Gandhi National Rural Employment Generation Scheme implemented in India has become a farce. It spends more on advertisement and false bills rather than the work executed in rural areas.

Food security can alone solve most of the problems in India and other developing countries and can restore peace everywhere. Food security can save millions from starvation deaths; it can render peace to all extremely poor people.

In India, most of the poverty alleviation schemes are political in nature and deviate from economic principles. These poverty alleviation programs result in corruption, no work culture, pilferage, wastage and anti-people. The government should scrap all these schemes. It should give monetary help directly to the poor people and farmers. The Government of India should not procure Paddy (Rice with husk) at fewer prices from the farmers and cannot distribute at 3 INR per Kg to prove its social responsibility.

When the pay of government officials, elected members of Parliament and Assemblies in India was increased thrice in 2006, the procurement price of cereals should have been increased thrice. It was not increased at par with a political purpose. This disparity has created problems in agriculture in India.

Food Security is possible when peasants get justice by the government. Food security is not possible by contractors, bureaucrats, politicians, and industrialists and NGOs. Import of grains from foreign countries could award food security temporarily but it would cause subordination to a foreign country forever.

The budgetary support on subsidy in agriculture should be invested in farmers and poor families directly through their Bank Accounts.

So these countries must follow pro-poor, pro-rural and pro-agricultural policies. Food security is possible when agriculture becomes a profitable enterprise.

Supply of essential commodities through public distribution system, guaranteed employment generation schemes and subsidies in fertilizers, seeds, pump sets or tractors for poverty alleviation of the poor are creating large-scale corruption in all developing countries. These programs are political rather than economic.

The World Bank programs are intended to enrich the Bank rather than to assist the poor people residing in developing countries. The World Bank is responsible for less investment in education and healthcare. The World Bank praises the corrupt officials and awards bank loan for 40 years for non-viable projects.

Foreign debt increases corruption, poverty, hunger, number of cheats, lawlessness and widens rich-poor gap. A portion of foreign assistance reaches the terrorists or Maoists through contractors and engineers.

Subsidy in agriculture should be abolished in all countries. The absolute hungry people should be provided cereals in raw form free of cost up to two quintals of cereals to check starvation deaths.

In Orissa state (India) 126 peasants committed suicides in 2009 -2010 and the Directorate of Agriculture confirmed that the peasants committed suicides for family problems. Is the department authorized to study family problems? The ill–fated persons committed suicides when they could not repay back bank loan and private loan invested in agriculture. Corruption, inefficiency and politicization of the government departments have caused these un-time deaths. So an exemplary punishment could have been awarded to the Directors of Agriculture, Horticulture, Agricultural marketing, Animal Husbandry, Fishery, Agriculture University, and Irrigation department with dismissal of their services. Or at least, the government could have paid condolence for their un-time deaths.

In short, Food security is possible by increasing the income of the people. It does not rest upon Gross Domestic Product of the country. People need peace. But the governments try to remain in power by corrupt practices, martial law, or war. The funding institutions should consult the opposition members and local economists before sanction of credit.

Each state must prepare 'Master plan for agricultural markets'.

High cost investments such as mega irrigation dams, rural roads, buildings for poor, warehouses and cold storages, research buildings, air-conditioned vehicular facilities for officers, high salary for government employees and social safety nets etc call for maximization of foreign credit. But these funds pass into wastages and pilferage.

Investments in agriculture should be for crop production and marketing to strengthen food security, farmers' welfare and creation of employment in agriculture.

If the developed countries desire to assist the hungry people of the world, they should find ways to help the peasants, farmers, artisans and hungry people.

The governments must ensure one bank account to each voter and allow the senior citizens pensioners' benefits and a lump sum grant for disease or deaths. The government may directly grant some amount for crop grown or crop failure or climate failure each year in lieu of subsidy. The government should deposit the amount in the accounts of beneficiaries. A farmer cannot commit suicide as long as he has money in his account.

Food security is possible if agriculture becomes a profitable enterprise. Free food makes everyone a beggar. Charity must be free from obligation.

India should priorities birth control to reduce population growth. It should go for one-child norm and late marriage. India should adopt pro-poor, pro-rural and pro-agricultural policies.

Subsidy in agriculture should be drastically cut or simply it should be abolished. But free gifts should continue, such as tube-wells for drinking water purposes or tanks as water reservoir for common use. The world can achieve food security if all countries prioritize agriculture and allied subjects.

A good plan would increase income of the farmers, peasants and other rural households and award food security to all. And it is possible.

Food security can award brotherhood, inculcate humanity and restore WORLD PEACE provided rural poor are gainfully employed and farmers are satisfied with their occupation.

Charity is a religious activity. Charity gives satisfaction to the donors and recipients. Charity cannot be traded. Charity cannot be deposited in bank. It is a human activity. Let all people be awarded food security and peace. It is the gateway to WORLD PEACE. And it is possible.

Views of Mahatma M K. Gandhi

Sixty five years ago, Mahatma M. K. Gandhi (1947)[111] in his post-prayer speech said:

The system of control and rationing in his opinion was unnatural and un-business like. They had plenty of fertile land; there was enough water and no dearth of manpower. Why should there be food shortage under these circumstances? The public should be educated to become **self-reliant**. Once they knew that they had got to stand on their own legs, it would electrify the atmosphere. It was well known that fright took a

[111] M K. Gandhi (1947), " Food Shortage and Agriculture", Navajivan Publishing House, Ahmadabad, 1949,P. 57: Speech in Birla House, New Delhi, Harijan, October 10, 1947 and October 19, 1947

larger toll of life than actual disease. He wanted them to shed all fear of calamity if they took the natural step of **self-help**. He was convinced that removal of food control would not result in a famine and deaths by starvation. In another speech, he said that rationing has very limited use if any. If the producers were left to themselves, they would bring their produce to the market and every one would get good and eatable grain.

In short, it is necessary that all food insecure countries must try to produce their food requirements as a top priority agenda. And the farmers can produce more than the requirement of food grains in the country, if they are in peace. The farmers can produce more than the country's demand, when farming becomes a profitable enterprise and a successful profession.

THE END

Appendix 1

Members of the Committee on World Food Security

(As on November 3, 2006)[112]

A Afganistan, Albania, Algeria, Angola, Argentina, Armenia, Australia, Austria, Azerbaijan,

B Bangladesh, Belarus, Belgium, Benin, Bhutan, Bolivia, Brazil, Bulgaria, Burkina Faso, Burundi,

C Cameroon, Canada, Cap Vert, Central African Republic, Chad, Chile, China, Colombia, Congo, Costa Rica, Cuba,Côte d'Ivoire, Croatia, Cyprus, Czech Republic,

D Democratic People's Republic of Korea, Democratic Republic of Congo, Denmark, Dominican Republic,

E Ecquador, Egypt, El Salvador, Eritrea, Estonia, Ethiopia, European Community,
F - Finland, France

---

[112] Report of the 32nd Session of the Committee on World Food Security, October 30 to November 4, 2006, Appendix B

G - Gabon, Gambia (the), Germany, Ghana, Greece, Guatemala, Guinea, France, Gabon, Gambia (the), Germany, Ghana, Greece, Guatemala, Guinea, Guinea-Bissau, Guyana,

H - Honduras, Hungary,
I – Iceland, India, Indonesia, Iran, Islamic Republic of, Iraq, Ireland, Italy,

J - Japan, Jordan,
K - Kenya, Kuwait, Kyrgyzstan

L - Lebanon, Lesotho, Liberia, Libyan Arab Jamahiriya Lithuania, Luxembourg,

M -Madagascar, Malawi, Malaysia, Mali, Mauritania, Mauritius, Mexico, Moldova, Morocco, Mozambique,

N - Netherlands, New Zealand, Nicaragua, Niger, Nigeria
Norway

P – Pakistan, Panama, Papua New Guinea, Paraguay, Perú, Philip pines, Poland, Portugal

Q - Qatar
R - Republic of Korea, Romania, Russian Federation

S - San Marino, Saudi Arabia, Senegal, Serbia, Seychelles. Sierra Leone, Slovakia, Slovenia, Solomon Islands, South Africa, Spain, Sri Lanka, Sudan, Sweden, Switzerland, Syrian Arab Republic (the)
T – Thailand, Tonga, Turkey,
U – Uganda, Ukraine, United Kingdom, United Republic of Tanzania, United States of America, Uruguay
V - Venezuela (Republic of Bolivar)
Z – Zambia, Zimbabwe

AUTHOR INDEX

+++++

SUBJECT INDEX

*****

A MOVEMENT FOR A PEACEFUL WORLD

AUTHORS

Professor Suresh Chandra Mallick (b 1944) was a faculty member of the OUAT, Bhubaneswar (India) during 1968 - 2004. He is a researcher, writer, thinker and social worker. He is an Agricultural Economist with specialization in Agriculture, Poverty, Marketing, Policy and World Peace to motivate people's involvement in peace process. He held the post of Vice President, Indian Society of Agricultural Marketing during 2003 - 05. At present, he is the Chairperson of the Institute of Development Studies & Policy Research, Bhubaneswar.

Pritam Mallick (1975–2006) was extremely noble, friendly and knowledgeable and possessed extraordinary memory. He received B.A. (Honors) from Utkal University, M.A. from Central University, Hyderabad and M. Phil. Degree from JNU and completed Ph. D. courses in JNU. He was a specialist in Monetary Economics and Econometrics. He remembered the Oxford Dictionary and Roget's Thesaurus to master English literature. He acquired deep knowledge in Astrology, Palmistry, Mathematics and Statistics. He contributed enormously for WORLD PEACE manuscripts as co-author. But his heavenly demise occurred on August 4, 2006.